Tiki Road Trip

WITHDRAWN

A GUIDE TO TIKI CULTURE IN NORTH AMERICA

BY JAMES TEITELBAUM

FOREWORD BY SVEN A. KiRSTEN

SANTA
MONICA
PRESS

SANTA
MONICA
PRESS

Published by:
Santa Monica Press LLC
P.O. Box 1076
Santa Monica, CA 90406-1076
1-800-784-9553
www.santamonicapress.com
books@santamonicapress.com

Printed in the United States. Second Printing – May 2003.

Santa Monica Press books are available at special quantity discounts when purchased in bulk by corporations, organizations, or groups. Please call our Special Sales department at 1-800-784-9553.

ISBN 1-891661-30-2

Library of Congress Cataloging-in-Publication Data

Teitelbaum, James, 1967-
        Tiki road trip : a guide to Tiki culture in North America / by James
        Teitelbaum ; foreword by Sven A. Kirsten.
                p. cm.
        ISBN 1-891661-30-2
        1. Restaurants–Decoration–United States–History–20th century. 2. Bars (Drinking
        establishments)–Decoration–United States–History–20th century. 3. Art, Polynesian
        Influence. 4. Decorative arts–United States–Foreign influences. I. Title.
        NK2195.R4T45 2003
        747'.8571'097309045–dc21

                                    2003002373

Cover design by Shag

Interior design by Ann Buckley. Special thanks to Don Brown and Kat Borosky.

Table of Contents

FOREWORD BY SVEN A. KiRSTEN 8

INTRODUCTiON 10

BEFORE WE HIT THE ROAD 17

Classification System 19

Our Criteria 20

UNiTED STATES

Alabama 24

Alaska 24

Arizona 24

Arkansas 28

California 29

Colorado 86

Connecticut 89

Delaware 89

Florida 89

Georgia 103

Hawaii 104

Idaho 111

Illinois 112

Indiana 134

Iowa 135

Kansas 136

Kentucky 136

Louisiana 136

Maine 137

Maryland 137

Massachusetts 140
Michigan 147
Minnesota 149
Mississippi 150
Missouri 150
Montana 150
Nebraska 151
Nevada 153
New Hampshire 162
New Jersey 163
New Mexico 167
New York 170
North Carolina 176
North Dakota 176
Ohio 176
Oklahoma 184
Oregon 185
Pennsylvania 194
Rhode Island 195
South Carolina 196
South Dakota 196
Tennessee 197
Texas 202
Utah 204
Vermont 205
Virginia 205
Washington 210
Washinton, D.C. 220
West Virginia 223
Wisconsin 223
Wyoming 225

CANADA

Alberta 226

British Columbia 226

Manitoba 230

Ontario 231

Quebec 234

INTERNATIONAL

Australia 238

Belgium 239

Chile 239

Cuba 244

England 245

France 247

Germany 248

Greece 250

Italy 250

Japan 251

Mexico 253

Norway 253

Spain 253

Sweden 256

Switzerland 257

Tahiti 257

Virgin Islands 258

INTERNATIONAL TRADER VIC'S LOCATIONS 258
DRINK RECIPES 260
GLOSSARY 270
HAWAIIAN VOCABULARY 282
PHOTO CREDITS 285

Acknowledgements

A book like this can never be truly complete. The Polynesian influence on American popular culture is nearing its 75th year, and counting *all* of the Tiki influenced locations that have ever existed in America – let alone the rest of planet Earth – is an impossible task. This book is the result of 12 years spent trying, but no one man could do it alone.

In 1994, I began using the internet to aid in my search, creating "The Tiki Bar FAQ" which I posted to the UseNet. In 1995, I took things a bit further when I created the Tiki Bar Review Pages on the world wide web (www.tydirium.net). Over the past eight years, many people have sent me data on new and old Tiki Bars worldwide. A portion of this book is based on that information, and this book would therefore not have been possible without the assistance of these particular Tiki gods. The most significant contributions (of raw data, detailed texts, and sharp images) are from the following dedicated urban archaeologists:

Duke and Amy Carter, Lorrie and Doug Akins, Jane Murray, Dana Sixty, Elena Cambio, Kevin Crossman (world-wide Mai Tai expert), everyone at the Tiki Central (especially Hanford Lemoore, Mig Ponce, Bruce Woodbury, Woofmutt, Dean Curtis and Timothy Haack), Octavio, Chris Jepson, Ginger Dzerk, John Trivisonno, Tom Hemmen, David Bartell, Matt Gold, DAC Crowell, Al and Shelley Knepper, Mike Skinner, Shan Finnerty, Mark Bello, Dave and Colby Vasta, Dietrich Kempski, Julie Thompson, and the inestimable Otto Von Stroheim.

Triple extra Aloha goes to Sven A. Kirsten, who has provided a wealth of knowledge and advice, not only to me, but to seekers of the Tiki everywhere, to Shag for his speedy and brilliant cover art, and to Dana: there were many, many Tikis and many, many road trips between our blue-lit dawn on a chilly Chicago morning, and our pink-lit dusk at the paradise of Anakena. We'll always have Rapa Nui....

Updates, corrections, annecdotes, love letters, historical information, debates, gifts, and other Tikicentric data can be sent to the author at: tikibars@yahoo.com

Mahalo!
James Teitelbaum

Foreword

by Sven A. Kirsten

As the American Tiki is an endangered species, the Tiki bar is its reserve. That is why this present work represents a valiant and highly necessary effort. This labor of love, a gargantuan undertaking to find and catalog all the remaining Tiki sanctuaries, will undoubtedly raise awareness for the rarity of these last examples of authentic Tiki pop culture. Together with other recent publications that fuel the current Tiki revival, *Tiki Road Trip* should also help to inspire new entrepreneurs to again establish urban islands in the image of those classic Tiki Temples (as recent examples in New York, Las Vegas, and London demonstrate). And as individual appreciation of Tiki is on the rise, home Tiki bars are again being erected in rec rooms all over the country. The golden age of the Tiki bar might never return, but it's recognition as a unique American pop culture phenomenon will no longer be denied.

Why is this a desirable situation? We all know that the cliché of the South Sea island as earthly Garden of Eden was just an idealization, and that reality is much more complex. But our rational mind has sped by and left behind our emotional self, which still needs to believe that there is an escape to a Shangri-La. The Tiki bar is the perfect hideaway to playfully indulge in this need, even though we know that it is all make believe. Every city needs such a tropical oasis.

HALA KAHIKI, River Grove, IL

And what is this strange fascination that the figure of Tiki has invoked in the past, and is again today?

German ethnologist Karl Woerman remarked about Tikis: "Once you have seen them, you are haunted as if by a feverish dream...." This is obviously what happened to James Teitelbaum, sending him on the fervent pursuit that led to the present work. It is uncanny how this quote seems to apply to many contemporary artists today. The Tiki has an archetypal power that is inspiring to creative minds, and his image has recently reappeared in fashion design, illustration and in popular cartoons like *Sponge Bob* and *The Simpsons*. It defies analysis, but once encountered, the Tiki image is not to be erased.

Upon publication of my *The Book of Tiki*, in which I documented the history and Golden Age of American Tiki culture in the 1950s and 1960s, some novices to the phenomenon saw all the colorful imagery and happily expected to find a fully functioning Polynesian paradise just around the corner of their neighborhood. I had not fully clarified that more than 90 percent of the Tiki havens in my book no longer exist, having fallen victim to the changes in taste and political correctness, and that *The Book of Tiki* was a socio-historical documentation, *not* a restaurant guide.

URBAN ARCHEOLOGIST AT WORK

This book *is* a restaurant guide, but not in a purely consumerist sense. The criteria present in the search for a Tiki establishment are quite different than those for any other restaurant. Humility in the face of the rarity of the few remaining Tiki temples is a good attitude. Do not expect epicurean sensations, and if you want friendly family service, go to IHOP. This is urban archeology, and if the carpet is stained and the blowfish lamps are mummified from 40 years of nicotine, appreciate the place as if it was King Tut's tomb; it is not supposed to be Starbucks. When Paul Gauguin arrived in Tahiti, civilization in the form of French colonialism had already tainted this Polynesian paradise, but he was fascinated by the melancholy atmosphere of decay in Papeete, detecting "the blurred surface of some unfathomable enigma." This sense of paradise lost, of *temps perdu*, is an integral part of enjoying the musky darkness of an old, authentic Tiki bar.

Today's inability to appreciate the quality of patina, the wear and tear that tells there is a history to a place, has resulted in bland and generic environments without individual character. In contrast, one of the basic concepts of the Tiki bar is clutter, a dense jungle comprised of different artifacts and materials from exotic cultures, the jetsam and flotsam of the Seven Seas. Just like in the early museums that inspired the Surrealists, these collections of objects are not didactically organized, but thrown together to form a layered environment that creates a sense of mystery. A good Tiki bar is like a good movie: you have to revisit them to get the sense that you have seen it all. If the cocktails are good and they play exotic mood music, even better. And some actually *do* good food and service.

Introduction

What is a Tiki bar?

Good question.

Put simply, a Tiki bar is a bar with Tiki in it.

So, what is a Tiki?

And why would you want one in a bar?

Those are slightly more complicated questions.

Put into extremely broad terms, "Tiki" is a generic description for any of a wide variety of stone or wood carvings created by Pacific islanders.

Put into the terms of popular culture, Tiki is a design aesthetic that symbolizes an idealized way of life. The concept of Tiki conjures up romantic fantasies of tropical islands, exotic cultures, and easy living.

Unfortunately, that fantastic tropical island doesn't actually exist, but a long legacy of entrepreneurs has spent most of the twentieth century trying to create an approximation of it for those of us who remain landlocked.

DON THE BEACHCOMBER'S, 1950s, Waikiki

Shortly before World War I, the so-called "Golden Age of Travel" began when transportation by ship (and later by air) entered the financial grasp of many Americans and Europeans. Journeys to exotic South Seas destinations became the rage for the well-to-do. Years later, new bars and nightclubs began to pop up everywhere, and many of them attempted to capture a South Seas flavor. Bob Brooks is largely credited with opening the best of the bunch, the legendary Seven Seas. His Hollywood hot spot was decorated with palm trees and black velvet paintings of exotic beauties from primitive Oceanic islands.

These paintings are noteworthy, as they were created by Edgar Leeteg, an American expatriate living in Moorea, Tahiti. Often called the American Gaugin (more for his lifestyle than his art), the painter was something of a *bon vivant*, cultivating an exaggerated reputation for excess drinking, for fighting, and for bedding his exotic Tahitian models. He died in a motorcycle crash in 1953, but left behind a legacy of about 1700 black velvet paintings.

EDGAR LEETEG PAINTING

In 1934, one Earnest Raymond Beaumont Gantt rechristened himself Donn Beach, and opened the first of his many Don the Beachcomber restaurants. It was just two blocks away from Seven Seas. Many credit Don the Beachcomber with developing the Tiki bar as we know it today. He took the Seven Seas' concept, and added all manner of flotsam, anything a beach comber might find washed ashore: fishing floats, nets, starfish, sea turtles, and pufferfish. To this array of ephemera, he added artifacts such as spears, masks, clubs, and (most importantly) idol figures from far and varied islands throughout Polynesia, Micronesia, and Melanesia.

Don had thusly introduced the Tiki to the bar, and history was made.

The pan-Oceanic decor of most subsequent Tiki bars recognized no boundaries, and diverse art from Hawaii, New Guinea, the Cook Islands, Samoa, New Zealand, the Marquesas, and Rapa Nui (Easter Island) was fused together into a new mainland hybrid that was simply called "Tiki." It wasn't about authenticity, it was about escapism. As long as it was exotic and Oceanic, it fit. In these pre-politically correct times, no one worried about how the islanders them-

DON THE BEACHCOMBER AT WORK

selves might have reacted to these mutated effigies of their deities or ancestors ending up nailed to the end of a bar.

HAWAII HILTON, 1960s

Things reached a fever pitch when Victor Bergeron jumped onto the bandwagon. He transformed his first restaurant, Hinky Dinks, into Trader Vic's, adding more Tikis, better food, and more potent drinks. Bergeron was legendary for his hospitality, his generosity, and his skill at inventing exciting new food and drink recipes. The Trader Vic's chain is arguably the most successful Tiki bar chain in

UNKNOWN TIKI BAR, 1960s

history, and is still going strong to this day.

After the Second World War, the full-on Tiki invasion of the U.S.A. began in earnest. G.I.s who had actually been in the South Pacific flocked to Don's in droves, Hawaii became a state, and Thor Heyerdahl completed his famous Kon-Tiki expedition. By the early 1950s, the Tiki bar was a bona fide national phenomenon, with several lush and mysterious new Tiki-themed taverns, nightclubs, and restaurants opening up in just about every town in America.

Given that both Don and Vic had food as well as drink in their master plan, a faux-Polynesian cuisine was contrived. Stumped for any authentic island dishes to serve (short of "long pig"), plenty of fish made it to the menu. Pineapple, coconuts, and pork were found in enough quantity on Hawaii to make them per-

WESTWOOD MUGS

manent staples for any restaurant laying claim to the growing Polynesian fad. When in doubt, just add pineapple to whatever it was you were serving, and you could add "Hawaiian," "Islands," or "Polynesian" to the name of the dish. Chinese food was still somewhat exotic to Americans at that time. The Cantonese and Hunan dishes that we take for granted at fast food stands nowadays were still sufficient to impress people 60 years ago, so they served to round out the menu.

These palaces of pretend paradise would also need new libations. The martini would later become the symbol of the space age bachelor pad, but that was still in the future. Beer would never do, and the standard highballs were just too ordinary. Something new and tropical had to be created. Something with lots of exotic fruit, plenty of ice, and a great deal of rum. Don created the Zombie and the Missionary's Downfall, while Trader Vic concocted the world's first Mai Tai Roa Ae. Other enigmatically named drinks followed, such as the Suffering Bastard, Planter's Punch, Dr. Fong of Tahiti, and the Samoan Fogcutter. Ceramic mugs in the shape of Tikis began to appear, and before long they became souvenirs to take home.

LES BAXTER'S *THE SOUL OF THE DRUMS*

Not all proprietors could afford to collect authentic Oceanic artifacts with which to decorate their establishments, so Tikis and other items of decor were carved, with varying degrees of authenticity, by companies such as Oceanic Arts, Witco, and Orchids of Hawaii.

The music of Hawaii provided a workable soundtrack at first, but just as the decor molded the gods of many far off lands into a fantastic mongrel called Tiki, a new hybrid music was called for too. It fell to Martin Denny, Arthur Lyman, Les Baxter, and a few others to take the mysterious music of many lands, run it through a blender full of rum and jazz, and emerge with a sound that was just as contrived and phony (but ultimately pleasing) as the decor and the chow. It was dubbed "Exotica," after the title of Denny's first LP, and arranged with vibraphones, congas, and birdcalls, it was the perfect soundtrack for the Tiki bar.

Denny's recording of the song *Quiet Village*, written by Baxter, became a huge hit. The Tiki bar now had a concept, a drink, a menu, and a soundtrack. By the 1960s you couldn't leave your house without stumbling over a Tiki bar, and

MARTIN DENNY GROUP

then stumbling back home after a notoriously strong Suffering Bastard. Tiki then left the bar, and permeated the decor of motels, apartment buildings, strip clubs, bowling alleys, massage parlors, mini golf courses, nurseries, and even an entire town in Texas.

So what happened to it?

Well, like all fads, Tiki eventually died. That said, it lasted for a solid 30 years, which is far longer than most other fads last. By the mid-1970s, Tiki bars were closing at an alarming rate. Someone had figured out that the whole thing was rather tacky, and one by one the great Tiki monuments across the US of A fell to the call of the wrecking ball.

STEPHANI & MELANIE SNEAD 1973

Rock and roll music replaced Exotica, and it seemed that all interest in going to a place referred to as a "lounge" in order to actually *lounge* – that is to say: *relax* – had vanished in favor of a new hard-partying sensibility in night life cultures that the ages of disco, and then punk, and then techno served to solidify.

By the 1980s, Tiki palaces were few and far between, many of the remaining ones were in states of disrepair, and interest in maintaining them was near zero...except in California. For children growing up in California, Tiki style has always been a part of everyday life. Even with the amount of Tiki we have lost in the past 30 years, Tiki still permeates California. Not so in the midwest, where this humble author was spawned in the late 1960s.

Unlike my cousins in California, my midwestern exposures to Tiki were few and varied, and it was only by a fluke that my interest in the subject developed at all. Throughout my teens and early twenties, I became interested in both art and anthropology, and thereby developed a love for authentic Oceanic art. Separately, and based on different sets of circum-stances and stimuli, I developed an affinity for the aesthetic appeal of 1940's and 1950's American culture (the cars, movies, clothes, art, architecture, design, and even the furniture from this era). One fateful evening while longing for a drink during a trip to Florida, these two completely unrelated interests came crashing together. I pulled open the door to a dark and gloomy looking bar. Inside this smelly old watering hole was a world of adventure like I'd never seen. There were Oceanic carvings...from the 1950s! In a bar! All of the classic Tiki bar criteria were present that day (you'll read about them throughout this book), and an obsession was born.

Popular culture likes to recycle itself, and it was there-fore inevitable that sooner or later Tiki would make a come-back. As my fascination with Tiki grew, so it was with oth-ers. A fellow in San Francisco by the name of Otto von Stroheim started a magazine called *Tiki News* around the same time (1994) I launched

WAIKIKI, CHICAGO, IL 1948

my web site, "The Tiki Bar Review Pages" (www.tydirium.net). A serious clique of Tikiheads was gathering in California (of course); smaller groups popped up in places like Chicago and Montreal. John Trivisonno, kingpin of the Montreal group, started a magazine of his own, *The Mai Tai*. By 1999 there was even a thriving Tiki message board on the internet at Tiki Central (www.tikiroom.com).

Artists of no small repute began to incorporate Tiki into their work, including (but by no means limited to) Mark Ryden, Coop, Duke Carter, and of course Shag. Tiki mugs went from 50 cent thrift store kitsch to hot internet auction collectibles. People such as Wayne Coombs and Bosko began to carve new Tikis to meet a growing demand. After 25 years of nothing but closing Tiki bars, new ones began to open − although with the changing times, few could truly be called lounges. Aloha shirts became popular again. Urban archaeologist Sven A. Kirsten penned *The Book of Tiki*, a lavish and excellent coffee table book illustrating the com-

ALOHA LOUNGE 1970s

plete history of American Tiki culture, and bringing the phenomenon to the masses for the first time in a generation.

By the late 1990s, I was mapping out itineraries for road trips that would take me through Tiki-filled towns, visiting every Tiki bar I possibly could. I endured stares from drunken customers as I photographed the walls and ceilings, took notes about my drinks, and begged for souvenir menus. Readers of "The Tiki Bar Review Pages" embarked on similar quests, and informed me of the results. The fruit of all of this odd behavior is now in your hands.

So, armed only with this book, you now have the knowledge and the power to explore Tiki bars on four continents, and to drive from one side of America to the other without having to cross more than two states to get a decent Mai Tai. What more do you really need? Only this advice: Don't drink and drive.

Aloha!

James Teitelbaum

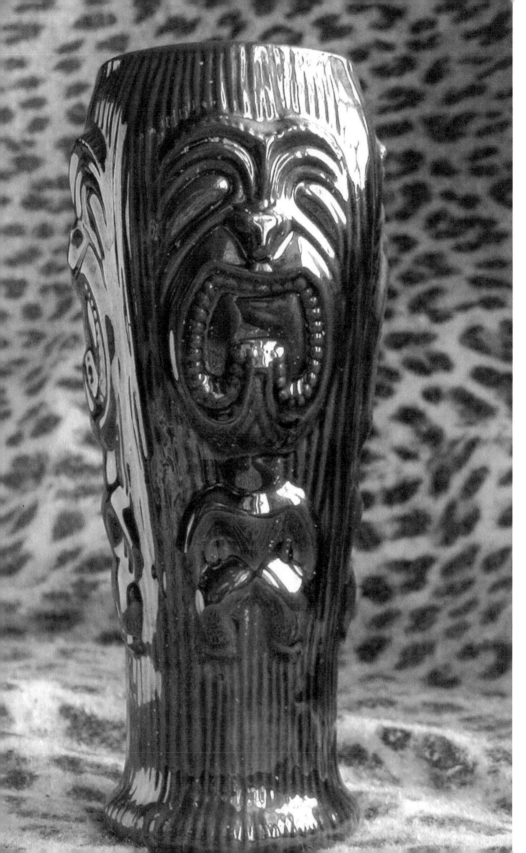

Before We Hit the Road

ORGANIZATION, TERMS, AND CONVENTIONS USED IN THIS BOOK

Reviews are divided into sections for each of the United States and Canadian provinces, as well as for International destiniations. Reviews are listed alphabetically within each state. In cases where states have several large cities (each with locations worth visiting), the cities are listed alphabetically, and reviews for specific locations are alphabetical within the city.

Certain states feature an additional alphabetical listing for locations that exist but remain unreviewed ("More Tiki Sites to Explore"), and some contain a lengthy alphabetical section for locations that have closed ("Tiki Sites Permanently Closed"). Why is this latter section included, and in such detail? Several reasons. First, so that if you hear about one of these places, you don't go looking for it. Or, perhaps you are interested in checking out the ruins of an ex-Tiki bar to see what is there now. Most importantly, these sections provide a history of the Tiki bar, putting the remaining locations into perspective as part of a larger cultural phenomenon. No other source has attempted to collect evidence of all of these monuments into one place before. Ideally this book is not only a travel guide to the Tiki bars of the present day, but a time-warp into the Tiki bars of the past as well; a catalogue of not only what is, but what was.

The major sites also include a row of "TiPSY Factor" icons, which provide an indication of the overall "Tikiness" of any given location; these icons are *not* a comprehensive rating of the site, but rather an indication of the amount of Tiki decor only.

There are several general terms which cover broad ranges of concepts used extensively throughout this book. We use the term "Tiki bar" to refer to

CLIFTON'S PACIFIC SEAS

any establishment that serves tropical drinks (also called Tiki drinks). Many of these places are also restaurants, and they're often *primarily* restaurants. To stretch things even further, some of them are beauty parlors or bowling alleys.

The term "Tiki bar," however, is a useful all-purpose phrase for the types of places we're exploring in this book.

The term "Tiki mug" refers to any glass or ceramic drinking vessel, with or without a handle, created to look like a Tiki. Additionally, novelty vessels shaped into forms other than Tikis are also recognized as Tiki mugs.

ROCK-A-TIKI LOUNGE, Chicago, IL

Popular examples include hula girls, bamboo shoots, skulls, shrunken heads, and the enigmatic Dr. Fu Manchu.

The term "TiPSY Factor" is an acronym created by this author which stands for "Tikis Per Square Yard." The term has entered the general lexicon of Tikiphiles and urban archaeologists in recent years, and refers to the actual number of Tiki carvings present in any given Tiki bar. The TiPSY Factor also includes items that are not actually Tikis, but which enhance the atmosphere of the Tiki bar. These items might include other non-Tiki Oceanic carvings (masks, spears, shields, clubs), taxidermy sea life (turtles, pufferfish, starfish), glass fishing floats, paintings with tropical themes, nets, and outriggers suspended from the ceiling. In

general, a TiPSY Factor described as large is more desirable. This means there's more stuff in the room, and in Tiki bars, clutter of a Polynesian nature is good! The more the better.

TIKI LOUNGE, Modesto, CA

CLASSIFICATION SYSTEM

In order to give you a better idea what each Tiki bar we are going to visit is like, we have subdivided them into several categories.

Type I – Classic Tiki Bar

The Classic Tiki Bar is a bar built before the 1970s that is decorated with a high TiPSY Factor, and serves tropical drinks in an exotic environment. It may be an open air establishment on a beach, or a windowless retreat from city life hidden in an urban metropolis. Some of them are old dive bars, others are well-maintained and classy. A further subdivision of this category is the "Florida Tiki Bar," which is found all over the East Coast. The Florida Tiki Bar is usually just a small bar with a thatched roof sitting near some water. It rarely, if ever, has any actual Tikis in it at all, and its tropical drinks are almost never made according to traditional recipes.

Type II – Fine or Casual Dining with Polynesian Atmosphere

The best example of this genre is Trader Vic's, particularly the Emeryville, CA and London, UK locations. This is top-notch food, served up in an exquisitely designed Polynesian setting. Even if it weren't a Tiki hotspot, this would still be an excellent place to eat. Often adjacent to a hotel.

Type III – Chinese Restaurant with Tiki Lounge

The title says it all. An astounding majority of the remaining Tiki locations are essentially Chinese restaurants with a Tiki Lounge in the back. Many of them are worth a look.

LUAU, Beverly Hills, CA

KAHIKI, Columbus, OH

Type IV – Tiki Mecca

A Tiki Mecca is a palace designed with one thing in mind – making you forget. A Tiki Mecca does everything in its power to transport you to an idealized South Seas Paradise, complete with strong drinks, good food, beautiful gardens, and exotic decor. A floor show featuring gorgeous hula dancers, brave fire knife dancers, traditional music, and thunderous log drummers is featured. Everything that Types I and II have plus more. Sadly, these are disappearing fast. Perhaps less than five remain.

Type V – Neo-Tiki

Typically erected in the past five to seven years, with some level of Tikiness in the decor. Usually, the owners are Tikiphiles, and often display their own collections of Tiki artifacts. Emerging artists like Bosko or Wayne Coombs join the venerable Oceanic Arts in providing the Tikis.

Type VI – Non-bar or Restaurant

Mini golf courses, apartment buildings, retail stores, motels, museums, beauty parlors, strip clubs, hardware stores...anything with a Polynesian Pop flavor that doesn't serve food or drink as their primary function.

Type 0 – Any of the Above, but Don't Bother!

Reserved for a few of the most wretched Tiki locations on the map, these establishments are embarrassments to Tiki culture enthusiasts.

OUR CRITERIA

ORCHIDS OF HAWAII R-3 MUG

Some people may find it strange that we will spend a comparatively small amount of time actually discussing the food served in some of the restaurants reviewed in this book. While a good meal certainly enhances the Tiki bar experience, one must keep in mind that the Tiki bar aficionado is largely concerned with the whole of the escapist experience. So, the decor, the drinks, the music, the architecture of the building, and even the attire of the staff are all as important as the food.

Also keep in mind that for the context of this book, we are reviewing the various locations listed herein in the context of their Tikiness. Any given restaurant might serve great food and have an awesome staff, but we are looking – again – for a complete escapist experience, and will judge each place we visit according to that criteria.

What are our criteria?

What makes a Tiki bar great?

Glad you asked!

HAWAII HILTON, 1960s

Drink Quality

Clearly, any bar must have good drinks, but this is of particular importance in a Tiki bar. At the *very least*, we need quality rum (most classic Tiki drinks are rum-based), fresh juice, a skewer of pineapple, and a paper umbrella. Things get better if the drink is made to order (as opposed to being dumped out of a jug of pre-fab drink mix), and is served in a mug that looks like Lono, Ku, a Moai, or even a mermaid. If the libation of choice is served up in a big volcano bowl with a flaming shot of 151 in the center, this is better still, and if the mug is a souvenir to keep, we have reached nirvana. Just make sure that you're dealing with 151 in the center of that volcano; some bars use lighter fluid. We've seen people trying to extinguish the flame early in order to siphon that extra shot of rum down into the drink. Lighter fluid causes a nasty hangover.

Architecture

The very best Tiki bars have been constructed in stand alone buildings that have the look of an exaggerated Polynesian dwelling, or in some cases, an entire small village. The architecture of a Tiki bar, inside and out, is of vital importance in perpetuating the illusion that the patron is on a far off island. Most Tiki bars are free of windows, so that no reminders of the outside world may leak in to shatter the effect. Places like the

MAI KAI, Fort Lauderdale, FL

Mai Kai in Fort Lauderdale, Florida have labyrinthine tropical gardens on the property, complete with waterfalls, streams, torches, and fearsome Tiki god effigies poking out from among the foliage. The Tonga Room in San Francisco has a pool in the center of the room into which a simulated rainstorm effect pours down every half hour. The Kahiki in Columbus, Ohio, had a towering arched roof, reminiscent of an outrigger. These elaborate architectural curiosities are one of the many things that make a good Tiki bar stand out from the bland strip malls that populate the American tarmac of the modern era.

DON THE BEACHCOMBER, 1950s, Waikiki

Music or Entertainment

At the very least, the management should be playing music of either a traditional Hawaiian variety (Caribbean music or reggae does *not* work), or some classic Exotica (Martin Denny, et al.). Upping the ante a notch, a small band is even better. The ultimate, which is still possible to find, is a full Polynesian floor show consisting of live music, hula dancers, fire dancers, log drumming, and more. The Mai Kai in Fort Lauderdale, Florida as well as Bali Hai in Santiago, Chile both still feature elaborate dinner shows.

EXOTIC FEATURES

Bombay Curries with Prawns 3.00
Mild True Indian curries in cream sauce, served with rice, fried banana and glaced pineapple.

Fried Chicken Tahiti 3.00
Slow cooked, basted with honey, topped with toasted coconut, fried banana and glaced pineapple.

Fried Abalone 2.40
Tenderized tropical Mexican Abalone. Fried in butter.

Mahi Mahi 2.40
Native white fish of the Hawaiian Islands. Filet and grilled in egg batter. Served with fruit garni.

Teri Yaki New York or Tenderloin Steak 4.30
Steaks marinated in soy, fresh ginger, garlic, and saki. Done to your satisfaction.

SERVED WITH POTATOES, TOAST
SALAD AND DEEP FRIED BANANA
SPECIAL — FLAMING BANANA

Food

The food to be found in the Polynesian restaurants (included under the blanket term "Tiki bar" in this book) varies widely. Some excellent Tiki bars such as Hala Kahiki in River Grove, Illinois serve no food save for pretzels and fortune cookies. Other worthy establishments such as Portland, Oregon's Alibi have traditional American dishes. There are dozens of Tiki bars remaining that have been converted into Chinese restaurants, with varying degrees of quality.

The best of the Polynesian restaurants have full menus of semi-exotic cuisine assembled from all over the Pacific Rim. The Trader Vic's chain has outstanding food, worthy of a visit even for those who are not Tiki aficionados.

Staff

As in any business, we expect the staff to be friendly and accommodating. Men should be clad in Aloha shirts, and women in muumuus or sarongs. They should have an appreciation and an enjoyment for the atmosphere in which they work, and be knowledgeable about the drinks, the food, and to at least some degree, the historical relevance of the cultural phenomenon they are helping to keep alive.

TiPSY Factor

The TiPSY Factor, (an acronym for "Tikis Per Square Yard") is essentially a reference to the density of the decor in any given Tiki bar, and works hand-in-hand with the architecture. A Tiki bar with many Tikis and other appropriate artifacts is said to "have a high TiPSY Factor," while relatively sparse decor equals a "low TiPSY Factor." Ultimately, what makes any old bar into specifically a "Tiki bar" is the decor. We like to see as many effigies of Polynesian Gods and as much beach bum flotsam as the owners can squeeze into the room.

Please note that this term is not easily quantifiable, is never clearly defined, and is rather freely used. As the reader explores more and more Tiki bars, an intuitive understanding of the term should develop. To guide the intrepid urban archaeologists towards higher TiPSY Factors, each of the reviews will include between one and five icons representing the TiPSY Factor present. This is not an overall rating of the establishment, simply an indication of the quality and quantity of the exotic elements on display. Note that the designation "NR" ("Not Rated") is used for the handful of Tiki locations in the book whose TiPSY Factor has not been verified.

TIKI COVE, Fairbanks, AK

ALABAMA

There are currently no Tiki bars open in Alabama.

ALABAMA TIKI SITES PERMANENTLY CLOSED

Tiki Supper Club, Mobile, AL

ALASKA

There are currently no Tiki bars open in Alaska.

ALASKA TIKI SITES PERMANENTLY CLOSED

Tiki Cove, Mecca Bar, 549 2nd Ave., Fairbanks, AK
This candy-apple red Moai mug was created locally in
Fairbanks, possibly for the Tiki Cove (see picture).

ARIZONA

BiKiNi LOUNGE • 1502 GRAND AVE., PHOENiX, AZ

(602) 252-0472

Category I
CLASSIC TIKI BAR

TiPSY Factor

Conveniently located across the street from a teen
half-way house that used to be the Bali Hi motel, Bikini is a
classic Tiki bar that hasn't aged well. The Kon Tiki in Tucson
may have been opened by the same person back in the
1960s.

DRiFT SOUTH PACiFiC FUSiON • 4341 N. 75TH ST., SCOTTSDALE, AZ

(480) 949-8454

Category V
**NEO-TIKI
RESTAURANT**

TiPSY Factor

Opened in October, 2002, this restaurant is a fusion of
1950's and 1960's design and the island style of the traditional Tiki bars of the same era. Drift serves tropical drinks
in Tiki mugs, and has a South Pacific-influenced menu. The
owners have been "researching the history of Tiki for several years in order to get it right."

TRADER VIC'S • SCOTTSDALE, AZ

Peter Seeley, grandson of Victor Bergeron, announced in late 2002 that a new Trader Vics is planned in Scottsdale as one of at least five new North American locations. Watch your local press for details.

(213) 669-9381

Category II
FINE DINING

TiPSY Factor

NR

KON-TiKi • 4625 EAST BROADWAY (AT SWAN), TUSCON, AZ

Located in a shopping center on Broadway, the sign for Kon-Tiki is a true marvel, one of the better remaining vintage Tiki bar signs of all-time. Approaching the building, one passes through a small "forest" area, which serves to effectively separate the Kon-Tiki from the rest of the nearby shops. A few Tikis and a small bridge over a pond lead to big set of doors; the sign above reads "Welcome to Paradise."

(520) 323-7193

Category I
CLASSIC TIKI BAR

TiPSY Factor

The inside of the Kon-Tiki would be amazing if they hadn't installed sports TV and neon Bud signs behind the bar. If the doormen didn't wear little walkie talkies so as to be able to respond instantly to brawls. If the bartenders didn't typically suggest a character in a Cohen brothers' movie. If there weren't Jaegermeister machines behind the bar. If the music wasn't AC frickin' DC. A venerable Tiki Palace, the Kon-Tiki could be a contender for a top ten Tiki bars list, if it wasn't for the staff's obvious indifference towards maintaining the treasure they don't seem to be aware of having.

The Kon Tiki's actual history is hard to discern: one bartender places the Kon Tiki's vintage at "1962, I think." A doorman is more of a historian claiming "oh about 20 years, maybe 25" (putting it's vintage in the late 1970s). A hostess just glared, as though she had been asked what her (considerable) age was.

KON TIKI, Tucson, AZ

KON TIKI HOTEL, Phoenix, AZ

KON TIKI, Tucson, AZ

Said bartenders are real salesmen when it comes to the Mai Tai; according to them, the drinks are "ok...good...decent...." The 'Tai comes in a tall glass, it is red, and it is pretty much a disaster. The Scorpion comes in a hefty fishbowl-looking thing, like a huge brandy snifter. It basically tastes like some sort of weird rummy screwdriver. Orange in color, it is probably just rum, orange juice, and maybe some pineapple juice...but it *will* get you sloshed, complete with monster hangover.

Many of the drinks in the well-illustrated vintage menu are pictured in exotic Tiki mugs, including "A Drink of the Gods," which used to come in a mug with a kneeling hula wahine on the front, and "Kon-Tiki" written in "Chinese-style" letters above her in relief. Too bad all of the drinks come in standard glassware now, but it is nice to see that the most expensive drinks on the menu are still only five bucks.

The four big rooms are all jam packed with monster Tikis. There are probably two dozen Tikis in the three to seven foot tall range at Kon-Tiki, but they have all been painted bright colors to hide graffiti. The designers made extensive use of fishing floats, nets, and bamboo, which cover every inch of the place. Individual thatch-roofed Tiki huts along one wall ensure your party's privacy. On another wall are the coveted 1960's Sears paintings *The Pearl of Wisdom*, and the well-known painting of the creepy blue-faced Chinese girl by Tretchikoff. Another large room, visible through glass windows set into the back of the bar, contains about eight parrots and macaws. It is a pleasant surprise that the parrot cage has been maintained...given the state of the rest of the Kon Tiki, one might expect that this area would have been turned into a dance floor by now. Aquarium lovers will like the salt water aquarium in the lobby, right next to the unique "shy Tiki" (as he seems to be covering his...Tiki...with a look of panic on his face).

If it weren't for the lack of decent music, the rowdy crowd, the run-down decor, the crummy drinks, and the indifferent staff, the Kon-Tiki could very well be an all-time classic Tiki bar. But it isn't.

MAGIC CARPET GOLF • 6125 E. SPEEDWAY, TUSCON, AZ

Magic Carpet is a miniature golf course from the 1970s featuring a 30-foot-tall Moai. Stairs inside the Easter Island effigy enable explorers to perch themselves on the observation platform on top of Mr. Moai's head in order to observe the birdies.

(520) 885-3691

Category VI
OTHER

TiPSY Factor

MORE ARIZONA TIKI SITES TO EXPLORE

Aloha Motel, 445 N. Arizona Ave, Chandler, AZ (480) 963-3403
Two Tikis and a great crossed spear sign.

Cocomo Joe's, 28244 N. Tatum Blvd., Scottsdale/Cave Creek, AZ (480) 538-8008
Good atmosphere, if a bit pricey. Very good seafood, good music, serviceable drinks ($6), festive crowd.

Sunset Steakhouse & Tiki Lounge, Florence Highway, Coolidge, AZ (520) 723-3997

Tiki Hut, 8939 E. Indian Bend Rd., Scottsdale, AZ

Tiki Lounge, Coolidge, AZ

ARIZONA TIKI HOTELS, APARTMENTS, AND TRAILER PARKS

Hawaiian Gardens Apartments, Phoenix, AZ

Kon Tiki Mobile Home Village, 555 West Warner Rd., Chandler, AZ (480) 963-3655

Peoria Polynesian Village Trailer Park, 10951 N. 91st Ave Peoria, AZ

Sands West apartments, Phoenix, AZ

Tiki Tai Mobile Village, 5745 W. Maryland Ave., Glendale, AZ (623) 939-6090
Rumor has it they recently scrapped the Tiki theme.

Tiki Motel, 2649 N. Oracle Road, Tucson, AZ (520) 624-0956

ARIZONA TIKI SITES PERMANENTLY CLOSED

Islands, The, 4839 N. Seventh Blvd., Phoenix, AZ (just south of Camelback Rd.)
Decorated by Oceanic Arts, it featured a custom souvenir Tiki mug in a Hawaiian Kukailimoku style.

Kon Tiki Hotel, 24th St. and Van Buren, Phoenix, AZ
Razed in 1997.

Pago Pago, 2201 Oracle Rd, Tuscon, AZ
Pago Pago's whimsical matchbooks featured a wahine wearing nothing but a lei, being ogled by a cartoonish cowboy with a lasso.

Polynesian Massage & Spa 963 E. Curry Rd. (near Scottsdale and Curry), Tempe, AZ
Was once a Tiki palace of some kind, but later went strip/massage under the name Seven Seas. The building still exists, and is worth a drive-by.

Traders, The, Phoenix, AZ

ARKANSAS

We have no evidence of any Tiki bars, past or present in Arkansas.

KON TIKI HOTEL, Phoenix, AZ

CALIFORNIA

ALOHA SHARKEEZ • 52 PIER AVE., HERMOSA BEACH, CA

Aloha Sharkeez does indeed have Tropical decor. There are some Tikis and hula girls airbrushed onto the signs in front of the building, but you do not want to visit this place. Imagine the lamest possible knucklehead frat boy beer bong bar, but with bamboo. Some of the bartenders do not even know how to make the Mai Tai boldly mentioned on the menu, but this is probably for the best: it is five bucks, it is served in a plastic cup, and it has less than one shot of bottom shelf rum in it (dumped over something from a plastic jug). 'Nuff said.

(310) 374-7823

Category O
DON'T BOTHER!

TiPSY Factor

(Don't) look for their other location in Santa Barbara (415 State Street), or their Baja Sharkeez affiliates in Manhattan Beach (3801 Highland) or Newport Beach (114 21st street).

Dano's Beach Grille, around the corner from Sharkeez (at 1301 Hermosa Ave.), has some Tikis on their outside patio decor. Seems like a nice place to eat.

BAHOOKA • 4501 N. ROSEMEAD BLVD., ROSEMEAD, CA

Opened in 1967 by WWII Navy vet and Kelbo's bartender Jack Fliegel (no relation to the founding member of the Banana Splits), the original Bahooka location in West Covina closed in 1980. By that point, a second location had opened (in 1976), which still survives today. Fliegel's wife and daughters (Darlene, Stacy, and Samantha) still run the current Bahooka, which is crammed full of artifacts salvaged from various shipyards by Jack himself.

(818) 285-1241

Category II
CASUAL DINING

TiPSY Factor

Bahooka is a huge place (over 10,000 square feet), with maze-like corridors housing more tropical and nautical artifacts than one could ever hope to examine in just one visit. All of the usual Tiki bar accouterments are present, including scores of blowfish, exotic lanterns, original glass fishing

BAHOOKA, Rosemead, CA

floats, and taxidermied sea turtles. Look for one seriously huge Hawaiian-style Tiki leering down at you as soon as you walk in the door. Also look for two Tiki poles on either side of a vintage post office window in the main room, and a print by The Pizz on the wall. That's about it for actual Tiki gods, but don't be fooled by a statistic: the Bahooka definitely feels like a classic Tiki bar in every sense, even if Lono and Pele took a vacation while Bahooka was being built.

Bahooka means "hut," and each of Bahooka's high-backed booths is separated from its neighbor by an aquarium, making each booth totally private and isolated from the next – like your own little Tiki hut. Cared for by a full-time aquarium specialist named Renardo, Bahooka's one hundred and four aquariums are home to such long-time residents as Pacu (since 1977), and until very recently, Bubbles, a giant Gourami who passed away at the ripe old age of 26. Darlene and Stacy have declined to comment on whether or not Bubbles was the guest of honor at a recent Bahooka fish fry (just kidding; we're sure Bub got a decent burial).

Bahooka history includes appearances in the films *Riptide* and *Fear and Loathing in Las Vegas*.

The drinks are great, and there are no less than 63 of them on the nicely illustrated menu. Sitting at the bar (which is an aquarium in itself; you eat on the glass top with little mudskippers bopping around under your elbows), try the Mai Tai, Scorpion, and Cozmo, all favorites done right. Insider tip: order a Hand Grenade (not on the menu), and to go a step further, ask for it "with the pin pulled" for an extra float of 151 rum on top.

The food is good and well prepared. The sliced ham is excellent, the fried shrimp yummy, the barbecue chicken flavorful, and we have heard reports of people driving 50 miles for Bahooka's ribs.

If you sit in a booth, try to get seated in the section attended to by the infamous Go Go. She will reportedly accommodate almost any "flaming" request you may have. Meaning, if you want it on fire, Go Go is your gal. Flaming drinks? Kid stuff! We are talking flaming clam chowder, drinking water, salad...whatever you want. After a couple of Fog Cutters, things can get very interesting. Call ahead to make sure she is there.

BAHOOKA, Rosemead, CA

Bahooka sells a nicely designed t-shirt, with art based on the work of Mark Ryden.

CACAO • 11609 SANTA MONICA BLVD., LOS ANGELES, CA

Cacao is a small hipster coffee house in Los Angeles. The decor is about 75% Tiki and about 25% grey aliens/psychedelic sci-fi. Tiki masks can be found on the walls; some of them appear to be by Bosko. Exotica LP covers framed in bamboo provide additional retro-Tiki hipness, and the actual coffee bar is covered in bamboo. Hula girls, travel stickers, and a Tiki-decorated menu complete the theme. Cacao also hosts art shows. They open at 5:00 P.M. every day. Worth a quick peek if you're in L.A. and need a caffeine and/or Tiki fix.

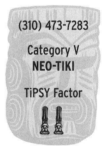

(310) 473-7283

Category V
NEO-TIKI

TiPSY Factor

CACAO, Los Angeles, CA

CALIENTE TROPICS RESORT • 411 EAST PALM CANYON DR., PALM SPRINGS, CA

(866) HOT-9595

Category VI
OTHER

TiPSY Factor

Designed by the legendary Ken Kimes, and opened in 1964, this 90-room resort was the 38th of Kymes' 45 hotels (five were Polynesian themed). Resort visitors could dine at a Sambo's coffee shop, the Reef Lounge (slated to repoen in 2003), the Congo Room steakhouse, and the Cellar lounge. During the Caliente's heyday, the Rat Pack, Elvis, and Victor Mature were frequent visitors, but the property fell into decline through the 1970s and 1980s, changing ownership multiple times. Once on the verge of being destroyed, the property was bought and remodeled in 2000. Although the rooms themselves are now fairly common hotel rooms (albiet with Hawiian floral print beadspreads and tropical lithos on the walls), the owners have seen fit to preserve the Tiki decor for the remainder of the resort grounds. Large A-frame roofs, rock walls, and plenty of bamboo – as well as a good number of Oceanic Arts Tikis – make this a place you will want to visit.

Note: Caliente was host to a large gathering of Tiki worshippers in 2002 that may become an annual event.

CALIENTE TROPICS RESORT, Palm Springs, CA

CALIENTE TROPICS RESORT, Palm Springs, CA

DAMON'S • 317 N. BRAND AVE., GLENDALE, CA

Damon's opened at 118 S. Central Street in 1937, and moved to its current location in 1990. Located just a few feet from the street, Damon's facade is promising, with plenty of thatch and bamboo, a colorful Tiki pole, and no windows. A lack of windows is a key architectural feature in any classic Tiki bar, since a lack of windows is also a lack of reminders that the "real" world is just a few yards away.

(818) 507-1510

Category II
FINE DINING

TiPSY Factor

Damon's heavy doors lead into a dark entryway, and then into two spacious dining rooms. While there is definitely a fair amount of bamboo present (augmented by floral seat cushions and carpet, plenty of aquariums, and a generally exotic atmosphere), you'd be hard pressed to find any of the most exciting Tiki bar elements, such as carved Tiki gods, blowfish, or Tiki mugs at Damon's. The only actual Tiki in evidence is near the hostess stand, and at about 18" tall, it isn't much to write about. There are a few nice vintage Hawaiiana prints above the arch leading to the bar area, and the murals on the back wall of the bar area are interesting, too. They were done in 1987 by Bettina Rakita Byrne in the style of Eugene Savage.

A collage of newspaper clippings about the original location can be found near the solitary hostess stand. The collage is notable not only for the information on the original Damon's location, but for some great 1930's-1950's advertising preserved alongside the Damon's articles.

DAMON'S, Glendale, CA

The bar manager mixes up a mean Lava, the house drink. Basically a Mai Tai with a splash of something red that seeps into the drink like (you guessed it) hot lava, it is unique, and pretty strong. All of the drinks are made fresh. The actual Mai Tai is a little bland, but not bad. Made with traditional ingredients, it comes garnished with a cherry, a pineapple chunk, and the obligatory umbrella. The Blue Hawaiian stinks, but it is tough to find one that doesn't. The novelty is the color, and few Tikiphiles usually bother with the wretched things.

Your Mai Tai may be interrupted by a football game on the television in the bar (which sometimes drowns out the faint traces of exotic music barely audible on the muzak system).

The crowd at Damon's is mostly families and middle-aged couples, and the place definitely feels more like a typical modern restaurant than a classic Tiki bar. Steak and potatoes is the fare. Lots of seafood too, and although the TiPSY Factor isn't anything special, the food is very good, and priced fairly. Given the pricey nature of the Trader Vic's over in Beverly Hills, Damon's might be your best Los Angeles choice for a good meal in a quasi-Tiki atmosphere.

DON THE BEACHCOMBER'S • CALIFORNIA ADVENTURE, 1776 SOUTH DISNEYLAND DR., ANAHEIM, CA

In order to provide parking lots for their newest theme park, Disney bulldozed two classic Tiki motels (the Pitcairn and the Polynesian Hotel) plus a small town's worth of other atomic era buildings. The good news (possibly) is that the theme park in question – California Adventure – contains a reasonably accurate resurrection of a Don the Beachcomber restaurant. Vintage Beachcomber collectibles are on display, and neo-Tiki decor is from Oceanic Arts and Bosko.

(714) 781-4565

Category V
NEO-TIKI

TiPSY Factor

ENCHANTED TIKI ROOM • DISNEYLAND, ANAHEIM, CA

Opened on June 23, 1963, Disney's famous Tiki-Tiki-Tiki-Tiki-Tiki Room is still open, and includes colorful singing Tikis, birds, and plants. The Enchanted Tiki Room was Disney's first animatronic attraction. Talking Tikis in a style

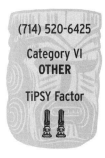

(714) 520-6425

Category VI
OTHER

TiPSY Factor

evocative of New Guinea or New Caledonian carvings (which in this case are curiously named after Hawaiian gods –Lono, Pele, etc.) entertain visitors waiting in line. They are of course, colorfully painted. The Tahitian Terrace (with its waterfall and floor show) is long gone, the soundtrack of the show has been "updated," and the Polynesian aspects of Adventureland continue to shrink, so go have a peek while you can.

ENCHANTED TIKI ROOM, Anaheim, CA

GALLEY RESTAURANT • 2442 MAIN ST., SANTA MONICA, CA

(310) 452-1934

Category II
FINE DINING

TiPSY Factor

Established 1934, this classic restaurant bears mentioning since it is the oldest restaurant in Santa Monica, and maintains a South Pacific nautical theme. Vintage memorabilia (menus, napkins, etc.) fill a display case outside (which also includes inexplicable but welcome pictures of Betty Page), and you've got to love the mermaid above the door.

Inside you'll find grass hut booths, hula girl cocktail napkins, weird nautical stuff, a mermaid room, and tropical drinks — but no actual Tikis. The food is steaks and seafood, with an emphasis on the steaks.

ISLANDS • 101 E. ORANGE GROVE AVE, BURBANK, CA

(818) 566-7744

Category II
CASUAL DINING

TiPSY Factor

The Islands is a rather nondescript Hawaiian/tropical themed restaurant. There are few if any Tikis to speak of, but the general atmosphere does conjure modern-day images of Hawaii. Their $4.25 Mai Tai is made with more or less traditional recipes and is quite strong. The staff are clad in Aloha shirts.

LAVA LOUNGE • 1533 N. LA BREA AVE, HOLLYWOOD, CA

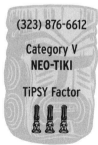

(323) 876-6612

Category V
NEO-TIKI

TiPSY Factor

The Lava Lounge, a hep little bar in Hollywood, easily manages to seem exotic, even though there is a distinct lack of actual Tiki gods present. All of the walls are covered with — guess what — chunky black lava rock, and dim red light seeps from lanterns hung along each of the walls. Pinholes in the black ceiling are made to look like stars, and with a little imagination, the Lava Lounge becomes an outdoor Tiki bar under the stars at the base of a volcano, rather than a small pub in a strip mall in Hollywood.

The drinks are expensive, but pretty darned good. The bartenders have an excellent grip on the tropical drinks theme, even if the recipes are non-traditional.

There always seems to be a few vintage cars in the parking lot, and you will usually find a cross-section of Los Angeles swing, rockabilly, and lounge hipsters in the handful of booths near the front of the bar.

One caveat: they have live music six nights a week. Even if you love to hear bands, one must understand that the Lava Lounge is a small place, and the little stage in the corner isn't really adequate to contain most acts. As a result, the volume of even the most conservative of acts becomes detrimental to the conversation, relaxation, and flirtation in which you might otherwise indulge.

That aside, some of the bands (such as the Jazz Jury and the Blue Hawaiians) are really good, and seeing them in such close quarters might be right up your alley. The choice is yours, but if you want to support neo-exotic culture in L.A., definitely peep out the Lava Lounge.

ROYAL HAWAiiAN • 331 NORTH COAST HWY., LAGUNA BEACH, CA

Royal Hawaiian has existed in Laguna Beach since the 1940s. The bar is small, but well-decorated with Tikis carved by Milan Guanko. The house specialty is the very strong Lapu-Lapu (pineapple and Meyer's). The food is good, and inexpensive; the ribs are said to be the best on the planet (perhaps Bahooka would dispute this?). One used to be able to find four large Tikis carved by Andres Bumatay outside of the building; sadly, only two remain.

(949) 494-8001

Category II
FINE DINING

TiPSY Factor

Urban archaeologists may also want to investigate Crystal Cove, a stretch of beach just north of Laguna. This quasi-ghost is home to a bunch of vacant bungalows from the deco era along the beach. One has a huge Tiki outside.

SAM'S POLYNESIAN (AKA SAM'S SEAFOOD) • 16278 PACIFIC COAST HWY, HUNTINGTON BEACH, CA

(714) 592-1321

Category II
FINE DINING

TiPSY Factor

This Tiki hotspot is a favorite amongst Los Angeles Tiki aficionados, but could be easily missed by those not in the know. The main restaurant area, a bar, and two banquet rooms are all decorated in full-on tropical splendor. The banquet hall is awesome, with a huge waterfall, and booths done as huts lining the edges of the room. They also have a Polynesian revue. The Hidden Village, the lounge within Sam's Seafood, is considered a must-visit by many Los Angeles Tiki authorities.

A former location existed at 3901 East Coast Highway, Corona Del Mar, CA

SAM'S POLYNESIAN, Huntington Beach, CA

SAM'S POLYNESIAN, Huntington Beach, CA

TAHiTi • 7910 WEST 3RD ST. (CORNER OF FAIRFAX & 3RD), LOS ANGELES, CA

Very classy, rather expensive, and definitely neo-Tiki, Tahiti serves what is termed "world cuisine." The interior boasts high-back leopard skin booths, peacock feather chandeliers, and starfish on the walls of the men's room. The dining room floor is a giant map of the Pacific Ocean. A courtyard is decked out with a blue tile waterfall, thatch umbrellas, and bamboo furniture. One Tiki (about two feet tall) oversees the entrance to the restaurant. A Tiki-themed bar will be open by the time you read this.

(323) 651-1213

Category V/II
NEO-TIKI/
FINE DINING

TiPSY Factor

TiKi Ti • 4427 SUNSET BLVD., LOS ANGELES, CA

(213) 669-9381

Category I
CLASSIC TIKI BAR

TiPSY Factor

Tiki Ti is a tiny but excellent Tiki bar in Silverlake, just east of Hollywood. Ray Buhen, the man responsible for Tiki Ti, was a local legend among Los Angeles Tikiphiles. Ray was a bartender at Don the Beachcomber's in Hollywood as far back as 1934, and also worked at Seven Seas, the Luau, the Tropics, and at the Beverly Hills Trader Vic's. Ray opened Tiki Ti in 1961, and maintained it until his death in September of 2001.

Fortunately, his son and grandson (Mike and Mike Jr.) have kept Tiki Ti in business.

Tiki Ti is only open Wednesday through Saturday. The decor of the cozy and diminutive bar is strictly authentic South Pacific. Hand-carved Tikis, backlit with eerie orange lights, loom over the half dozen booths, while the bar fronts an exotic fluorescent waterfall. Martin Denny provides the soundtrack, as is properly befitting any good Tiki bar.

TIKI TI, Silverlake, CA

Look for rattan stools along the L-shaped bar (which seats 12), above which hang blowfish lamps, a lamp made out of a turtle, Tiki statuettes, and license plates from all over the world (including Guam and Peleliu). Total capacity is less than 40, and 30 people feels crowded.

Ray kept many of his best recipes secret, choosing to mix from a variety of unmarked bottles, leaving the patron bewildered by his mixing magic. As his son and grandson share his zeal, these recipes are sure to remain safe for years to come. Some of these recipes are Donn Beach concoctions, and Tiki Ti may be the only place keeping these libations alive.

The drink menu features 42 rum cocktails (such as the Tuba Cola, the Never-Say-Die, and the Sumatra Kula), 10 vodka cocktails (including the Princess PuPuli), and a variety of gin, tequila, and other mysterious concoctions. All drinks are $8 to $10, except for a couple of particularly nasty concoctions (that's a good thing), one of which seems to have spawned the theme song of the place. The drink is served in a stemmed mug of liquors, into which the bartender then, with much pomp and ceremony, drizzles an alarming amount of tequila. Each tequila bottle is capped with a bull-head pour spout, so when the bartender begins to pour, the entire bar erupts into a chorus of "Toro, toro, toro!" until the deadly cocktail is complete.

Tiki Ti is a must visit. We truly believe that the Tiki Ti comes closest to preserving the authenticity and spirit of the Tiki bar as envisioned over 50 years ago. Check it out while you can — only time will tell how much longer this piece of history will hang on.

TRADER ViC'S • 9876 WiLSHiRE BLVD., BEVERLY HiLLS, CA

The Trader Vic's chain is one of the cornerstones of Tiki culture. First opened in 1938 by Victor Bergeron, the original Oakland Trader Vic's was a largely successful attempt to imitate and improve on the concept of the Tiki bar/Polynesian restaurant hybrid developed by Don the Beachcomber.

(310) 276-6345

Category II
FINE DINING

TiPSY Factor

While Don's restaurants have all vanished, as have other chains spawned by additional imitators (such as Stephen Crane's Kon Tiki Ports), Trader Vic's is still going strong all over the world. At its peak, Bergeron had 14 Trader Vic's locations in North America; however at this time there are only five (with five new locations planned, however). Interestingly, as the Trader Vic's sites have closed in the U.S. and Canada, new ones have sprung up in places as diverse as Thailand, England, the United Arab Emerates, Japan, and Germany.

Trader Vic's in Beverly Hills opened in August of 1955 as The Traders. The outside is very impressive, a quintessential example of mid-century architecture, complete with Polynesian motifs sculpted into the concrete, and a few towering Tiki gods guarding the door. Most of the Tikis seem to have been exiled to the parking lot however; you will see very few inside anymore. Over the years, some of the Trader Vic's locations remaining in America have toned down their Tiki decor, and have begun to focus on a more conservative upscale yacht club image. In certain Vic's, Marquesian Tiki poles have been replaced with ships in bottles, Maori wall ornaments have given way to Currier and Ives prints of schooners, and Leeteg paintings have been mothballed to make way for sailing club pennants. In the Beverly Hills location, virtually all of the remaining Tiki action is in the bar; the restaurant has been more or less cleansed of Tiki.

TRADER VIC'S, Beverly Hills, CA

There are two amazing paintings near the bar area depicting warring Polynesian tribes. The somewhat violent works of art seem incongruous in the conservative restaurant, but they are highlights of the otherwise tame decor.

Sitting at said bar on a good night, you will be given excellent and attentive service by long-time bartender Jack Leoung, who makes an amazing Suffering Bastard. Rumor has it that Jack has a notorious and rare original Hinky Dink's drink menu, featuring a few dozen drinks rarely heard of or consumed by modern day Tikiphiles: Rum-Dum. Madame Pele (for two). Auku-Tiki. Rum Giggle. One can only dream....

If you come for dinner, remember that you are in Beverly Hills. You will be expected to show up dressed nicely; your Aloha shirt will *not* be considered festive. As is the case with all of the Trader Vic's restaurants, the food is excellent. Given the upscale location, this isn't really surprising; you can expect to find a fairly affluent crowd dining

with Lono (or his memory, at least). With that in mind, it is
not surprising that young hipsters seeking a fun time
in a classic mid-century bar will not always be welcomed
warmly. If that's your goal, go to Tiki Ti....

TRADER VIC'S, Beverly Hills, CA

MORE THINGS TO DO IN LOS ANGELES

L.A. is a Mecca for googie, retro, kitsch, and hipsterdom. One could write an entire book about Los Angeles sites that (while not strictly Tiki) would appeal to Tikiphiles, googie enthusiasts, and urban archaeologists. Here is a very small selection of new and old favorites to get you started:

Oceanic Arts (12414 Whittier Blvd., Whittier, CA 90602-1017 (562) 698-6960)

OA's awe-inspiring warehouse is open to the public. They sell Tiki mugs and other gift items, plus hundreds of actual Tiki carvings in all shapes and sizes. We heartily recommend a stop at this Mecca for Tiki. This is where the decor for a great many of the classic and modern Tiki bars listed in this book comes from, and walking around their warehouse full of thousands of Tikis in all shapes and sizes will permanently alter your brain. If you're lucky, you may meet owners Leroy Schmaltz or Bob Van Oosting, who have been carving Tikis since 1956. Look for some googie architecture in the vicinity, including a liquor store (Bailey's Beverage Corner) near the boy's correctional school(!).

OCEANIC ARTS, Whittier, CA

They are open 8:00-4:00 on weekdays, except for a lunch hour at noon, and 10:00-1:00 on Saturdays, except holiday weekends.

CP Prop House (1107 Bronson (at Santa Monica Blvd.), Santa Monica, CA)

Drive by this address and look for four huge Moai statues that were created for a Laverne and Shirley reunion episode, but eventually not used.

OCEANIC ARTS, Whittier, CA

Nightlife:

Good Luck Bar (1514 Hillhurst Ave. (323) 666-3524) is decorated in 1950's Chinese style, and they have tropical drinks too. **Bigfoot Lodge** (3172 Los Feliz Boulevard (323) 662-9227) in Los Feliz has a must-see Pacific Northwest theme. **Pann's** (6710 La Tijera Blvd. (323) 776-3770) is the ultimate example of a classic googie coffee shop, immaculately preserved. **The Derby** (4500 Los Feliz Blvd (323) 663-8979) is still the nexus for the swing scene in Los Angeles; Royal Crown Revue did legendary early gigs here, and the bar was seen in the movie *Swingers*. Sadly, they are no longer an all-swing club; call for details.

Shopping:

Wacko (4633 Hollywood Blvd. (323) 663-0122), just around the corner from Tiki Ti, is your best bet for finding new (as opposed to vintage) Tiki stuff in L.A. The building also houses the legendary **La Luz de Jesus** art gallery, which has shown work by Shag, Ryden, Coop, and other artists who use Tiki themes. The nearby intersection of **Sunset and Hyperion** is a good place for some vintage shopping. The corner of **Melrose and La Brea** is another starting point for shopping; from there you have a solid mile (at least) of stores ranging from very cool to very lame. Lots of vintage Tiki. South of Los Angeles, in Hermosa Beach, is a pricey little store called **Aloha Cruz** (802 Hermosa Ave. (310) 374-6224), who carry an astounding array of vintage Hawaiiana and surf ephemera, but they are *very* expensive. There are a few vintage clothing stores on the same street.

MINNIE'S RESTAURANT • 107 MCHENRY AVE., MODESTO, CA

(209) 524-4621

**Category III
CHINESE
RESTAURANT**

TiPSY Factor

The Chinese restaurant with a Tiki lounge added to the back room is a grand tradition in the Tiki bar idiom that also includes Chef Shangri La (Chicago area), Omni Hut (Smyrna, TN), Jasmine Tree (Portland, OR), Mai Tai Lounge (Omaha, NE), and many, many others. Opened in 1953, Minnie's fits comfortably into this genre, and while it contains no real surprises, there are still plenty of reasons to head over to Modesto for a look.

Minnie's is easily identified by two big Tikis in front of the restaurant. The seating area is decorated in the usual Oceanic Arts style, with the same war clubs, masks, Tiki poles, and blowfish that we have seen so many times, but which never seems to bore us. Minnie's also has a rather large collection of foxy wahine artwork, both on black velvet (not Leeteg) and painted on framed boards. Throughout the restaurant and the bar, you can find almost a dozen lovely islander gals enhancing the atmosphere.

The food is pretty bland, with nothing about it that we can truly recommend. Conversely, there is nothing we might warn you away from either. The sizzling chicken platter arrives steaming mightily on a cow-shaped skillet, so at least it earns a few points for presentation. The white rice that most people would expect to be included with this dish is an à la carte item.

MINNIE'S RESTAURANT, Modesto, CA

The lounge is decorated with the aforementioned nude wahines, a moderate TiPSY Factor, and tons of weird ephemera behind the bar. The Mai Tai, Zombie, and Rum Runner are reasonably priced (good), made with traditional recipes (good), strong (good), but made with very cheap liquor (bad), and not blended well (bad). The result is a trio of drinks which all could rank extremely high, if the bartender used a better grade of rum and bothered to shake them up. Redeeming their drink menu is the house specialty,

the Jerk. Invented by owner Peter Mah, this drink is a sort of pink daiquiri, made with strawberry sherbet. The bartender pours a healthy dose of 151 rum right into the long and thick straw just before serving it up. Tasty and strong.

MINNIE'S RESTAURANT, Modesto, CA

TiKi LOUNGE • 932 MCHENRY AVE., MODESTO, CA

(209) 577-9969

Category I
CLASSIC TIKI BAR

TiPSY Factor:

The Tiki Lounge is located in a stand-alone building next door to the Tropics Motel in Modesto (one of five Tiki motels designed by Ken Kymes; this one opened in 1962). It consists of a small fenced-in patio area, home to some huge plants, and a long, narrow A-frame building. Walking through the front door, you'll see a large L-shaped booth to the left, which surrounds a fireplace. Beyond that (also on the left) is the bar. On the right is a row of a half dozen booths, covered by a dried grass awning. To the rear are the "powder rooms," accessible through a hallway decorated with a big volcano mural.

The booths are upholstered in dark leather, and at one time they each contained a phone. Apparently, the Tiki Lounge was a favorite mobster hangout in decades past, so in order to discourage the riff raff from making their deals in this particular would-be paradise, the phones were removed from the "offices" in which they were once installed.

The area behind the bar is chock-full of groovy artifacts, including a collection of Tiki mugs, many of which are

TIKI LOUNGE, Modesto, CA

vintage and valuable, and four very nice paintings of exotic wahines frolicking in tropical environments. Plenty of vintage Hawaiian shirts, and a few Oceanic Arts shields and masks (in their eastern Melanesian style) round out the classic collection of clutter. A neon sign featuring a palm tree and the holy word "Tiki" adds a more modern feel to things. Our normal anathema to neon in Tiki bars is temporarily suspended. A collection of custom stickers made for the bar by Randy, an nine-year veteran bartender, decorates every other possible blank space. Ask for copies of his latest design.

Stephanie, another veteran bartender, may soon be a member of your favorite Tiki bartenders club. After sampling her Mai Tai (which is pretty far removed from the classic recipe but a great drink nonetheless), ask for her own creation, the Witches Brew (equal parts Vodka, Midori, Malibu or Parrot Bay, Cranberry juice, and OJ, with a splash of grapefruit).

A favorite one-two punch (a Scorpion and a Zombie) are both made with what seems close to the traditional recipes. The Zombie is red in color, and very strong. The Scorpion does indeed contain quite a sting, and includes a secret ingredient that is retrieved from a back room.

The Tropics Motel next door does not disappoint either. Four Tikis in the 15 foot tall range populate little gardens in the parking lot, and another resides in the office. The pool has a substantial Tiki guy on the safety rules sign, but the gigantor Tiki seen in old promo pictures of the motel is sadly long gone.

TIKI LOUNGE, Modesto, CA

Given the proximity of the motel, the Tiki Lounge, and Minnie's Restaurant to each other, it is very conceivable that one could spend a satisfying evening exploring just a few blocks of McHenry street in Modesto: dinner and a quick drink at Minnie's, and then a drive down the street for drinks galore at Tiki Lounge, and then (no need to drive) a Tiki-themed motel right next door. Not bad. Not Mai Kai. Not Hala Kahiki. But not bad.

TIKI LOUNGE, Modesto, CA

BALi HAi • 2230 SHELTER ISLAND DRiVE, SAN DiEGO, CA

(619) 222-1181

Category II
FINE DINING

TiPSY Factor

The Bali Hai is a good example of 1950's atomic age architecture. In a departure from the traditional A-frame so often seen in Tiki style, the Bali Hai looks more like some sort of UFO transported out of Tomorrowland, crashed into a tropical isle, and covered with dried palm leaves by the natives. In the early 1950s, the Bali Hai was *the* place to go in San Diego: the two-level building sported a floor show, terrific food, classic Mai Tais, and an amazing panoramic view of the bay. No less a legend than Arthur Lyman had a regular gig at the Bali Hai.

Rechristened "Sam Choy's Hawaii at the Bali Hai," the restaurant is still open for business, although it has lost some of its splendor. The floor show is long gone, drinks are no longer served in Tiki mugs, and the TiPSY Factor is rather small – although a glass case full of Hawaiian war clubs is noteworthy. A five-foot tall sculpture of the enigmatic and whimsical headhunter known as Mr. Bali Hai stands watch outside of

BALI HAI, San Diego, CA

the front door, and a Tiki mug created in his image has been widely imitated. The original mug (with the unique lid) is one of the cornerstones of any good Tiki mug collection. Mr. Bali Hai has been given so many coats of paint that he is almost unrecognizable. Also look for an incongruous sculpture of a chef, known as "The Goof" on the very top of the spire that crowns the building's roof.

The drinks are still rather good, as is the food. Although barely a Tiki bar anymore, the Bali Hai is still a fine place to take in a good meal, and the view of the bay can't be beat.

BALI HAI, San Diego, CA

HUMPHREY'S HALF MOON INN • 2241 SHELTER ISLAND DR., SAN DIEGO, CA

Virtually across the street from the Bali Hai is the Half Moon Inn, opened by Stephen Crane. Easily found by looking for its immense A-frame, Humphrey's is another fine example of mid-century architecture right on San Diego's picturesque bay. While the TiPSY Factor is fairly low, Humphrey's does have a Polynesian atmosphere, although the excess and camp value that best exemplifies the Tiki spirit is not really to be found there. Like the Bali Hai, the Half Moon Inn has a great view of the bay. The wait staff is attired in Hawaiian shirts. The food is excellent. Look for some Tikis "borrowed" from the Kona Kai by the pool.

Also on Shelter Island are the Kona Kai (remodeled around 1995), and the Shelter Island Marina Inn. Both were once seriously Tiki; little remains now.

(619) 224-3577

Category II
FINE DINING

TiPSY Factor

ISLANDS RESTAURANT, HANALEI HOTEL (RED LION/BEST WESTERN), 2270 HOTEL CIRCLE NORTH, SAN DIEGO, CA

The Islands opened circa 1966. It is stocked full of artifacts supposedly carved by direct descendants of King Kamehameha. These treasures were originally part of the decor of the Outrigger restaurant in Los Angeles, which had closed down by the time the Hanalei opened. Artifacts from Stephen Crane's Luau also made it to the Hanalei in 1979.

In the past, one could wander through a labyrinthine Polynesian paradise, consisting of a bar, two dining rooms, and a private meeting/banquet room (full of Maori artifacts), all decorated with an outstanding TiPSY Factor. One may speculate as to whether or not putting the Maori artifacts in the meeting room was done with the intent to create the essence of a Maori men's house. The corridors themselves were equally inviting, and the overall effect was such as to make the entire ground floor of the hotel feel like one large, maze-like room.

(619) 297-1101

Category II
FINE DINING

TiPSY Factor

And what a room it was! Imagine rock walls, and low ceilings painted black. Imagine Tikis ranging from a few inches tall all the way up to ceiling-scraping behemoths, aquariums, nautical artifacts, a spiffy rock fountain with Tikis embedded into the concrete, bridges over a running indoor stream, and a lava rock waterfall in the dining room. Most of the areas were divided by waist-high fences supported by carved Tiki posts. Little bridges stretched over the stream snaking its way in, around, and through the various rooms. The tables were made of authentic Monkey Pod. There was a small outrigger hanging from the ceiling along with a fair amount of bamboo framework. They also had a gorgeous vintage Chinese chandelier, which has since been damaged. Not strictly Tiki, but very cool.

Moving through the premises and through a door to the outdoor pool area today, a nearly life-sized Moai stands guard over the kidney-shaped pool. Proceeding into the base of the rear tower of the hotel, one finds a gigantic atrium with dense foliage, a gazebo, another stream full of Koi, and more Tikis hiding in the palms. This rear tower was added circa 1980, at which time a High Priest from Hawaii came by to bless the building.

Unfortunately, when Best Western remodeled the building in 1997, they seemed to have decided that a more conservative image was needed. Their excellent and distinctive vintage "Hanalei" sign, easily visible from the freeway, was replaced with a generic Best Western sign.

ISLANDS RESTAURANT, San Diego, CA

The meeting room still has the Maori-styled artifacts on the walls, and the main dining room was largely untouched during the remodeling. The fountain in the hallway still exists, as well as the rock wall dribbling water into large clam shells in the dining room. However, these rooms comprise less than half of the Islands' original floor plan. The actual bar area was stripped of Tiki, and redecorated in a hideous mauve and floral motif.

With the bar and corridors largely de-Tikified, the overall impact of the Islands Restaurant has diminished considerably. Some remaining artifacts in the redecorated rooms are blandly hung along the white walls at regular intervals as if they were pastel still-lifes purchased wholesale from a hotel decor warehouse. These Sepik, Marquesian, and Hawaiian-inspired artifacts deserve better.

Robbed of all personality, the spirits living in the bar have also given up on the Tropical Drink menu. The new bartenders do not seem to have been adequately trained in the arcane art of making decent drinks. The modern Islands Room Mai Tai is a pinkish-red syrupy, sugary mess.

Slightly better are the Scorpion (served up in a big plastic seashell; the cherry brandy in it gives it a sweet taste with a hint of chocolate) and the Zombie (orange in color, and packing quite a wallop). The Blue Hawaiian (a drink usually consumed for novelty value more so than taste), is almost tolerable at the Islands Room, and this is therefore a step above most Blue Hawaiians. Blue drinks!

In spite of the renovation, the Islands is still San Diego's best Tiki spot, and is well worth a visit.

ISLANDS RESTAURANT, San Diego, CA

TRADER MORT'S LIQUOR STORE • 2904 SHELTER ISLAND DR., SAN DIEGO, CA

(619) 224-3771

Category VI
OTHER

TiPSY Factor

Trader Mort's is right on the corner of the street that will take you into Shelter Island. It is a tiny liquor store on a moderately busy intersection. The little building was definitely designed with a mid-century Polynesian look in mind, and plenty of palm trees and a few big Tikis adorn the outside of the structure. Inside, one can find the usual selection of libations, as well as a small deli area for fresh sandwiches to go. A few Tiki masks decorate the walls inside. Just be careful while taking pictures – you have to stand in the middle of a busy intersection to get the most desirable shots!

MORE THINGS TO DO IN SAN DIEGO

Red Fox Room (2223 El Cajon Blvd. (619) 297-1313), is a swanky 1960's piano bar within a steak house (think martinis, red leather, and people singing along with an ancient piano player). Also make time for **Pacific Shores**, a very hip little vintage bar in the Ocean Beach area, which also home to some antique malls and hipster stores (Tiki abounds). The **Hillcrest** neighborhood is an excellent place to observe some amazing art deco architecture. In Oceanside, look for the **California Surf Museum** (308 N. Pacific), which includes a Tiki that was supposedly stolen back and forth between rival surf gangs in the 1950s.

BAMBOO HUT • 479 BROADWAY (NEAR KEARNEY), SAN FRANCISCO, CA

Adjacent to (and owned by) the Hi-ball Lounge, Bamboo Hut is a newish Tiki bar that sits comfortably among the strip clubs that populate that particular section of Broadway Street in San Francisco. It is an easy walk from Chinatown and the City Lights Bookstore. Note that they are open Wednesday through Saturday only.

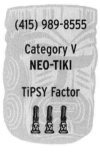

(415) 989-8555

Category V
NEO-TIKI

TiPSY Factor

The room is deep and narrow, with a long bar running the entire length. The side of the room opposite the bar seems to be designed to leave as much open space through the center as possible, giving the potentially cramped room a more spacious feeling. Towards the back is a cluster of three booths with a big blowfish hanging over each of them, and to the left of the front door (as you enter) is a big fountain with a huge Tiki head suspended over it. This monument apparently dates to 1948, lending some vintage authenticity to the Bamboo Hut. There are some smaller Tikis, drums, plants, and other stuff rounding out this door side "Tiki Garden." The bar itself is designed in bamboo 'n' thatch, and in spite of the semi-sparse TiPSY factor, the place succeeds in feeling exotic.

BAMBOO HUT, San Francisco, CA

A collage of bizarre artifacts behind the bar is a must for a good Tiki bar, and Bamboo Hut is well on its way towards accruing the requisite clutter. But, the signed photos of Britney Spears and some random stripper might best be left at home in the owner's bedroom. That said, a collection of Tiki mugs is accumulating on the same shelf, so things are indeed underway.

BAMBOO HUT, San Francisco, CA

The bartenders tend to be a bit inattentive. This might be because they would prefer to be alone with Britney, or perhaps it is because they clearly have no idea how to concoct a good Tropical Drink. Wretched. All of 'em.

For a neo-Tiki bar, the Bamboo Hut seems to be doing a bang-up job on all aspects except for the drinks. We definitely recommend a visit, but stick to beer or traditional cocktails. You might also want to be cautious about visiting on the third Thursday of each month; they advertise "Rockin' Like Dokken – classic metal and rock 'n' roll." Not *exactly* the Arthur Lyman Group, but close.

HAWAII WEST • 729 VALLEJO ST. (NEAR STOCKTON), SAN FRANCISCO, CA

(415) 362-322

Category I
CLASSIC TIKI BAR

TiPSY Factor

Hawaii West is a little beat up, but still worth a visit. Right near Chinatown, Hawaii West is also walking distance from Bamboo Hut.

The front half of the tiny bar is sparsely decorated with beer ads, neon, a TV, a pool table, and some other run-of-the-mill bar junk. However, if you move towards the back, you will find a small Tiki bar. The roof over the bar is thatched, there are a half dozen Tikis in the two-to-four-foot range (including one of those fiberglass United Airlines' Hawaii vacation promos – you know the one!) and even a stone fountain that takes up most of the wall opposite the bar.

The bartender mixes up a serviceable Mai Tai. No one seems to know how long the place has been open, but one gets the impression that it has been at least a few decades – the thatch over the bar is really old looking, and those United Airlines Tikis are hard to get these days.

The jukebox does have a moderate amount of older music – mostly Rat Pack stuff more than any real Hawaiian music or Exotica. Contemporary hits round the box out.

HUKILAU • 1581 WEBSTER ST. (IN THE ISUZU RESTAURANT), SAN FRANCISCO, CA

A bar opened and operated by true locals from Kauai, Big Island, and Oahu, now living in San Francisco. Hukilau has a Tiki club, with private Tiki mugs for paid members. Decor is Hawaiiana.

(415) 440-HUKI

Category V
NEO-TIKI BAR

TiPSY Factor

NR

HUKILAU ISLAND GRILL/ALOHA LOUNGE • 16TH & O, SACRAMENTO, CA

Their ad depicts a hula dancer, surfboards, and a Tiki god, but they have no Tiki statues or mugs. The Zombie is $5.75, Daiquiris, Blue Hawaiian, Rum Runner, and Mai Tai are $4.75 each. The food is similar to what you would get at any diner ($6.95 for the Islander burger).

(916) 444-5850

Category II
CASUAL DINING

TiPSY Factor
0

HULA'S • 622 LIGHTHOUSE AVE, MONTEREY, CA

Lots of vintage stuff. Bamboo and lauhala matting. Hawaiian music and Martin Denny. The food is fantastic, featuring luau-style pork, fish from Hawaii, lots of mangos, papayas, coconut, ginger, and macadamia nuts. Excellent fresh fish crusted in coconut and "island style" ribs. Decor is very good with a few small Tikis, surfboards, thatch and bamboo on all the walls, some great old photos/ads (including a great framed Matson Line reproduction). One caveat: they do not have a liquor license. Beer and wine only. The menu art features pictures of classic Polynesian restaurants: the Luau, the Mai Kai, and others.

(831) 655-4852
(HULA)

Category II
CASUAL DINING

TiPSY Factor

KALEO CAFE • 1340 IRVING (BETWEEN 14TH & 15TH AVE. IN THE SUNSET DISTRICT), SAN FRANCISCO, CA

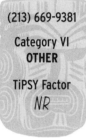

(213) 669-9381

Category VI
OTHER

TiPSY Factor
NR

Opened September 9, 2000. A coffee house with a twist; the owners regularly dance the hula and play Hawaiian music. Their haupia pie with toasted coconut and macadamia nuts is said to be divine.

TEMPLE BAR • 984 UNIVERSITY AVE., BERKELEY, CA

(510) 548-9888

Category II
CASUAL DINING

TiPSY Factor

The backbar was built in 1849, brought to San Francisco before the 1906 earthquake, and has been in its present location since 1990. Temple Bar features a wide array of live Hawaiian music and Pacific Islands cuisine. Drinks (in the $5 range) include Hawaiian Golden Sunrise (passion, orange, guava juices, Jose Cuervo Gold, floated with grenadine), Kanaka Mai Tai (rum, pineapple and orange juices with grenadine), Honolulu Cooler (vodka, 7-up, orange juice and midori), and Blue Hawaii (rum, Blue Curacao, pineapple juice with a splash of cranberry juice). Look for their Luau the first Sunday of each month (beginning at 3:30 P.M.) featuring acts such as the 17-member Royal Hawaiian Ukulele Band.

TRADER VIC'S • 9 ANCHOR DR., EMERYVILLE, CA

(510) 653-3400

Category II
FINE DINING

TiPSY Factor

The original Trader Vic's in San Francisco and Oakland are long gone, so this location (their current flagship store), is as close as you will get to visiting the home of the Mai Tai. Pay that toll, cross the bay bridge, and prepare for an amazing Tiki experience, an amazing dining experience, and the best tropical drinks anywhere.

Pulling into the parking lot, a mandatory (but free) valet drives your car away, leaving you to contemplate a cluster of three large Tiki gods on a little tropical island located in the middle of the circular driveway. These are of a grey colored wood, and done in a traditional Hawaiian style. The entranceway features a big sign with a Victor Bergeron quote, and the first of many, many original works of art that can be found throughout the restaurant.

Inside and to the left is a lounge area and the bar. Straight ahead and down a short hallway are the main dining rooms (and the pair of huge antique Chinese ovens in which all of the food is prepared). Beyond that are the Captain's Cabin and Deck (a private dining room) and an outdoor dockside bar. To the right is the Captain Cook Room, a larger banquet/conference style-room with an incredible mural on the far wall. To the right of the mural is a glass case running the length of the wall with all kinds of paintings, wood carvings, fishing nets, and a giant sea turtle. This room is often closed to the public, but do make an effort to see it.

In the main dining and bar areas, there is also plenty to see, and every turn brings new surprises to the Poly Pop aficionado, to lovers of art, and to junior anthropologists. Look for a big black snaggle-toothed Tiki god in the hallway, a trio of huge anatomically correct "light bulb head" Tikis throughout the restaurant (these are Marquesian), and several Maori artifacts. Oceanic artifacts are everywhere (from New Caledonian masks to Hawaiian temple images to New Guinea shields and wall ornaments), along with glass floats in nets, Orchids of Hawaii lamps, carved wooden fish, a walrus skull, stuffed marlins, and a diving helmet. Exposed beams in the high ceiling allow plenty of space for all the various items which are on display and give the dining room a spacious feel.

TRADER VIC'S, Emeryville, CA

Art fans will appreciate the plethora of original works scattered throughout the building. A gorgeous black velvet painting of a Tahitian wahine hangs on the side of the bar near the hostess area. This can be seen on page 44 of the book *Leeteg of Tahiti*. There is an original Leeteg in the dining room farthest from the front. You will have to work to find it; it is in the left hand corner near a mirrored section of the wall. In addition to the Leeteg, one can view the original art used on vintage Vic's menus, and a dozen other works in various mediums. How many other Tiki bars have so much art on their hands that they can afford to hang an original charcoal of a Tahitian maiden in the men's room? Making things even, look for the awesome Zombie charcoal in the ladies' room. Speaking of this less than exciting part of the establishment, said men's room is wallpapered in real tapa cloth. A sea turtle above the bar is painted with a dedication to "our boys" lost in war, and a list of Hawaiian sounding names.

It can be argued that other Tiki bars also have huge collections of artifacts on display, but the difference is that with the possible exception of the Mai Kai (Ft. Lauderdale), few of them have *authentic* artifacts or original artwork on display; these other places all have (often terrific) fakes. Make sure you take a tour before you start drinking!

Trader Vic's Emeryville is a bit different than most Tiki bars or Polynesian restaurants in that it is nice and bright inside, with plenty of big windows providing magnificent views of the bay on which it is located. One almost expects some Maori to come paddling up in an outrigger to say hello!

TRADER VIC'S, Emeryville, CA

The food is great. Bill Taw (the dining room Captain) and Hoy (a Vic's waiter for *decades*), are extremely attentive and can be counted on to accommodate all of your needs. Hoy left Dai-Tune (a small village near Canton) in 1951 and has been at Vic's ever since. Too cool.

The Norwegian Salmon is really good. Cooked in the aforementioned Chinese ovens, it is moist and delicate and retains its flavor well. It is served with mashed potatoes and asparagus. The grilled seafood platter is very good too. Consisting of salmon, sea bass, and prawns, it is served on spinach with a seafood sauce. The Singapore Noodle is also a favorite; thin noodles with a nice flavor. Ask for chopsticks!

And now the moment you've been waiting for, dear lushes. Drinks ahoy!

The bar itself has about a dozen seats, and there are plenty of tables scattered around the lounge area. A small, quiet, and talented jazz combo began providing evening entertainment in 2002. They do have a television in the bar, but at least the TV is located in a corner where you can't even see it from most of the lounge.

That hurdle overcome, a Mai Tai to end all Mai Tais is the only order possible. Trader Vic's Mai Tai is $8, and worth every sheckle. It comes in a large old-fashioned glass, silk screened with some Trader Vic's artwork. It is prepared with lots of crushed ice, various rums, lime juice, and Trader Vic's Mai Tai mix. The ingredients are shaken and then poured into the glass. It is topped with mint leaves, a swizzle stick skewering a pineapple and cherry, and the leftover lime rind. Due to the plethora of ice, the drink is very, very cold. If that doesn't convince you, let us once again remind you that you will be drinking it, more or less, in the place where the king of all tropical drinks was invented.

But here's the kicker — ask for a "San Francisco" Mai Tai (or a Mai Tai made "the old way"). Vic's excellent and very talented bartenders will conjure up a drink suitable for Makemake himself. Made from Victor Bergeron's original recipe, it contains no prefab mix; it is all fresh and mixed from scratch. Containing Appleton and St. James Rum with a topper of Demerarra, it is one serious drink! Fruity, refreshing complex, and strong – everything a truly awesome cocktail should be!

We would be remiss in failing to mention the rest of the extensive drink menu. This thing has to be seen to be believed. The drinks are pricey, but you'll very rarely see such an exhaustive array of quality tropical drinks. There are also monthly specials, often in souvenir glasses. The Scorpion comes in the traditional bowl-shaped goblet with a real gardenia floating in it. It is tasty and strong. The real flower adds some class. The Zombie comes in a tall, thin glass. Red in color, it is garnished with the standard pineapple/cherry/mint combo. Worth a try. Planter's Punch is a darker red, garnished as above. In the words of artist Rene J. Cigler: "It's a little carnival on your tongue!" Kamaaina comes in a coconut-shaped mug that you can keep. Garnished with a mint leaf, it has a flavor in keeping with its container. The Samoan Fog Cutter comes in a tall, vase-shaped mug with Polynesian village scenes on it. Refreshing. The description of Trader Vic's Grog on the menu claims that it is served in a "Manly Mug." In reality, it is served in a tall and curvy 1980's-looking girlie glass with a black base. An orange drink garnished with a cherry; it is strong and delicious, but not necessarily manly.

Keep in mind that Trader Vic's is more of a restaurant than a night spot, so it closes rather early. Go there now.

TRADER VIC'S • 4269 EL CAMINO REAL, PALO ALTO, CA

(650) 849-9800

Category II
FINE DINING

TiPSY Factor

Opened in 2001, the first new North American Trader Vic's to open in decades has an alarmingly low TiPSY Factor. The food and drinks live up to the high standards exhibited in all of the other worldwide Trader Vic's locations, but we hope that the five upcoming North American Trader Vic's locations will make more of an effort to model themselves on the outstanding Emeryville location.

TONGA ROOM • FAiRMONT HOTEL, 950 MASON STREET (BETWEEN SACRAMENTO AND CALiFORNiA STREETS), SAN FRANCiSCO, CA

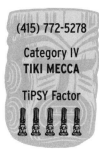

(415) 772-5278

Category IV
TIKI MECCA

TiPSY Factor

The Tonga Room has been through many changes over the years. When the Fairmont Hotel first opened, the room was Norman Hall, a banquet room. In 1929, it became the Terrace Plunge, the recreation area and swimming pool for hotel guests. In 1945, it became the S.S. Tonga, and the entire large room was decorated to look like the deck of a cruise ship, with the pool in the center. When Tiki became the rage, the room was transformed into what remains one of the most amazing of the surviving vintage Tiki bars. Records indicate that Tiki had crept in by the late 1940s, and by the late 1950s it was officially named the Tonga Room and Hurricane Bar. Oceanic Arts updated the room once again with a major revamp in 1967.

When you walk in to the hotel from the steep hike up Mason street, you'll immediately find a little Tiki garden at one end of the hallway, near the elevators that would take you to the hotel lobby. Entering the Tonga Room, one encounters large Tiki statues, a "cliffside" bar, and a dance floor made to look like the deck of a schooner. The actual bar area is towards the front of the establishment, and has a nice rocky motif to it. A huge and dreaded TV in the lounge area serves only to knock a few points from Tonga's final ranking, and is the only object in the room that distracts from the vintage appeal.

TONGA ROOM, San Francisco, CA

The Tonga Room might have taken a few cues from Disney's theme parks when designing their room. The ceiling is very high, and painted black. Strategic lighting on the row of mushroom-shaped Tiki huts enclosing the tables along the right wall, and the single large Tiki hut adding privacy to the seating on the left wall, make one feel as though they are in a small Polynesian Village at night. The effect is very good.

Completing the atmosphere is the much-ballyhooed large square pond (the ex-swimming pool) that dominates the center of the room. There is a small shack on a "floating" platform in the center of the pond, and a simply dreadful band performs there nightly. The platform usually rests near the back of the pool, and when the band begins, it "floats" out to the center on a track. Every half hour, thunder effects replace the music, while strobe lights simulate lightning, and a series of sprinklers around the perimeter of the pool gush forth a rectangle of "rain." This bi-hourly event is unique among remaining Tiki bars, and is the Tonga Room's chief claim to fame. Further aquatic details include giant tridacna shells submerged in the water.

TONGA ROOM, San Francisco, CA

The decor in the Tonga Room is nothing short of amazing, and for that reason alone, it definitely deserves its reputation among the top remaining vintage Tiki bars. But, the quality of the service, the drinks, and the food vary wildly and can often be disappointing.

For an establishment that is part of an elegant classic hotel, you would think that they'd be able to serve some decent food. The Cantonese fare they offer is mediocre, no better than what is served up at any Type III Chinese restaurant at one third the price.

The drinks (at $8-$10) are hit and miss, depending on which bartender is working. The colorfully illustrated drink menu is full of classics (Mai Tai, Blue Hawaii, Temi Temi Ubangi, Tonga Itch, Scorpion, Zombie...), but they are sometimes mangled quite severely. At one point the Hurricane came in a mug that you could keep, but those days have vanished. The Bora Bora Horror is perhaps the most aptly named.

During Happy Hour, Tonga Room offers similar drinks for $4.95. Served in little coconuts, and (only) half filled with some foul and seemingly alcohol-free concoction, they are no bargain. Mr. T says: "I pity the fool who spends ten clams for these drinks during regular hours!"

On the topic of Happy Hour, it lasts from 5:00 to 7:00 P.M., Monday through Friday. They have an appetizer buffet (that was free for many years, but is currently $6) that offers pot stickers, chicken wings, noodles, egg rolls, and the like. After Happy Hour, a $3 entertainment fee (and a one drink minimum) is added to your bill.

This entertainment fee is presumably for the band, who have gone far past "cool" bad, or kitschy bad, and into the realm of just plain awful. The three piece ensemble offers up 1970's light pop tunes, and an inexplicable version of "YMCA" that will make you want to leave the room immediately. What a horrible waste of a unique vintage bamboo covered bandstand in the middle of a lagoon in a classic Tiki bar! How about an Exotica combo of vibraphone, congas, and string bass? A few Les Baxter and Martin Denny classics mixed with some jazz and Hawaiian standards, performed live in this outstanding environment, would almost make the food bearable, and would be something any person of taste would be glad to pay far more than $3 to see.

In spite of these seemingly harsh criticisms, we suggest that you definitely go to Tonga Room! It is with few peers as a surviving retro/Tiki artifact, and is a shining example of the mid-century Tiki vibe. But expect hit-or-miss drinks, to be annoyed by the band, and for god's sake man, don't eat the food!

TONGA ROOM circa 1940s, San Francisco, CA

TRAD'R SAM • 6150 GEARY (NEAR 26TH), SAN FRANCISCO, CA

(415) 221-0773

Category I
CLASSIC TIKI BAR

TiPSY Factor

Trad'r Sam might have been opened in 1939 (or 1937, depending on who you ask). It is a smallish place, mostly dominated by a large, kidney-shaped bamboo bar with plenty of flotsam and clutter above and behind it. There aren't any actual Tikis to speak of, but there are enough accouterments hanging about to make the place feel exotic. For example, you'll notice exactly one token glass float. The photo of a middle aged man behind the bar is *not* Sam. Around the edges of the single room are an array of booths decorated with a collection of beat up vintage bamboo sofas, and chairs with great 1940's floral patterns on the graying cushions. These little seating areas are loosely segregated by bamboo arches, each bearing the name of an exotic island: Tahiti, Hawaii, Samoa, Hilo, Kauai, Guam, and Maui.

The jukebox in the corner spews forth modern rock and pop hits, a selection ranging from Tool to Billy Joel; there is no Martin Denny in sight. A Louis Armstrong disc almost helps, but it is not quite enough.

Trad'r Sam is typically full of kids in their early 20s making out on the sofas. Beer bottles and other debris often litters the floor. You may feel like you're at a frat party rather than a Tiki bar. In past years, Trad'r Sams always had a nice mix of college kids, local alcoholics, hippie types who had wandered over from Haight Street, avant-garde artsy hipsters, neighborhood toughguy gearheads, and a couple of old-timers who first went there while on leave from fighting the Japanese. Reports indicate that around 1996, a local newspaper listed Trad'r Sam's as an "in" place to go. Overnight, Sam's had become jam-packed "with idiots in $1000 black leather jackets drinking Heinekens." It seems that their younger siblings have since taken over.

The Planter's Punch is flat tasting, but moderately strong. It is served up at room temperature in a tall thin glass, barely garnished, and seems to be made of Hawaiian

Punch poured over bottom shelf rum. Neither shaken nor stirred.

The Mai Tai is also strong but harsh. It is orange in color, and served in a tall glass. It is garnished with an orange slice, a cherry, and an umbrella. It is difficult to drink – each sip reminds one more of battery acid than anything else. Red Lectroids, then, might enjoy it. We can't state with certainty that patrons are given the same glassware with successive drinks, but it seems possible. The adventurous might want to try the P-38, which is a giant snifter full of everything the bartender can find behind the bar, including ice cream, several typically incompatible liquors, and something that tastes like industrial strength drain opener. It is definitely more interesting than the previous libations (and is served to parties of four).

In spite of the loud clientele and lack of any sort of relaxing environment, Trad'r Sam is worth at least one visit, if just for its historical significance, and for a glance at the presumably undrinkable drink menu, which consists of about 40 different (identical?) concoctions.

TRAD'R SAM, San Francisco, CA

ALPHiE'S • 5725 HOLLiSTER AVE., GOLETA (15 MiLES NORTH OF SANTA BARBARA), CA

(805) 683-1202

Category II
CASUAL DINING

TiPSY Factor

Outside, notice the intricate Maori-style carved poles. Inside is a vintage Tiki restaurant full of Hawaiian and Tahitian carvings mixed with some African artifacts. There is an outrigger canoe hanging from the ceiling, a stuffed turtle, and some paddles on the wall. The Maori motifs are repeated on the interior. Alphie's serves no alcohol (it is, after all, a breakfast place), and the tasty if incongruous Italian menu items are all given Hawaiian names (Wahine, Kahuna, etc.). Open from 6:00 A.M. to 2:00 P.M.

CHUCK'S OF HAWAii • 3888 STATE STREET, SANTA BARBARA, CA

(805) 687-4417

Category II
FINE DINING

TiPSY Factor

In business since 1967, Chuck's is essentially a steak house with no real Tiki to speak of. The staff wear Hawaiian print shirts, but that's as far as Chuck indulges in homage to his homeland. There is a nice selection of wines, and we are told the steaks are awesome. Chuck has further locations in his homeland.

HARBOR HUT • 1205 EMBARCADERO, MORRO BAY, CA

(805) 772-2255

Category II
CASUAL DINING

TiPSY Factor

The Harbor Hut in Morro Bay was once much more Tikified, but has fallen on dull times. It is just an average quality seafood restaurant, but you can see the former greatness. The building is a mid-century classic design, and there are a few large Tikis outside. Inside, you'll find very restrained nautical decor. The only almost-tropical drink they have is their "special." It is served in a huge glass mug (about 30 oz.) with a plastic monkey hanging off the side. It is much too sweet, but with a fair amount of booze. There is a take-out fish and chips place on the property called The Little Hut.

MORE CALIFORNIA TIKI SITES TO EXPLORE

Aloha Joe's (aka Aloha J's), 27497 Ynez Rd., Temecula, CA (909) 506-9889
A Tiki mug exists that provides evidence that Aloha J's exists.

Bamboo 2 U & Tikis Too (retail store), 1015 S. Coast Hwy., Oceanside, CA 92054 (760) 754-6996
The owner's name is Judy Swain. Pricey, but with a good selection of Hawaiian ephemera. Look for a few large wooden Tikis outside.

Grass Shack (coffee shop), San Clemente, CA
Exit I-5 at El Camino Real, go right and keep an eye out 100 yards or so on the right for the giant carved Tiki in front.

House of Tiki, 1860 Newport Blvd., Costa Mesa, CA, 92627 (949) 642-TIKI
Described as an overpriced surf shop.

Java Lanes Bowling Alley, 3800 East Pacific Coast Highway, Long Beach, CA 90804 (562) 597-5558

Java Lanes Bowling Alley, 2075 Solano Street, Corning, CA 96021 (530) 824-4844

Leilani, 1425 N. Blackstone, Fresno, CA (559) 237-6101

Luau, The, 1663 Fulton, Fresno, CA (559) 237-4722
The incredible googie-Tiki sign is the only reason you'll want to stop at the Luau.

Ports of Call Village, Port of Los Angeles, San Pedro, CA
Part of a "Ports of the World" theme village; it is open but run down.

Punahele Island Grill, 2650 Judah St. at 32nd Avenue (in the Sunset District), San Francisco, CA (415) 759-TARO

Purple Orchid, 221 Richmond Street, El Segundo, CA 90245 (310) 322-5829
A neo-Tiki nightclub, said to contain a reasonable TiPSY Factor ("ten Tikis noted on site"), attractive bartenders, and good drinks, all of which are steadily improving (unlike the music − loud rock).

**Ron Jon Surf Shop (and cafe) in "The Block,"
20 City Blvd. West, Orange, CA (714) 939-9822**
They have a full bar, but the Mai Tai is said to be lacking. A dozen full sized Tikis by Wayne Coombs guard the wetsuits and surfboards.

Salton Tiki, Salton Sea, CA
Salton Sea is about 50 miles south of Palm Springs. It's the largest inland saltwater body of water in California. It is practically deserted, like a beach ghost town.

Tiki Bar, The, 1700 Placentia Ave., Costa Mesa/Newport Beach, CA (714) 548-3533
Once a notorious punk rock club.

Tiki House, 1152 Garnet Ave., Pacific Beach, San Diego, CA (858) 273-9734
A little beer and wine joint owned by Dave and Dale Miller, which recently celebrated it's twentieth anniversary. There is a worthwhile sign outside, and some neat Tiki masks inside. However, those are about the only features that are Tiki. Otherwise it is a typical watering hole, and is small and crowded.

Tiki Lounge, 7910 W Third Street, Los Angeles, CA (323) 651-1213

Tiki Room/Yesterdays, in the Art Colony on 2nd St. (across from the Glasshouse) Pomona, CA
The outside wall is red with a painting of a Tiki.

Tiki's Hawaiian Massage, 1978 California St., Berkeley, CA (510) 848-4767
Not very friendly to Tiki fans.

Tiki Theatre, 5462 Santa Monica Blvd., Hollywood, CA, 90029 (323) 466-4264
Just a few blocks from Tiki Ti, you might spot the Tiki Theatre. Despite the fact that it says "Live Nude Girls" on the marquee, there are no live girls to be had. It is simply (at least at this point) a porno theater. Are there Tikis inside? If you find out, please let us know. None of our affiliates have had the courage to brave the $8.00 admission charge and the belligerent doorman.

Tiki Tom's, 1535 Olympic (near Main), Walnut Creek, CA (925) 932-9202

Opened June 2001, this is a trendy spot with a little bit of classic Tiki appeal, some Hawaiian decor, but a more African feel than anything else. The drink menu is reportedly decent, with Trader Vic's-type recipes. Show up for the Live Hula Shows and South Pacific music groups during dinner on Friday and Saturday evenings. Tiki Tom's also features live jazz on Thursdays, and occasionally on Sundays and/or Wednesdays as well. Caveat: multiple televisions showing sports ruin the atmosphere.

Tonga Hut, 12808 Victory Boulevard, North Hollywood, CA (818) 769-0708

A blue collar dive where trucker types play darts. There's a large Moai inside, along with some plastic jungle foliage.

Victor Bergeron, Mountain View Cemetery, 5000 Piedmont Ave., Oakland, CA

The morbid and/or extremely respectful among you might want to know that Mr. Bergeron can be visited in the main mausoleum, Garden Terrace (lower level near the office), Crypt 357, Tier 3.

CALIFORNIA MOBILE HOMES, APARTMENT BUILDINGS, AND MOTELS

OPEN

Aloha apartments, 15515 Vermont, Los Angeles, CA

Nicely maintained building with few Tikis, but worth a peek. Or just move in!

Aloha Arms apartments, 5400 block of Rosemead Blvd., Pico Rivera, CA

Arne's Royal Hawaiian Motel, 200 West Baker Blvd., Baker, CA 92309 (760) 733-4326

Not much Tiki decor, but a decent example of a 1950's road-side motel nonetheless. You don't have many other choices if you're stranded in Baker....

Eli Kai apartments, 3845 226th St., Los Angeles, CA
Was this complex named after famed Tiki designer Eli
Hedley?

Exotic Isle apartments, Alhambra, CA
Recently remodeled and un-Tikified.

**Islander apartments, Gardena (south bay area),
Los Angeles, CA**
These apartments are in great shape. Several Tikis guard
the premises, and the building is clean and well-tended.
Look for a *horizontal* waterfall that shoots water in from a
slit high up the rock wall into a rock pool. This water then
runs under a bridge and down a second waterfall. The rec
room has a nice bar and a stone barbecue, watched over by
a wooden Tiki.

**Kapu Tiki apartments, 5400 block of Rosemead Blvd.,
Pico Rivera, CA**

**Kona Kai apartments, 22413 Ocean Ave.,
(near Sepulveda Blvd), Los Angeles, CA**
Built in 1965.

Kona Kai mobile home village, San Fernando Valley, CA
The biggest Polynesian trailer park in California.

**Kon Tiki Inn, 1621 Price St., Pismo Beach, CA, 93449
(805) 773-4833**
Also see Trader Nick's (closed). The Kon Tiki Inn is a nice
motel, right on the beach. It is a fairly modern building with
little architectural interest, and no Tiki decor present...any-
more. Records indicate that this has not always been the
case. Sigh....

Polynesian mobile home park, Santa Clarita, CA

**Polynesian Paradise apartments, Bakersfield, CA 93301
(661) 325-7469**
On McDowell road, just east of the Papago mountains in auto-
dealer row you'll find an Enterprise car rental with a huge A-
Framed roof that was once in the heart of a Tiki strip mall.
Behind the Jaguar dealership (south) you'll find the
Polynesian Paradise Apartments. Look for a giant black Moai.

Royal Hawaiian Motel, 1632 S. La Brea, Hollywood (Los Angeles) CA 90019 (213) 937-2049

As of 2000, this classic Tiki motel got a bit of a facelift with some exterior repairs. The one Tiki outside is looking pretty sorry, but Tiki is Tiki.

Samoa apartments, 5400 block of Rosemead Blvd., Pico Rivera, CA

Tahitian mobile home park, 15445 Cobalt Street, San Fernando/Sylmar CA (818) 367-7100

Tahitian Village apartments, San Fernando, CA

Tiki apartments, Arrow Rt., between Mountain and Euclid, off I-10, Upland, CA (253) 564-7707

Tiki Aloha apartments, 3505 Artesia Blvd. (near Yukon), Los Angeles, CA

The façade features two small A-frame arches, woven matting against the walls, and bamboo and rope sheathing on the columns.

Tradewinds Motel, corner of Mission Bay Dr. and Rosewood, San Diego, CA

Seven of their eight Tiki poles have been stolen, so drive by and pay homage to the last Tiki standing....

Tropics Hotels, Palm Springs, Modesto, Indio, and Blythe, CA

All opened by Ken Kymes, who also created forty other non-Tiki hotels in his career (cross reference: Tiki Bar in Modesto, and Caliente Tropics resort). Kymes' wife and son had an interesting career as well: they were professional con-artists, and are now currently incarcerated for murder.

CLOSED

Bali Hai Motel, 7041 Sepulveda Dr., Van Nuys, CA

Kamina Apartments, 13472 Leda St., Garden Grove, CA

This incredible complex, designed by Eli Hedley, featured an A-frame rec room supported by a twelve-foot Tiki totem pillar. It was bulldozed in early 2002.

Kona Kai Apartments (on Rosemead in Los Angeles area), CA

Kona Pali Apartments, in Northridge (Los Angeles area), CA

Outrigger Inn Motor Hotel, 5325 E. Pacific Coast Pkwy., Long Beach CA

Pitcairn Hotel, 11751 Harbor Blvd., Anaheim, CA
Designed by Heathcoate in 1961, demolished in 1998.

Pele Apartments, CA
Town unknown; business card exists.

Polynesian Village Apartments, Pershing Dr., near Manchester, Playa Del Rey, CA
Destroyed in 2001. The carver of the Tikis at the Polynesian Village also did the sister apartments of Kona Pali in Northridge and Kona Kai on Rosemead. It could have been Andres Bumatay. Designed by the kings of the California Coffee Shop, Armet & Davis, in 1962.

Shelter Island Apartments, CA
Once included large a Tiki installation, it is now de-Tikified.

Tropics Hotel, Rosemead, CA, (opened by Ken Kymes).

Waikiki Motel, 631 W. Katella Ave., Anaheim, CA

CALIFORNIA TIKI SITES PERMANENTLY CLOSED

Aloha Burger, Santa Barbara, CA
Had Tikis and puffer fish, and a wall with a painted beach scene. It would rain inside with thunder and lighting every few minutes. Closed around 1992.

Aloha Jhoes, Palm Springs, CA
Opened 1962.

Aloha Luau, 7272 E. Gage Ave., Commerce, CA

Bali Hai, 325 20th St., Oakland, CA

Beach Bum Berts, 605 North Harbor Drive, Redondo Beach, CA

Bora Bora Room, 16240 Ventura Blvd., Encino, CA
Photo evidence shows a fairly large Tiki bar with an extremely high TiPSY Factor. Decorated by Oceanic Arts.

Burma Trader, CA

Chi Chi Bar, Catalina Island
Claim to fame: old Martin Denny hangout.

Chi Chi Starlite Room, Palm Springs, CA

Clifton's Pacific Seas (Clifton's Cafeteria), 618 S. Olive St., Los Angeles, CA

Club Mandalay, 720 Washington St., San Francisco, CA

Club Royal Hawaiian, 960 Bush St., San Francisco, CA

Club Tabu, San Jose, CA
Matchbook shows a great deco-era building radiating a "nuclear" glow.

CLUB MANDALAY, San Francisco, CA

Club Tiki, Roscoe at Desoto, Canoga Park, CA

Coral Reef Lodge, Sacramento, CA
Razed in July, 2002 after being closed and fenced off for many years.

Don the Beachcomber, Corona Del Mar, CA

Don the Beachcomber, 1727 N. McCaden Pl., Hollywood, CA
This was the original location, built in 1933.

Don the Beachcomber, Marina Del Rey, CA

Don the Beachcomber, 1101 N. Palm Canyon Dr., Palm Springs, CA
This was Don's second store; the third was in Chicago.

DON THE BEACHCOMBER, San Diego, CA

Don the Beachcomber, corner of Vacation Rd. and Ingram, San Diego, CA

Don the Beachcomber, Santa Barbara, CA

Don the Beachcomber, San Jose, CA

Driftwood Room, Seventh and Broadway, Los Angeles, CA

Harbor Hut, Embarcadero, Morro Bay, CA

Hawaiian, The, 4645 E. Pacific Coast Hwy., Long Beach, CA

Hawaiian Paradise, 69 First St., San Francisco, CA
"San Francisco's exclusive cocktail lounge with Hawaiian atmosphere."

ISLANDER, Stockton, CA

Hinky Dink's, corner of 45th and San Pablo, Oakland, CA
Victor Bergeron's first venue, which later morphed into the inaugural Trader Vic's location. It's a vacant lot now, with nothing but a couple of palm trees left to mark the spot.

Holo Wai Miniature Golf (Kim's Family Restaurant), 574 S. Glassel, Orange, CA

Hukilau Exotic Polynesian Lounge, Long Beach, CA
"On the second deck of the captain's inn, located on the shore of the beautiful long beach marina." The Lord Menu Co. created an outstanding illustrated menu for the Hukilau in March of 1961, which was available to take home as a souvenir for $1.00. Thank the Lord for great Tiki bar ephemera!

Hula Hut, 9314 E. Whittier Blvd., Pico, CA

Island Cafe, 1031 Orange

Islander, The, 385 N. La Cienega Blvd., Los Angeles, CA
This building was raised several feet from the ground on a pole foundation, and it featured a "tropical rainstorm" in the planted areas along each side of the room every ten minutes or so. Closed circa the early 1970s; owner Tommy Lee (no relation to the Motley Crue drummer) died in September 2002. They had a nice square-ish souvenir Tiki mug. Another Islander was located at 6623 Pacific Ave. in Stockton, CA.

KELBO'S RESTAURANTS
(HOME OF THE HABIT-FORMING SPARERIBS)

KELBO'S, Los Angeles, CA

Java, San Diego, CA

Kai Kai, Whittier, CA
Located near (and decorated by) Oceanic Arts. Also featured a great menu design with a Hula girl looking out to sea while a Tiki slyly watches the wahine. The A-frame building which featured at least a dozen giant Tikis along the perimeter eventually became known as Dorian's.

Kapu Kai bowling alley (and Tahitian Fire Room), 8874 Foothill Blvd., Rancho Cucamonga, CA

Kelbo's Restaurants, (one on Pico Blvd. near Exposition, one on 1st and Fairfax) Los Angeles, CA
The one on Fairfax was good and dark, and it had lots of Tikis, running water, and similar appropriate decorations.

The barbecue was well-known, and the drinks were good. Now a strip club called Fantasy Island.

Kona Inn, 1901 Shelter Island Drive, Shelter Island, San Diego, CA

Kona Kai Bar, Western Blvd., Gardenia, CA
A nice looking sign still remains outside, but the inside has been gutted.

Kona Kai Club, 450 Yacht Harbor, Dr., Shelter Island, San Diego, CA

Kona Kai Motel, 1820 South West St., Anaheim, CA
"Walk to Disneyland," and "1/2 Block from Disneyland."

Kona Kove (in the Stardust Bowling alley), 1035 W. Walnut Creek Pkwy., West Covina, CA

Kona Lanes bowling alley, 2699 Harbor Blvd., Costa Mesa, CA
Slated for demolition in 2003. Run!

Kono Hawaii Restaurant, between Disneyland and the 405 freeway, Anaheim/Santa Ana, CA
Kono Hawaii is still standing, but has been closed and fenced-in for years. Their custom mug was a minimalist Marquesian.

Kon Tiki Restaurant and Motor Inn, Riverside, CA

Lanai, 4070 El Camino Real, San Mateo, CA
The Lanai was a full free-standing bar and restaurant. The inside was totally dark. Décor included fish netting, glass floats with all manner of sea creatures caught in them, many aquariums, high-backed chairs, and a mural

KONA HAWAII, Santa Ana, CA

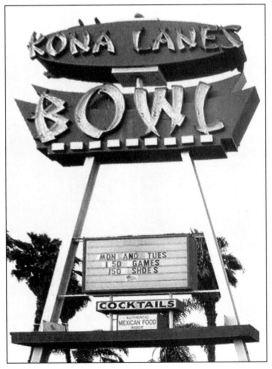

KONA LANES, Costa Mesa, CA

LANAI, San Mateo, CA

(which would change colors every few minutes) depicting a tropical horizon that ran the length of one L-shaped bar. The Sidewinder Fang was served in a giant fishbowl for two. They also had flaming drinks served in a custom souvenir Tiki mug. Their mug was light brown with sloping sides, and a dark Aztec-looking figure in darker brown relief on one side. After they closed in the early 1990s, someone bought up a lot of the Tikis and reopened in a cheezy strip mall. It fizzled after a year or two. The original building site is now a Red Lobster restaurant.

Lanai Liquors, 8 41st Ave., San Mateo, CA
Had one of the Lanai's Tikis out front. This Tiki, carved by Barney West, was sold to a collector in 2002.

Latitude 20, corner of Pacific Coast Highway and Ocean, Torrance CA
Razed in the early 1980s to make way for a mall.

Lei Lani, Californian Hotel, 35 State St., Santa Barbara, CA

LUAU, Beverly Hills, CA

Lilo Lounge corner of 18th and Connecticut, Potrero Hill, San Francisco, CA

Closed July 31, 2001. There was an overwhelming lack of appreciation for anything Tiki; instead, almost everybody in the crowd was bent on using tropical drinks as a catalyst to try to score with girls. The music was ordinarily downtempo/electronica stuff that, though not Exotica, actually worked fairly well.

Luau (formerly The Tropics), 421 N. Rodeo, Beverly Hills, CA

"Polynesian atmosphere and the finest food around. An experience."

LUAU, Beverly Hills, CA

Stephen Crane was a failed B-movie actor who was briefly married to Lana Turner and was later associated with Ava Gardner and Rita Hayworth. His first restaurant, the Luau (opened in 1953 and razed in 1979), was the template for Crane's later Kon Tiki chain. A spectacular full color menu advertised such concoctions as "Tonight or Never" ($1.25: dark rum, Demararra, lime, and honey), and "War Dod" ($2.50: "A lethal potent only for the lusty and fearless warrior").

As the Tropics (owned by Harry "Sugie" Sugerman), one piece of advertising art exists featuring two seductive Tahitian bathing beauties, and another features the legend (printed in and around a bare-breasted wahine) "Fine food, Exotic Drinks are a stand out at The Tropics."

Mai Kai Room (at Mar Vista Bowl), 12125 Venice, Blvd., Mar Vista, CA

Located within the still-standing Mar Vista Bowl, the Mai Kai Room, built by Armet & Davis circa 1961, was decorated in a googie-Tiki hybrid. Closed by the 1970s.

Mauna Loa, 6530 Sunset Blvd., Los Angeles, CA

Outrigger, The, Surf and Sand Hotel, 1515 South Coast Hwy., Laguna Beach, CA

Now "Splashes," a must to avoid!

OUTRIGGER, Monterey, CA

Outrigger, The (Mark Thomas's), Cannery Row, Monterey, CA

Closed in the early 1990s. Much of the decor ended up at the Islands Room in the Hanalei Hotel in San Diego. A unique greenish mug features a Cook Islands-like Tiki face; a pineapple-shaped mug with separate lid is hard to find.

Palms, 1010 E. Orangethorpe, Fullerton, CA

Pago Pago, Long Beach, CA

Polynesian Village

Containing the Tahitian Room, the Hawaiian Room, the Samoan Hut, and the Cannibal Cocktail Lounge.

Pomona Polynesia (apartments), Pomona, CA

Pub Tiki, 1718 Walnut

Reef Lounge, The, 1300 Munras, Long Beach Harbor, Monterey, CA

"Overlooking the Blue Pacific"

Royal Tahitian, Ontario, CA

Located within the city's municipal golf course.

Rudy Solario's Tiki Lounge
A custom mug exists with Rudy's name on the back.

Seven Seas (Bob Brook's 7 Seas), 6904 Hollywood Blvd., Hollywood, CA
Widely acknowledged as being the very first Tiki bar. First establishment to display Leeteg paintings.

Skipper Kent's, 1040 Columbus, San Francisco, CA
Featured a nice Moai mug (made by OMC) with an inscription on the bottom.

South Pacific, 850 S. Baldwin, Arcadia, CA
"Superb Cantonese cuisine. Exotic Polynesian drinks."

Surfside Lounge, Mission and 5th, Carmel by the Sea, CA

Tahitian Hut, 99 South Broadway, San Francisco, CA
"All star Tahitian entertainment," "French Dinners."

Tahitian Room, 3529 Torrance Blvd., Torrance, CA
Part of a small shopping center that also included a liquor store and a florist. Opened as early as the 1960s as the Tapo Room; bulldozed in late 2002.

Tahitian South Seas, 4th and Broadway, Santa Monica, CA
Opened in 1939 by Herman Klabunde. The bar was called the "Play Room," the restaurant was the "Rose Room." Interior walls were painted with South Seas murals and hula girls. A "Rain on the Roof" effect with sound, light, and running water was a memorable feature. Closed in 1947.

Tahitian, The, Ventura Blvd. just east of Laurel Canyon, San Fernando, CA
The Tahitian opened circa the mid-1950s, and it closed in the early to mid-1960s. Dim and windowless, it was the epitome of a classic Polynesian restaurant. Inside was a pond fed by a waterfall, and Tikis, pufferfish lights, colored net float lights, and outriggers hung from the ceiling. The Tahitian was one of the first casualties of the slow demise of Tiki in L.A.

PAGO PAGO, Long Beach, CA

Tahitian Village, 13519 Lakewood Blvd., Downey, CA

Hosting a motel, a 24-hour cafe, a travel agency, four banquet rooms, and Tiki Men's Salon, this 6.3 acre site was built in 1959, closed in 1995, and was razed in July 2000.

Tiburon Tommy's, 41 Main St., Tiburon (Marin County), CA

Closed around 1994, the building still exists, but it is in quite a shambles. Look for the unique double-decker A-frame over the entrance.

Tiki Bob's, Corner of Taylor and Post. St., San Francisco, CA

Opened by former Trader Vic employee Bob Bryant in 1955, and located near the site of the San Francisco Trader Vic's, Tiki Bob's seemed to offer a second rate alternative to Vic's upscale fare. The Tiki Bob character pole (repainted many times) is still in front of the property. The unique Tiki Bob mug (shaped like the pole) trades briskly among mug collectors, and was imitated by a bar in New Orleans, as well as by the producers of an Elvis movie as a give-away to the cast and crew. Tiki Bob's also had a less notorious mug sporting a Maori-like design.

TIKI BOB'S, San Francisco, CA

Tiki Bob's, Capitol Inn, Sacramento, CA
Part of a brief attempt to franchise, Bob Bryant's
Sacramento Tiki Bobs opened in the early 1960s and didn't
last long.

Tiki Bob's Mainland, 333 Bush St., San Francisco, CA
Part of a brief attempt to franchise, Bob Bryant's Tiki Bob's
Mainland offered lingerie fashion shows at lunch time.
Exotica, indeed.

Tiki Hut, 525 Sepulveda Blvd., El Segundo, CA

Tiki Island, 3743 S. Western Ave., Los Angeles, CA

Tiki-Jo, The, Miramar Hotel, Santa Monica, CA

Tiki Kai, (city unknown, matchbook cover exists)

**Tikis, The theme park, 1001 Potrero Grande Dr.,
Monterey Park, CA**
Opened by Danny Balsz in the 1960s, the park closed in the
1980s when the city revoked their entertainment license.
Balsz spent years building a new location in Lake Elsinore,
but it never opened. The property is now a paint-ball park.
The Tikis were sold to a store called The Sea, which closed
in 2000. Souvenir Tiki mugs with a "The Tikis" logo on the
back are fairly common. Their entertainment boasted a cast
of at least 20 performers wearing costumes more elaborate
than anything ever actually seen on Tahiti.

Tiki Town, 1579-A Solano Ave., Berkeley, CA
Was a vintage clothing store specializing in Hawaiiana.

**Tonga Lei Restaurant, 22878 Pacific Coast Hwy.
Malibu, CA. phone (213) 456-6444**
Gone by the 1980s.

**Trader Nick's, next to the Kon Tiki Inn, 1621 Price St.,
Pismo Beach, CA**
Originally had an A-frame entrance, and plenty of Tikis.
Several small remodeling jobs over the years gradually
eroded the TiPSY Factor, and when they finally closed in the
late 1990s, there wasn't much to choose from at their liqui-
dation sale.

TRADER VIC'S, 1965, San Francisco, CA

Trader Ric's, Pismo Beach, CA

Trader Vic's:
Many of the U.S. Trader Vic's locations were built for hotels, who paid Trader Vic's a sum of money to build the restaurants, and a percentage of the gross to manage them. The hotels eventually got tired of paying the fees, and opened their own restaurants. Trader Vic's plans to reopen at least five more locations across the U.S., this time maintaining sole ownership.

Trader Vic's, 200 Cosmo Place, San Francisco, CA
Opened 1951, Closed 1994. Peter Seeley, grandson of Victor Bergeron, announced late in 2002 that a new San Francisco Trader Vic's is planned as one of the new Trader Vic's locations.

Trader Vic's, 6500 San Pablo Ave., Oakland, CA
Hinky Dink's morphed into the initial Trader Vic's literally overnight.

Trade Winds, 1st and Wall, CA
Included The Palm Room lounge.

Tropicana Lanes/Kon Tiki Room Cocktails, 11163 S. Prarie Rd., Inglewood, CA

Tropic Isles (Herman's...), 3329 Washington Ave., Venice, CA
Another of Herman Klabunde's five restaurants.

Tropics, The (see Luau, above)

Tropics Room at the Tropicana Motel, Fresno, CA

Waikiki Club, Santa Catalina Island
"In Avalon – it's the Waikiki!"

Zombie Hut, 5635 Freeport Blvd., Sacramento, CA

Zombie Village, 65th and San Pablo, Oakland, CA
Right across the street from the original Trader Vic's/Hinky Dink's.

TROPICS, Beverly Hills, CA

COLORADO

SURFSIDE 7 • 150 NORTH COLLEGE AVE., FT. COLLINS, CO

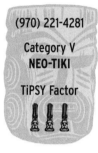

(970) 221-4281

Category V
NEO-TIKI

TiPSY Factor

Surfside 7 should appeal to all fans of everything and anything retro, with the emphasis on Tikis, surf, and Hawaiiana. The owner is also the proprietor of a vintage clothing store in Denver, so he has a pretty good line on top notch vintage items and he certainly uses those connections to their fullest. One wall of his bar sports a row of old surfboards covered with cool old photos; above them are a row of very excellent 1950's skateboards and a bunch of Tiki mugs. The bar itself is bambooified (bamboozled?), and decorated with a half dozen elongated Tiki masks. Along the right wall is a row of booths, each of them sporting an amazingly rare vintage rayon Aloha shirt (under Plexiglas) above it. The vintage drum kit above the door is impressive too.

SURFSIDE 7, Ft. Collins, CO

Great bamboo furniture (with the original tropical-themed upholstery intact), occupies a riser by a front window, along with some retro lamps and tables. Very cozy. The jukebox (vintage, of course) covers a wide array of musical idioms: punk, old soul, rockabilly, Exotica, and some surf. Thumbs up on the juke.

The local version of a Scorpion has a limit of one firmly enforced. But, there's nothing to say that you can't have that one truly powerful concoction before, after, or during a half-dozen other drinks. Try 'em all! They're good, and good for you.

And... how many other Tiki bars have custom painted toilet seats?

Gotta love it.

ALOHA GLORIA'S • 313 NORTH MAIN ST., PUEBLO, CO

Upon hearing that a Tiki bar in Pueblo had been turned into a strip club, all of a sudden the word "Exotica" took on a whole new meaning.

Most of the Tiki action at Aloha Gloria's is outside. There are a couple of medium sized Tiki poles, and a few Oceanic Arts masks carved in a style similar to ones seen on New Ireland. There are virtually no traces of Tiki inside the venue, as all of the walls are now covered with rather grimy mirrors. Part of one wall is still covered in good ol' thatch and bamboo, and a lone Tiki stands in the corner, but if you look in any other direction, all you will see is a run down strip club.

Tropical drinks? Surely, you jest.

One possible tidbit of intrigue: a dark stairwell leading to a basement. There is a chain and a "Do Not Enter" sign across the top of the stairs, and it is so dark at the bottom that one can only see halfway down. But the handrails are bamboo... is it possible that the lower level is an off-limits Poly-Paradise? Maybe it is a party room, or perhaps this is where the old Tikis of yesteryear are stored. Peering down into the depths, one can almost *smell* the Tikis down there.

Alas, one doesn't cause trouble in strip clubs, because the gorillas they hire as bouncers are probably not interested in Tikiphiles' particular brand of urban archaeology, and probably wouldn't listen to anyone trying to tell them that their real motive for sneaking into the basement had nothing to do with the girls dancing on the stage upstairs. For fear of landing in a heap on the sidewalk, we suggest curbing your normally fearless and intrepid snoopiness for the evening.

(719) 545-8468

Category VI
OTHER. VERY
OTHER.

TiPSY Factor

ALOHA GLORIA'S, Pueblo, CO

COLORADO

COLORADO SITES PERMANENTLY CLOSED

Bali Hi Lounge, 432 18th St., Denver, CO
"Tropical Mixed Drinks, Exotic Food."

Don the Beachcomber, Hilton Hotel, Denver, CO
Formerly The Traders. Closed the night before the space shuttle *Challenger* exploded.

Tabu, 7111 E. 5th Ave., above the Velvet Room, Denver, CO
Opened circa 1997. Essentially a dance club with a little bit of almost-Tiki decor, and a Bosko carving by the front door.

Tiki Boom Boom, 1865 N. Academy (at Lasalle), Colorado Springs, CO
This dance club came and went within a year or so in the mid/late-1990s.

Tommy Wongs Island Restaurant, 4851 E. Virginia, Denver, CO
The original closed in the mid-1970s. It was reportedly on the same scale as the Kahiki (Columbus, OH) or the Mai Kai (Ft. Lauderdale, FL). The pool had a waterfall cascading into it, lit with red and orange light (to suggest lava flow), and gas jets on the surface to create flames on the water.

Traders, The, Denver, CO
Interestingly, this particular restaurant which took the name The Traders does not appear to have been a part of the early Trader Vic's sub-chain which used the name The Traders. Even more puzzling is that this Traders seems to have moved to the Hilton to become part of the competing Don the Beachcomber franchise.

Trader Vic's, Cosmopolitan Hotel, Denver, CO
Built 1954, and opened as "The Outriggers." Some early Trader Vic's franchises were opened as "The Traders," and others were opened as "The Outriggers." It seems that all eventually became simply Trader Vic's.

CONNECTiCUT

We have no evidence of any Tiki bars, past or present, in Connecticut.

THINGS TO DO IN CONNECTICUT

Timexpo Museum, 175 Union St., Brass Mill Commons Mall, Waterbury, CT

Check out the life-sized Moai replica in front of this museum dedicated to the history of Timex watches and clocks. The museum's owners were friends of Thor Heyerdahl, so they dedicated a whole floor to the Kon-Tiki expedition. It traces the route of the Kon-Tiki (and Heyerdahl's other voyages). The exhibit includes another (smaller) Moai, and replicas of artifacts discovered on Easter Island. Look for the cool Moai watch in the gift shop.

TIMEXPO MUSEUM, Waterbury, CT

DELAWARE

We have no evidence of any Tiki bars, past or present, in Delaware.

FLORIDA

BAHi HUT LOUNGE • 4675 NORTH TAMiAMi TRAiL, SARASOTA, FL

Opened in 1954, the highly rated Bahi Hut supposedly serves "the most lethal Mai Tai on the map". Their Sneaky Tiki and Mai Tai have used the same secret formulas since they opened in 1954. They are mixed fresh each morning from seven kinds of fruit juices, and what doesn't get used that night gets dumped. The current owner (Tim) worked there as a kid, and took over the business when the original owner retired. The secret drink recipes were passed along as well. Don't miss the giant Tiki fork doorhandles, panels of fiberglass with Tiki prints on them, great kitschy old paintings, and vintage bar napkins from an original massive 1960's batch, replete with an incredible mid-century modern architect's drawing of the Bahi Hut.

(941) 355-5141

Category 1
CLASSIC TIKI BAR

TIPSY Factor

MAi KAi • 3599 NORTH U.S. 1, FORT LAUDERDALE, FL

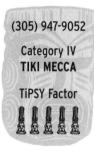

(305) 947-9052

Category IV
TIKI MECCA

TiPSY Factor

Driving down the flat and ugly highway through the scorching Florida sun, past endless strip malls, lunatics with sub woofers in their trunks, and ugly corporate office buildings, the Mai Kai springs out at you like an oasis in this concrete wasteland. Words cannot do it justice; the effect is of a small village on a perfect tropical island. There are multiple small huts, supported on bamboo legs over lush tropical foliage, and waterfalls flowing into ponds and streams. Several huge Tikis watch over the scene, almost as tall as the high-arched roof with the proud Mai Kai sign perched on top.

Pulling into the driveway, you'll see Bora Bora (a private party/meeting room) on the right, and the main restaurant on the left. A valet takes your car away for free. If you want to park yourself, the cost is $2.

MAI KAI, Fort Lauderdale, FL

Mai Kai was designed in the mid-1950s by George Nakashima, whose name should forever be revered by Tikiphiles with no less enthusiasm than Donn Beach and William Westenhaver. Mai Kai opened to the public in 1956. The seven rooms on the main dining area (Samoa, Lanai, Tahiti, Tonga, Hawaii, New Guinea, and Moorea) are each decorated with authentic artifacts from these islands, collected by Mai Kai's founder in the 1940s and 1950s. The usual Oceanic Arts material rounds out the decor, which has just about the highest TiPSY Factor imaginable. To begin to describe all of the ornaments present would be time consuming, but suffice to say, the uniqueness and sheer quantity of the pieces in the Mai Kai collection make it the best anywhere. The authenticity of so many of the works of art just make it that much better.

MAI KAI MYSTERY GIRL, Fort Lauderdale, FL

Our only gripe is that one particular Tiki in the gardens has been all too obviously emasculated to appease the more prudent tourists – we don't suspect you'll see Michelangelo's David spayed any time soon! This is art, people!

The Mai Kai is run like an old supper club, with two shows per night. If you arrive early, you'll wait in the bar area for the next seating. The bar is designed to look like the lower deck of a ship. Gas lamps, rope, nets – all the things you might expect to find on an old galleon. A sprinkler system provides a continual "rainstorm" cascading down the windows, partially obscuring the gardens that in turn block any view of the real world outside.

If the decor is awesome, the girls tending bar are more so. All dressed in bikini tops and matching mini-mini-mini sarongs, these lovelies take your drink orders and deliver them to the mixologists secretly concealed in a back room. There isn't a bottle in sight. After a short wait, the potions appear as if out of nowhere, and are delivered to your table.

Two negatives about the Mai Kai Mai Tai: the color and the price. Red, and ten bucks. For the price of a sawbuck, this had better be one helluva drink, red or not. Served in a medium-sized collins glass, garnished with a mint leaf, a

MAI KAI, Fort Lauderdale, FL

giant pineapple chunk, and a real flower, it is of moderate strength. Definitely a good drink, but we'd need to see at least three bucks lopped off the price before we could truly rave about it. The drinks are categorically arranged as "mild," "medium," or "strong." The "medium" and "mild" drinks are a little cheaper.

The K.O. Cooler, Zombie, Jet Pilot, Shrunken Skull, Yeoman's Grog, and the Barrel O' Rum have all been sampled by our team. All of the drinks are expertly blended and tasty. However, of these, only the Mara Amu comes in an actual Tiki-shaped mug, and this is also the only mug you can keep on the entire extensive drink menu. They do sometimes run out of this mug. The Cobra Kiss, the S.O.S., the Black Magic, and the Kona Coffee Grog also come recommended.

The gift shop looks like the interior of a Balinese Temple. Added in the late-1960s, the decor was apparently scavenged from an unidentified movie set. There is quite a selection of stuff to be found within the shop, but the quantity doesn't mean quality. Retro-Tikiphiles won't find all that much of real interest. Look for a t-shirt with a selection of drinks displayed on it, Aloha shirts, and costumes identical to those of the waitresses in the bar.

The chow menu is exhaustive, and will likely cater to almost any taste. Many exotic favorites are featured, of course. Thai has replaced Cantonese as the exotic food of choice for many Americans, and Mai Kai has updated the menu to reflect this. There are also plenty of old-skool Chinese dishes, and many other selections as well. The entrees are great, and the portions are fairly generous. The PuPu Platter is disappointing; it resembles four different types of brown lumps, all pretty much indistinguishable from one another.

The floor show is outstanding, and executed with style and professionalism. Three female dancers and two men, backed by a six-piece band, perform an array of traditional island dances with grace and accuracy. The nifo'afi is exciting, and the hulas are spellbinding. The Mai Kai performance is a bit slicker, with a better stage and slightly more skilled performers than most. You will be billed $9.95 per person for the show.

MAI KAI, Fort Lauderdale, FL

Walking through the dining rooms after your meal and show, you may wish to proceed to the gardens. On the way, you will pass two large black velvet paintings. Leeteg signed a lot of his work, but these have no signatures. Given the quality of these two pieces, and the authenticity of many of the other objects in the Mai Kai, we would be surprised if they had been the work of anyone but the Master himself.

Beyond these, there is a door that leads outside, and into paradise. A series of paths wind through a tall, dense, and lush garden, filled with trees, plants, flowers, occasional tables, fountains, streams, bridges, and lots of Tikis and other carvings. One can spend quite a bit of time exploring these paths.

If you want a small cozy lounge, the sort of place that immediately springs to mind when listening to your Arthur Lyman records, the reposeful Hala Kahiki is still number one. But if you are looking for a full-blown experience – the custom designed building, the floor show, the food, the whole package – Mai Kai is doubtlessly the best remaining establishment of its kind.

They also offer a Mai Kai club card that costs $10 and saves you 25% off food and drinks as well as 50% off the show price for two people. A good deal.

SWANNY'S TiKi BAR (AT DAY'S INN) • 2201 NORTH FEDERAL HWY., FT. LAUDERDALE, FL

(954) 566-8303

Category 0
DON'T BOTHER!

TiPSY Factor
0

Floridians have quite a different definition of a "Tiki bar" than the rest of the country. As far as they're concerned, any open air bar with a thatched roof near the water is a Tiki bar. There doesn't have to be a Lono or Ku replica within a day's canoe trip for Floridians to slap "Tiki bar" on their signage. It has come to the point where you can walk into a so-called Tiki bar on the south east coast and get looked at funny for questioning a lack of actual Tikis!

In interviewing the staff, the bartenders had no idea what we were talking about when we asked why there were no Tikis in this Tiki bar. When we started talking about "tacky modern reproductions of ancient Polynesian fertility gods," they thought we had flipped. The beer is served in plastic bottles.

The **Tiki Bar** at the Parkside Motel, 4510 N. Ocean Drive (A1A) near Ft. Lauderdale, FL is identical.

BAMBOO LOUNGE • 4849 W. HWY 192 (AT SR 535), KISSIMMEE (ORLANDO), FL

This ramshackle bar was opened by WWII Pacific theatre veteran Bruce Muir (who died in 1999). The TiPSY Factor has diminished over the years, but the general clutter, bamboo trim, and a few extant Barney West-carved Tikis make it your best bet in central Florida. The house drink – the titular Big Bamboo – contains "rum, rum, rum, and stuff."

(407) 396-2777

Category I
CLASSIC TIKI BAR

TiPSY Factor

FLORIDA RESORTS, HOTELS, AND MOTELS

Aku Tiki Inn/Aku Tiki Traders, Best Western Hotel, 225 S. Atlantic Ave. (A1A), Daytona Beach, FL (386) 253-8338

The incredible Moai sign in front of the building has made the Aku Tiki Inn an icon within Tiki Culture for at least 40 years. If nothing else, a drive-by is mandatory.

The tiny front office has a Tiki theme and some really great pieces of carved wooden furniture, but the adjacent Aku Tiki Traders Tiki Bar now hosts country line-dancing. The building's roof line is of Polynesian design and very attractive. Wall panels inside are decorated with Tiki images. Little else seems to remain of what was obviously designed as a Tiki themed and decorated hotel.

Banyan Resort, 323 Whitehead Street, Key West, FL (305) 296-7786

Hawaiian Inn, 2301 South Atlantic Avenue, Daytona Beach, FL (904) 255-5411

The Hawaiian Inn was owned by a man named Cohen in the 1960s. The Inn had a weekly luau, and custom designed Tiki mugs (one actually had a handle, another was a unique mustard-colored Maori design, and the ubiquitous Leilani mug showed up with the words "Hawaiian Inn" added at the bottom). Cohen sold the hotel to a man named Dodd who ran it until he died in 2000. Mr. Dodd didn't care as much for the show and thought running the bar was not worth the trouble; especially because the original Hawaiian show

AKU TIKI INN, Daytona Beach, FL

HAWAIIAN INN, Daytona Beach, FL

group were always staying up late partying and annoying the guests. Teauila's show took over after the first group was fired in the late-'70s. Teauila's show closed in the mid-1990s and returned in 2001 when the hotel was sold by Dodd's son and re-developed.

The Hawaiian Inn is a much larger hotel than the nearby Aku Tiki, newer and more heavily decorated with Tiki/Hawaiian art (primarily by Witco). The hotel boasts a "Tiki Room" for private events. The lobby is fantastic. Very nice murals are painted on several of the walls. There is a small outdoor Tiki bar by the pool and a lounge/restaurant inside that features the Hula show on Friday and Saturday nights. They have recently upgraded the show room with new light fixtures, an improved bar, a smouldering volcano, and more wall decorations. They also have a new drink menu containing many favorites.

Mandalay Motel, 16275 Collins Ave., Miami Beach, FL (305) 947-3427

Outrigger Beach Resort, 6200 Estero Blvd., Fort Myers Beach, FL (800) 749-3131

Outrigger Motel, 215 S. Atlantic Ave., Ormond Beach, FL (386) 672-2770

Polynesian Motel, 3635 South Atlantic Ave., Daytona Beach, FL (904) 767-1593
Barely any Tiki to be found here.

Polynesian Village, Walt Disney World, 1600 Seven Seas Drive, Lake Buena Vista, FL (407) 824-2000
This resort offers 853 guest rooms in eleven "longhouses," named Oahu, Hawaii, Bali Hai, Tahiti, Bora Bora, Moorea, Tonga, Rapa Nui, Samoa, Niue, Rarotonga, and Tokelau. The Great Ceremonial House (the main building of the resort) is certainly decorated with a tropical theme, including a spectacular Maori-style canoe prow by Oceanic Arts. First floor rooms have patios, third floor rooms have balconies, second floor rooms (in most of the buildings) have neither. Rooms begin at $200, and the better ones skyrocket to almost $500.

The resort is home the Kona Cafe, the more upscale 'Ohana (the dining room is crammed with Tikis) and its adjoining lounge, Tambu (which serves cocktails). The clear glass happy/angry Tiki mugs are $10. Drinks are $6.50-$7. Dinner is typically about $22 per plate. Also look for Captain Cook's snack shop (open 24 hours), the Coral Island Cafe (in the Great Ceremonial House), and the Barefoot Bar near the main pool. Like everything at Disney, the atmosphere in all of these places is a bit sterile.

The Luau Cove is where the nightly dinner show is held. For $47.80, you get all the food you care to eat, and a Polynesian revue.

In the actual theme park (reachable via monorail), look for the east coast remix of the legendary Enchanted Tiki Room. Talking Tikis entertain visitors waiting in line, parrots and plants join in song inside. Look for an array of eight-foot-tall slit drums (in a style more or less reminiscent of those found in Vanuatu) outside, plus Tikis in a style evocative of New Guinea or New Caledonian carvings (which are curiously named after Hawaiian gods — Lono, Pele, etc.).

Tahitian Resort (Best Western), 2337 U.S. Hwy 19, Holiday (Tarpon Springs), FL (727) 937-4121
An original Tiki site and still unchanged. Behind it is a Tiki themed condo; a Tiki office building next door is called the "Holiday Tower." A block north is the Tahitian Center strip mall. Behind the Tahitian Resort there is an old Tiki bar, but it is closed. The building is incredible.

MORE FLORIDA TIKI SITES TO EXPLORE

Bert's Bar, 4271 Pine Island Rd NW, Matlacha (Cape Coral), FL (239) 282-3232
Matlacha is a small fishing village (no gas station, no grocery store, four bars, and five bait shops). This bar is 60 years old and has a history to fill a book (part of it was a hotel in the 1940s-1960s, so you can guess the uses the walls have seen). Wrap that with old time barroom fights, a couple of deaths, and add the history of square grouper...

BUSCH GARDENS, Tampa, FL

Busch Gardens, 3000 E. Busch Blvd., Tampa, FL (813) 987-5660

There is a Tiki garden in this theme park, with some very large and very impressive Tikis in authentic Hawaiian and Sepik (New Guinea) styles. Unfortunately, the only Suffering Bastard in the place will be you, since you'll be drinking Bud Lite out of six ounce paper cups after riding the roller coasters.

Garden of Tiki Restaurant, 9770 Atlantic Blvd., Jacksonville, FL (904) 725-3123

Hona Luana Tiki Bar and Grille, 504 Tamiami Trail South (Hwy. 41), Venice FL (941) 483-3553

On the second floor of a building right on the water near a marina. A carver has his studio on-site (downstairs) and makes incredible Tikis from palm trees. It is a fairly light and "beachy" place, but interesting. Great t-shirts with a skull and cross-bones.

Jack Willie's Tiki Bar & Grill, 1011 St. Petersburg Dr., Tampa, FL (813) 854-1972

This may be the quintessential "Florida-style" (Anti-Tiki) Tiki bar. Their press reads: "Jack Willie's Original Tiki Bar & Grill is the Perfect Mix of Baseball & the Beach." This is as good a reason as any to avoid the place. Baseball is mentioned four times in the first paragraph, while Tikis, Polynesia, tropical drinks, and Exotic music are not mentioned anywhere. Get the picture?

Julians, 88 South Atlantic Ave., Ormand Beach (just north of Daytona Beach), FL (904) 677-6767

Massive A-frame Tiki entrance. Opened in 1967 and has not changed a bit since. Live music, strong drinks, and plenty of sea food.

Jungle Gardens, 3701 Bay Shore Rd., Sarasota FL (877) 861-6547

A highlight is an authentic Tiki acquired in 1961 from the south pacific island of Tatakoto. The island is now uninhabited, supposedly due to French nuclear testing in the 1960s. The Tiki carving represents an actual god, Tupaupau (the ghost), a fertility figure. The natives held a ceremony prior to carving the palm trunk. Once the carving was done, they had a feast with dance and chanting to bring the Tiki to life.

Mana Tiki, 1 Ave. A, Ft. Pierce FL (561) 460-4756

Located on the water in a marina. They have docks all around where you can see the fish and wildlife (including manatees?). They have a variety of great food ranging from appetizers to sandwiches to steaks to seafood.

Outrigger Lounge, 1623 West 15th Street, Panama City, FL (850) 769-7374

The bar is now called the Dolphin, but the restaurant is still called the Outrigger, and there are at least two very large Tikis within.

Polynesian Putter, 4999 Gulf Boulevard, Saint Petersburg, FL (727) 360-9678

Mini golf course.

Tiki Bar at Holiday Isle Resorts, mm 84, Key Islamorada, FL (305) 664-2321

This has been the "place to go" in the upper Keys for years. A favorite for spring breakers. Lots of memorabilia to be found. This is the Tiki bar where the Rum Runner was supposedly invented by a man known as "Tiki John."

Tiki Bar, Best Western motel, 614 Northwest Hwy 19, Crystal River, FL (352) 795-3171

Tiki Bar, Fawlty Towers Motel, 100e Cocoa Beach Causeway, Cocoa Beach FL (800) 887-3870

Tiki Island Golf, 1110 SW Ivanhoe Blvd # 23, Orlando, FL (407) 248-8180

The two mini-golf courses on the premises surround a four-story tall volcano that erupts when a hole-in-one is achieved on the last hole. The gift shop carries a selection of modern Tiki stuff. Plenty of Tikis decorate the courses, and one hole is located inside a darkened cave with an eerie Moai in it.

Trade Winds Lounge, 124 Charlotte St. Augustine, FL (904) 829-9336

Waterworks, 1133 Thomasville Rd., Tallahassee, FL (850) 224-1887

JUNGLE GARDENS, Sarasota FL

FLORIDA SITES PERMANENTLY CLOSED

Aloha, Coral Gables, FL
Their striking matchbook design sported a foreboding black mask on one side and an exploding volcano on the other.

Bamboo Gardens, Tampa, FL
Now a cheezy buffet, but some Tiki decor remains.

Beachcomber (Monte Prosser's), Dade Blvd. and West Ave., Miami Beach, FL
A vintage matchbook cover exists featuring a rather sinister looking tuxedo-clad Chinese host saying "Our humble thanks for your honorable visit" on one side, and a relaxing beach bum on the other. "Tropical Food, Exotic Drinks."

Beef 'n' Reef, Cocoa Beach, FL
This restaurant (as of the early 1970s) was said to have two dozen original Leeteg paintings and a dozen seven-foot tall carvings from Mai Tiki.

Castaway Beach Motel, 2075 S. Atlantic Avenue, Daytona Beach, FL

Castaways Motel, Miami Beach, FL

Club Bali, Biscayne Ave., between 7th and 8th streets., Miami Beach, FL
Featured cuisine by Delmonaco, no cover charge, and three shows nightly. The whole block has been demolished to make room for a sports arena.

Hawaiian Inn, 6200 Gulf Blvd., St. Petersburg Beach, FL
The building still stands, but the interior has been renovated.

Hawaiian Isles Inn Resort Motel and Tiki Lounge, 175th/176th Street, Miami Beach, FL
Was open in 1967. Located in the Sunny Isles section of Miami Beach, these side-by-side motels were in the heart of "motel row," 176th Street and Collins Avenue. The buildings are still there, though the motel has been completely remodeled and is no longer Tiki.

CLUB BALI, Miami Beach, FL

Hawaiian Village, 2252 N. Dale Mabry Hwy., Tampa, FL
Now a Days Inn. Their advertising included whimsical lettering saying "Tiki Lounge," and "Hawaii in Tampa," among illustrations of the building. The logo is similar to the Hawaiian Village in Waikiki, lending evidence that this might have been a part of a chain.

Heilman's Beachcomber, Clearwater Beach, FL

Hukilau, 1990 N. Roosevelt Blvd. (U.S. 1), Key West, FL
Closed in 2002. Some decor may remain. Look for the cool Tiki mosaic made out of what looked like colored bamboo tubes, and a Tiki by the main road in front of the restaurant, about 15 feet tall. The Hukilau Hurricane was fantastic. Hukilau really was the only Tiki establishment south of Mai Kai.

Islander Beach Lodge, N. Smyrna, FL
Seven story hotel with spectacular Polynesian-influenced architecture.

Kon Tiki Lounge at Harris' Imperial, ATA on the Ocean, Pompano Beach, FL
"World's Wondrous Dining Palace," became the Imperial Luau at happy hour. At least one of their seven-and-a-half foot tall Ku Tikis is now in the hands of a collector.

Kon-Tiki Oceanfront Camping Resort, St. Augustine Beach, FL
Among other things, this resort sold a swell decal depicting a stoic Moai.

Luau, The, Miami, FL
A big, Polynesian-themed restaurant, with flames, a fountain outside, and a hula show.

Polynesian Gardens, Indian Rocks Beach, FL
(see Tiki Gardens, below)

South Pacific, Miami, FL
Artifacts recovered from the South Pacific include a paddle-shaped swizzle stick.

Tahiti Bar, Miami Beach, FL
Advertising art featured a stern looking drummer and a bare-breasted hula girl.

TIKI GARDENS, Indian Rocks Beach, FL

Tahiti Motel, 16901 Collins Avenue (at 169th Street), Miami Beach, FL

In the Sunny Isles section of Miami Beach. Great motel with coral designs, lighted Tikis on the exterior and colored fountains. Tiki coffee shop. The hotel dates to the 1950s.

Tiki Gardens, 196th Ave. and Golf Blvd., Indian Rocks Beach (north of St. Petersburg), FL

"Tropical Paradise by Day, Polynesian Fantasy by Night."

Polynesian Gardens was originally opened by Frank and Jo Byers in 1955, behind The Signal House, Jo's jewelry store. After a 1963 fire demolished the original gardens and shop, the property was resurrected as the Tiki Gardens, which officially opened on May 9, 1964. This legendary Tiki Mecca expanded over the years into a 12 1/2-acre park, which included a 450-yard Polynesian adventure trail, the Wiki Wiki Lounge (opened May 14th, 1970), 10 gift shops, the 450-

TIKI GARDENS, Indian Rocks Beach, FL

seat Trader Frank's restaurant, Kahiki pier, and coral reef fishing. Animals abounded, including macaws, cockateels, harlequin birds, toucans, squirrel monkeys, and a Kinkajou. The entire park was designed by Jo, who had no architectural training, and relied (with no small measure of success) on what she called "a nesting instinct."

The electrical system was wiped out in a 1985 hurricane, and in 1988 the park was sold to Australian developers. By 1990, the site was beach access and parking lots. Some of the landscape features and canals remain, but all trace of Tiki has vanished. The astounding Tiki Gardens remains in the top echelon of best loved and most lovingly remembered Tiki sites.

Jo passed on in August of 1994, Frank followed in October of 1995.

Tiki Lounge, Hawaiian Village Motel, 2522 Dale Mabry Hwy., Tampa, FL

Trader Frank's, Tiki Gardens, Indian Rocks Beach, FL
(see Tiki Gardens)

Volcano Polynesian Restaurant, Highway 17, Winter Haven, FL
"A million dollar Polynesian showplace with restaurant and lounge only 4 miles from Cypress Gardens. See the erupting volcano with authentic lava rock and 30 foot geysers while sitting down to our quick and tasty $.95 cent lunch or our popular smorgasbord for only $1.75. Entertainment, dancing and shows nightly in our lounges. No admission or cover charge."

Waikiki Oceanfront Resort Motel, Miami Beach, FL
Located in the Sunny Isles section of Miami Beach in "motel row," 188th Street and Collins Avenue. Built in the 1950s. No longer in business as the "Waikiki."

TIKI GARDENS, Indian Rocks Beach, FL

Waikiki Supper Club and Lounge, 2301 S. Atlantic Ave. Daytona Shores, FL

GEORGIA

TRADER ViC'S • ATLANTA HiLTON, 255 COURTLAND STREET NORTHEAST, ATLANTA, GA

Very similar to the Vic's in Chicago. The Suffering Bastard, Honolulu, and Kava Bowl are noteworthy, the latter for the fresh gardenia planted square in the bowl. The kicker is the Zombie: a "lethal libation, a real dirty stinker."

While in Atlanta, visit the Little Five Points area, and look for **Blue Orchid**, a Hawaiiana shop (1129 Euclid Ave. 525-7261).

(404) 659-2000

Category II
FINE DINING

TiPSY Factor

Just down the street from there is the **Junkman's Daughter**, which also carries Tiki stuff (464 Moreland Avenue).

TRADER VIC'S, Atlanta, GA

HAWAII

A note about Tiki and Tiki bars in Hawaii...

Although Hawaii is clearly the birthplace of a majority of the Tiki iconography we have been exposed to in North America, Tiki bars of the sort we are striving to preserve and celebrate have become all but extinct on the Hawaiian islands. Although there are certainly Tikis to be found in abundance, the kitsch factor has diminished to the point of all but disappearing.

It has been theorized that perhaps Tiki bars in Hawaii are kind of redundant. It is like making a big deal out of a Thai restaurant in Thailand. It actually makes more sense to have Tiki bars on the mainland; if you're actually *in*

Hawaii (especially if you're native), there isn't much appeal to hanging out in a Polynesian-themed bar. On the mainland, it is endearing; there it's just annoying. That's the one theory, anyway.

Other theories for the decline in Hawaiian Tiki bars include rampant political-correctness, resentment by fundamentalist natives of their ancestral artifacts being used in a less than serious context, and the inexorable continuous renovations of the portions of Hawaii that tourists flock to. All of that said, there is *some* vintage Polynesian Pop to be found, not to mention plenty of exploration and education about *real* Hawaiian art, sculpture, and history.

LESLIE BROOKS, Hula Girl

HALEKULANi HOTEL (THE HOUSE WiTHOUT A KEY) • 2199 KALiA ROAD, HONOLULU, HI

While not a Tiki bar, frequent visitors to Hawaii seem to agree that the best Mai Tais on the islands (not to mention the best sunset views) are to be found in this elegant upscale hotel. The hula performance is also highly praised.

(808) 923-2311

Category VI
OTHER

TiPSY Factor
NR

KAANAPALi BEACH HOTEL • 2525 KAANAPALi PKWY., LAHAiNA, HI

Look for the huge Lono carving by their stand-alone outdoor Tiki bar. They claim to have the best Mai-Tai in Hawaii.

(808) 661-0011

Category VI
OTHER

TiPSY Factor

LA MARiANA SAiLiNG CLUB • 50 SAND ISLAND ACCESS RD., HONOLULU, OAHU, HI

Opened in 1952 by Annette Nahinu, La Mariana is *the* place to go for authentic Tiki and Hawaiiana on Oahu. When Tahitian Lanai closed, La Mariana rescued their most cherished Tikis and added them to a collection of artifacts culled from Don the Beachcomber's, the Tropics, Trader Vic's, Kon Tiki, and Tiki Hut.

(808) 848-2800

Category I
CLASSIC TIKI BAR

TiPSY Factor

La Mariana's multiple rooms are jam-packed with carefully maintained Tikis of all shape and description, bamboo floor to ceiling, glass floats, aquariums, an eight-foot indoor/outdoor waterfall, and the requisite pufferfish, all set against the lush foliage of Oahu and a view of the Pacific that can't be beat.

Sepik region New Guinea carvings line an outdoor path in front of a patio, while poles fashioned after Hawaiian-

LA MARIANA SAILING CLUB, Honolulu, Oahu, HI

style Tikis mark the entrance, which features beautiful woodworking. Skylights allow views of the exquisite greenery practically covering the buildings, or of the clear Hawaiian night sky.

La Mariana is best visited at night, when the floats are lit up, and the piano player fills the air with old Hawaiian songs. Friday and Saturday nights are usually booked solid, so make reservations early. Said to offer the best Mai Tai in Hawaii.

On the way from the airport into Waikiki, you turn right on "Sand Island Access Road."

MAMA'S FiSH HOUSE • 799 POHO PL., PAiA, MAUi, HI

(808) 579-8488

Category II
CASUAL DINING

TiPSY Factor

Competing with La Mariana on Oahu for the title of best vintage Tiki bar in Hawaii is Mama's Fish House. The drink menu contains not only the full name of each drink, but the location and date each was invented. The venerable Singapore Sling, in fact, goes back to 1900, according to Mama's menu. They might have the bast Mai Tai on the island. Mama's is located in a lush garden full of Tikis; look for Tasani (a local carver), creating Tikis out front.

ROYAL HAWAiiAN MAi TAi BAR • 2259 KALAKAUA AVE, WAiKiKi BEACH, HONOLULU, HI

The outdoor bar is a thatched roof and shellacked bamboo construction. They serve free plates of fresh pineapple. Said to offer the best Mai Tais in Waikiki, and the view is great.

(808) 923-7311

Category V
NEO-TIKI

TiPSY Factor
NR

TAHiTi NUi • RT. 56/KUHiO HWY (END OF THE NORTH SHORE), HANALEi, KAUA'i, HI

Auntie Louise has been running the bar, singing Tahitian tunes, and entertaining drifters for over 40 years at the Tahiti Nui. The drinks are strong and cheap, but the quality is variable. The Mai Tais are said to be the best in Hanalei. The atmosphere is old time Tahiti/Hawaii. The septuagenarian Happy Hawaiians band still play every Friday night. The decor is matting, masks, and fairy lights, with a resin bar set with Tiki motifs. The bar stools are fashioned out of Tiki statues. Look for the great pattern on the bar top, and the funny Tiki logo on their sign.

(808) 826-6277

Category I
CLASSIC TIKI BAR

TiPSY Factor
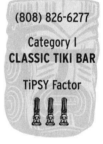

TiKi BAR • JOHNSON ATOLL, HI

Eight hundred miles southwest of Honolulu is a small island, home to only 1200 people. "The Tiki" gets a lot of business, as it is the only real bar on the island. No word on their Mai Tai.

Category I
CLASSIC TIKI BAR

TiPSY Factor
NR

SELECTED OTHER HAWAII DESTINATIONS

Bishop Museum 1525 Bernice St., Honolulu, HI (808) 848-4158

Princess Bernice Pauahi Bishop, the last descendant of King Kamehameha, was the wife of Charles Reed Bishop. He established the museum in 1889 to contain her extensive collection of Hawaiian royal family heirlooms. The museum includes countless artifacts, documents, and photographs about Hawaii and other Pacific islands. Bishop Museum is the biggest museum in Hawaii, and is the primary cultural history institution in the Pacific.

International Marketplace, Honolulu, HI

Martin Denny performed here regularly, and he was photographed here for an LP cover. Urban archaeologists will want to look for remaining traces of Trader Vic's.

Polynesian Cultural Center, 55 Kamehameha Hwy., Laie, HI (808) 293-3333

The Polynesian Cultural Center is a non-profit organization dedicated to preserving Polynesian culture. Opened in 1963, the center re-creates seven Pacific islands – Tonga, Hawaii, Samoa, Fiji, Tahiti, Marquesas, and New Zealand – on a 42-acre facility. Visitors may take narrated boat tours or foot paths through "island villages" (complete with song, dance, architecture, and more).

The PCC also offers the most authentic luau on the island of Oahu. The event is set in the company of a waterfall in a tropical lagoon. Also look for the "Horizons! A Celebration of Polynesian Discovery" show at night, the shopping plaza Treasures of Polynesia, and a bowling alley(!).

HAWAII SITES PERMANENTLY CLOSED

Ale Ale Kai, in the Hawaiian Village Hotel, Waikiki, HI

Decor by Oceanic Arts.

Barefoot Bar, Honolulu, HI

Dagger Bar (at Don the Beachcomber's), International Marketplace, Waikiki, HI (see below)
Martin Denny's most famous gig.

Don the Beachcomber, Waikiki Beachcomber Hotel, Honolulu, HI
On the current site of the International Marketplace.

From 1982 press: "(Excellent) fare, but with exotic accents thrown in, is served in an indoor, straw-lined, and South Seas-oned cave called Don the Beachcomber. The dining room is known for its rakish rum drinks. The food, however, is also interesting, and we heartily enjoyed our curry dish. The air-conditioning can be c-c-c-cold (we thawed our hands over a candle), and somehow we found ourselves whispering because the sound seems to carry (others across the room were creating a racket every time they shook a sugar packet). A newly installed waterfall might break the silence. It's also known for good pies."

Duke's, Honolulu, HI

Henry Kaiser's Dome Theatre, Honolulu, HI
Another place where Martin Denny performed regularly.

Kenoo Farm, HI
Guests could keep their Moai Tiki mug. Odd that a Tiki bar on Hawaii would feature a Moai Mug rather than a Lono or Kukailimoku style!

Kon Tiki Ports (Stephen Crane's), Sheraton Waikiki, Honolulu, HI
Stephen Crane's Kon Tiki chain went through several permutations. The original locations were simply called Kon Tiki, later stores were opened as Kon Tiki Ports, and his final restaurants were created as Ports of Call.

Crane's Honolulu store (one of the last to open) had a custom Tiki mug which was a dark brown Hawaiian-style with a trapezoid-shaped mouth.

Kokee's Lodge, Wiamea Canyon Park, Kawai, HI
Decor by Oceanic Arts included a big Maori-inspired sculpture behind the bar, which also housed a few Leeteg paintings.

Kona Inn, Kailua Island, HI

Kona Kai, Waikiki Sheraton, Honolulu, HI
Vintage press: "Ride up in its 'grass shack' elevator to a dramatic 'outdoors-indoors' layout. We passed up the Lobster Dean Martin, but the sweet-and-sour victuals we sampled were tasty and inexpensive."

Makihana Bar, Kokee Lodge, Kawai, HI

Mauilu Resort, Kihei, Maui, HI

Queen's Surf, Waikiki Beach, Honolulu, HI
"The most beautiful restaurant on the beach." "The best Hawaiian Luaus, $10 per person, Thursdays."

Shell Bar, Hilton Hawaiian Village, Waikiki, HI
Birthplace of Exotica, stomping grounds of Martin Denny, and home to the cast of the TV show *Hawaiian Eye!*

Skipper Kent's, Kona, HI
Featured a "weathered" tan Moai mug (made by OMC).

Tahitian Lanai (Spence Weaver's), in the Waikikian Hotel (see below), Honolulu, HI
A mostly outdoor bar with a huge, triangular, sloped roof, opened in 1939, closed around 1996. The legendary Lanai's Tikis went up for auction to the locals.

From 1982 press: "A very Polynesian theme is carried by the torch-lit old favorite called the Tahitian Lanai, just off the beach in the Waikikian Hotel. Try for a table in one of the little separate thatched huts along the walkway. This place is cosmopolitan with local overtones; the Hawaiian Dinner (about $8) is pretty good for its type, if you want to give it a whirl. The Tahitian Style Chicken, served in a coconut, was more our own speed. Some call the Tahitian Lanai a little corny, but what's sarong with that?"

Trader Vic's, International Market Place, Honolulu, HI
The restaurant is now the maintenance building for the International Marketplace.

Trader Vic's, South King Street, Honolulu, HI
Closed and replaced by above IMP location.

Peter Seeley, grandson of Victor Bergeron, announced late in 2002 that a new Waikiki Trader Vics is planned as one of at least five new North American Trader Vic's locations.

Tropics, Honolulu, HI

Waikikian Hotel, Honolulu, HI
From 1982 press:

"The modest, Polynesian-style Waikikian Hotel huddles between the Ilikai and the Hilton. It has loads of character, although we would never swim in the nearly stillwater Duke Kahanamoku Lagoon which forms its "beach." Free Tuesday Mai Tai party under the banyan tree; acres of palm trees and other tropical foliage; good, fresh-water swimming pool; locally famous Tahitian Lanai Restaurant; fun and camaraderie usually available in the Papeete Bar.

We like the 20-year-old part of the Waikikian, with rooms strung out in the 4 long, 2-story wooden Tiki Gardens buildings. Each unit there either opens onto the greenery on the ground floor, or onto a private lanai overlooking it all from the second deck. The accommodations themselves feature lots of wood, rattan, lauhala mats, overhead fans (not air-conditioning), sliding louvers, and other South Seas accouterments. In general, we don't like the shelters in the newer air-conditioned Tiki Towers building, many of which overlook the parking lot. And in the buildings we do like, there may be occasional complaints about revelers noisily departing the hotel's bar and restaurant. The Waikikian is getting a bit rough around the edges, but many still give it an 'A' for atmosphere. Let's hope they leave very good alone."

IDAHO

We have no evidence of any Tiki bars, past or present, in Idaho.

ILLINOIS

ALOHA MOTEL • 8515 S. CICERO AVE., AT 85TH STREET, CHICAGO, IL

(773) 767-3100

Category VI
OTHER

TiPSY Factor
0

... don't even bother.

HOE CHINA TEA • 4020-4024 W. 55TH ST., CHICAGO, IL

(773) 284-2268

Category III
CHINESE RESTAURANT

TiPSY Factor

Located near Midway Airport, this Mandarin and Cantonese restaurant (which advertises "The Best Chinese Food in Illinois"), has a colorful sign labeled "tropical drinks" in front, decorated with Tiki mugs and hula girls. Inside, one will find a single five-foot tall Hawaiian temple-style Tiki statue. A variety of Tiki mugs and a Tropical drink menu will certainly enhance your chow. Entrees are $7-$10, deluxe dinner for two is $25.95.

PAGO PAGO • THREE LOCATIONS (227 W. JACKSON, 316 S. WABASH, 126 N. WELLS), CHICAGO, IL

(312) 922-6686

Category ex-III
CHINESE RESTAURANT

TiPSY Factor
1 (for the billboard)

All three locations in this mythical chain of Tiki bars located right in the middle of the Chicago Loop still exist as restaurants (some under different names altogether), but they have all been *completely* de-Tikified. One of them has a very small bar area still made of bamboo, but without a Tiki mask or tropical drink in sight. The location at 316 S. Wabash still had some semblance of Tiki decor as recently as 1988, but the drinks are reported to have been poor. The incredible painted billboard remains, forming the last vestige of evidence. This holy relic is located on the north side of a building on Wabash Street, at about 300 South (near Jackson).

PAGO PAGO, Chicago, IL

Imagine walking around downtown Chicago back in the Tiki heyday, and having three Pago Pagos, a Kon Tiki Ports, Shangri-La, Don the Beachcomber, Jimmy Wong's, and Trader Vic's all within a square mile! You'd be hard pressed to go for a stroll without stumbling across (or into) a Tiki bar or four. Alas...

PARADiSE CLUB • 6900 BLOCK OF BELMONT AVE., CHiCAGO, IL

Just a mile or two from Hala Kahiki, Paradise Club is a great place to stop for one last beverage on the way home from HK.

Category I
CLASSIC TIKI BAR

TiPSY Factor

Paradise Club was once a full-on Tiki bar called Gracie Dee's Sneaky Tiki. Before that it was Gene Kamp's. At some point, perhaps the early 1980s, someone made a half-hearted effort to remodel. The result is a unique mixture of 1960's Tiki and 1980's black light day-glo, complete with a framed Pat Nagel poster behind the bar, right next to a Tiki fountain. A huge painted mural of a hula dancer on the side of the building is what may first lure you into Paradise, and one can see another mural painted on the rear wall of the bar's two small rooms.

Other surviving Tikiness includes several aquariums (one of which contains a pirhana), a display case full of shells, and lots of palm leaf and bamboo trim throughout the establishment. Even the light fixtures are early sixties post-atomic. A few Tiki mugs remain, lonely in another (mostly empty) display cabinet, and a few more can be seen behind the bar. A lone Witco piece remains by the front door.

Asking about Polynesian drinks, the typical customer is faced with some skepticism, but will be presented with a menu. This menu is jealously guarded by the (invariably gorgeous) bartenders, because they only possess *one* copy of the custom made tome. Pasted up into a scrap book, with one picture per page, are Polaroid photos of a reasonable array of Polynesian and Caribbean drinks.

PARADISE CLUB, Chicago, IL

Don't order one! They're not exactly up to standard, even if they are served in Tiki mugs. Rather, try one of the several varieties of Polish beer that Club Paradise sells at a very reasonable price. Why the Polish beer? The owners and most of the regulars are from the same Polish community you will occasionally encounter at Hala Kahiki. They are rather protective of their little bar, and it may take some work to gain acceptance into their sanctum. Their beers – Zywiec and Okocim – are excellent, so when in Rome... or Bora Bora... or Krakow...

ROCK-A-TiKi LOUNGE, 1942 W. DiViSiON, CHiCAGO, IL

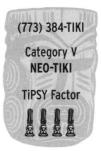

(773) 384-TIKI

Category V
NEO-TIKI

TiPSY Factor

Rock-A-Tiki Lounge was opened in November 2002 by Dion Antic, who also owns a handful of other hipster bars in the Chicago area. This trendy Bucktown spot will impress even the most jaded Tikiphiles, as careful attention has been paid to finer details in an attempt to have Rock-A-Tiki seem as true to the classic Tiki bar mileu as possible. The design staff (DSK Designs) has a firm grip on the classic Tiki concept, and have added quite a few beautiful little touches.

Custom murals (including some wonderfully politically incorrect nude hula wahines), pufferfish (lit from within in three colors), miles of bamboo (occasionally broken up by rock walls), a few dozen vintage table lamps, a salt water aquarium, and several rooms worth of bamboo furniture (scoured from Vintage Deluxe and every other antique store in town) give Rock-A-Tiki an authentic old-school Tiki bar feeling. Of course, several six-foot tall Tikis and a floor-to-ceiling Moai-ish "doorman" make the bar what it is. The carved Tiki poles (by Mai Tiki) that are used as bar stools are a great throwback to some of the best loved mythic Tiki bars of yore. Another row of carved Tiki poles, vintage Oceanic Arts-work in a Marquesian style, support the palm-frond

ROCK-A-TIKI LOUNGE, Chicago, IL

roof of the bar. The surface of the bar is a thick layer of Lucite poured over an array of seashells. The ceiling above the bar is painted with stars, further illuminated by vintage

Orchids of Hawaii lanterns. Requisite black velvet paintings line opposite walls in the front half of the room, which also houses three large booths.

The musical selections are mixed. Although there is some Exotica and surf music on the jukebox, loud rock music prevails on most nights. Given the local clientele – and the very name of the bar – this shouldn't truly come as much of a surprise to anyone. A DJ spins on weekends from a booth fashioned to look like a lifeguard chair, complete with Rock-A-Tiki life preserver.

Of the 50 beverages on the menu, about half are served in Dynasty Tiki Mugs, and are extremely strong. Variations on all of the classic tropical drinks are present, as well as a large selection of new libations. Hell in the Pacific, a Rock-A-Tiki creation, has a complex nutty flavor. The Frozen Bikini is a refreshing fruity daiquiri served on a Dynasty Lono mug. The Polynesian Lemonade comes in a cute, little, mini-Scorpion Bowl.

ROCK-A-TIKI LOUNGE, Chicago, IL

Some of the recipes could use some work, however. The $10 price tag per potion that seems fair at the Mai Kai or Trader Vic's doesn't always seem appropriate for Rock-A-Tiki. It isn't the amount of booze that makes a drink great (and worth an entire sawbuck per), it is the care and preparation that goes into the recipe. Drinks are only worth 10 clams if they are not only strong, but they taste great.

The food, on the other hand is an unqualified success. Almost everyone involved with Rock-A-Tiki recommends the coconut shrimp, and we found the grilled papaya salad to be healthful and delicious. The grilled ahi tuna BLT is a triple-decker, loaded with fresh chunks of succulent tuna and some fla-vorful wasabi mayo. Served with a mango salad, it complements the tropical drinks well.

ROCK-A-TIKI LOUNGE, Chicago, IL

As the only Tiki bar currently in existence on Chicago's north side, Rock-A-Tiki does an excellent job of resurrecting Tiki Culture in a town that once had almost a dozen Tiki bars within the city limits.

TRADER ViC'S • PALMER HOUSE HiLTON, 17 E. MONROE (CORNER OF WABASH), CHiCAGO, IL

(312) 726-7500

Category II
FINE DINING

TiPSY Factor

The Chicago Trader Vic's location (which opened in 1957 as The Traders – "created and supervised by Trader Vic's") lives on in the lower level of the Palmer House Hilton Hotel. The Palmer House is a gorgeous and very ritzy place to drop your bags for the night. As a result, the Trader Vic's is set up (like the Vic's in Beverly Hills), to cater to a pretty upscale and conservative crowd.

The food is outstanding, and the drinks are straight out of the (awe-inspiring) Trader Vic's recipe book. The Mai Tais at the Trader Vic's around the world can vary, since most are franchise operations. The manager at the Chicago restaurant has been with Vic's for nearly 40 years, and stays very close to the family recipe, using Appleton Gold and Dark rums.

TRADER VIC'S, Chicago, IL

After remodeling early in 2002, Vic's began a series of nightly specials. Depending on which night of the week you show up, you can get a Mai Tai, a Zombie, or several other classic drinks for $4 (half off), but the drinks themselves are not the "real versions" you'd get by paying full price. Proceed with caution. Pig out on free PuPus if you get there early on Friday.

Great food and drink are always welcome, but these things alone do not make a Tiki bar great. The theme at Trader Vic's Chicago is mostly American/European nautical. Flags, maps, model ships... Basically, it looks like any other upscale seafood restaurant, although we are impressed that they actually *added* some additional Tikis to the mix during the remodeling effort. This sprucing up unfortunately failed to rid the bar area of the two televisions; they may be variously tuned (sometimes simultaneously) to ESPN or an Elvis movie.

Of course we give Trader Vic's Chicago location respect for being one of the few surviving first generation Tiki bars, and the only one of the eight(!) classic Tiki bars in the Chicago Loop (the central business district) to have survived, and for that reason alone, all urban archaeologists will want to pay it a visit.

YOW BAR • LE PASSAGE NiGHT CLUB, 1 EAST OAK STREET, CHiCAGO, IL

Yow Low bartended at Trader Vic's in Chicago for 44 years. He is now retired, but can occasionally be found at his namesake Yow Bar. Opened in April 2001, the Yow Bar's decor is *not at all* Tiki, but the menu includes many of Low's Tropical Drink recipes, and is decorated with nice Tiki graphics. Aside from this incongruous drink menu, a lonely artifact of cool, the rest of the place is up-up-upscale, complete with dress code, snobby doorman, self-conscious fashionistas, and no, *you* cannot afford to be there.

(312) 255-0022

Category VI
OTHER

TiPSY Factor
0

MORE THINGS TO DO IN CHICAGO AND SURROUNDING AREAS

Barefoot Hawaiian, 1401 E. Oakton St., Des Plaines, IL (847) 699-7336

Barefoot Hawaiian is a group of hula dancers and musicians who perform all over the midwest. They have a retail store full of Aloha shirts, muumuus, and other Hawaiiana. They also participate in the astounding "Fires of Polynesia" show, a full-scale mobile floor show featuring five musicians, nine dancers, and a dozen huge Tikis (one of which talks!).

Novelty Golf and Game Room, 3650 W. Devon (just west of Lincoln Ave.)

Novelty Golf has a nice big Moai in the southwest corner of the course.

POLYNESIAN VILLAGE, Chicago, IL

Polynesian Village, 6845 W. Addison, Chicago, IL (773) 283-5567

This is essentially a banquet hall. There is no Tiki inside whatsoever. There had once been a fair amount of Tiki present, and the room could be divided into two halves, one of which would open up to the public as a Tiki bar on occasion. A drive-by will reward the obsessed with a photo op of the four black Tiki Poles that remain in the parking lot.

The Field Museum of Natural History, 1400 South Lake Shore Dr. (312) 922-9410

The Field Museum has an *extensive* collection of Oceanic artifacts, including a complete Maori meeting house that you can walk inside of. A must.

Nightlife:

Check out **Fizz** (3220 N. Lincoln Ave. just north of Belmont, (773) 348-6000) on Wednesday nights for Sneaky Tiki night. The bartender is really into the vibe, and will make you a drink served in a fresh pineapple or coconut. **Delilah's** (2771 N. Lincoln Ave. (773) 472-2771), is the coolest rocker bar in Chicago; the owner is a Tikiphile of the highest order. It may also be the only bar in the US of A that serves Pisco Capel in the amazing Moai-shaped bottle. **Holiday Club** (1417 N. Milwaukee (773) 486-0686), features an atomic cum Rat Pack décor, a great juke box, and a cool staff. The back room has a semi-tropical atmosphere. Take your Holiday on a weeknight, Yuppie desk-drivers stage their invasion on the weekends. **Club Lucky** (1824 W. Wabansia Avenue (773) 227-2700), is an excellent Italian restaurant just around the corner from Holiday, and is also decorated in an atomic-era motif. **Club Foot** (1824 W. Augusta (773) 489-0379) has cheap beer, no cover, and the most amazing collection of pop culture artifacts you will ever see. **California Clipper** is an amazing 1940's style club with live music and a beautiful Hawaiian room (open on selected nights).

POLYNESIAN VILLAGE, Chicago, IL

Shopping:

Vintage Deluxe (1846 W. Belmont (773) 529-7008) can usu-ally be counted on for some Tiki stuff, and plenty of other mid-century accouterments. Continue west on Belmont until Western Ave. for more vintage shopping (including Vintage Deluxe II and Danger City). **Lincoln Ave.** between Fullerton and Irving Park is another hotbed for vintage and antique shopping. Lots of atomic-era stuff; occasional Tiki. Rockers, goths, and modern primitives will want to walk a few blocks in any direction from the intersection of **Clark and Belmont,** while hipsters of all variety will like the **Wicker Park** intersection of North, Damen, and Milwaukee. Just south of there is Bucktown; look for **Right-On Futon** (1184 North Milwaukee (773) 235-2533). Owner Mark Bello always keeps some Tiki mugs on hand among the futons and lava lamps.

CHEF SHANGRI-LA • 7930 W. 26TH ST., NORTH RIVERSIDE, IL

(708) 442-7080

Category III
**CHINESE
RESTAURANT**

TiPSY Factor

Created by the former chef of Chicago's legendary Shangri-La (see closed locations below), the aptly named Chef Shangri-La was opened in 1976. Also a veteran of the Chicago Don the Beachcomber store and Fort Lauderdale's astounding Mai Kai, the charismatic Paul Fong has many stories to tell.

Chef Shangri-La consists of a main dining area, two smaller dining rooms, and a small lounge. There is a pretty fair TiPSY Factor, including a Koi pond, lots of bamboo, and plenty of Tiki gods, many with colored back lighting shining through carved-out eyes. Look for several larger Tikis (of the "Disney" variety – i.e. painted bright colors) outside. Tons of Orchids of Hawaii lanterns are present too. Note that Chef Shangri-La contains Tikis by all three major classic decorators: Witco, Orchids of Hawaii, and Oceanic Arts. They also have a Eugene Savage painting, the authenticity of which has been hotly debated by such experts as Sven Kirsten and Duke Carter. The Tiki decor is broken up a bit by traditional Asian/Chinese accouterments; the juxtapositions between the two styles is often fun to contemplate. The small but cozy lounge is dominated by a circular bar with a thatched roof.

One can't help but to be impressed with the strength of their Mai Tai. In fact, all of the drinks at Chef Shangri-La are

CHEF SHANGRI-LA, Riverside, IL

rather potent. Dr. Fong comes in the oft-seen happy/sad glass Tiki chalice. Port of Love is a Chef Shangri-La original, and their takes on the classic Scorpion, Zombie, Singapore Sling, and Flaming Virgin (on fire = good) are all faithful to the classic recipes. Most of these libations are a bargain at $4.25.

Polynesian Delight is a favorite menu choice ($8.45), and consists of "shrimps (sic), chicken and pork stir-fried with select vegetables." The South Sea Chicken ($8.25) is essentially sweet and sour deep friend chicken bits with some veggies; we'd pick the Polynesian Delight, given a choice. They also have a very generously portioned Sautéed Tofu with Vegetable ($7.95) for the vegetarians out there.

CHEF SHANGRI-LA, Riverside, IL

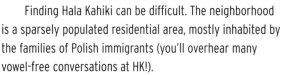

HALA KAHiKi • 2834 RiVER ROAD, RiVER GROVE, IL

Opened in 1966 by Rosa and Stanley Sacharski, Hala Kahiki has maintained every bit of the charm and authentic Tiki bar feel that it has possessed since day one. Hala Kahiki (loosely: "home of the pineapple") is one of the best Type I Tiki bars left in the world. It is not without flaws, but this little slice of paradise sequestered away in an unassuming shack in the suburbs of Chicago is a real treasure.

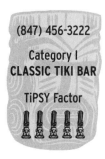

(847) 456-3222

Category I
CLASSIC TIKI BAR

TiPSY Factor

Finding Hala Kahiki can be difficult. The neighborhood is a sparsely populated residential area, mostly inhabited by the families of Polish immigrants (you'll overhear many vowel-free conversations at HK!).

The first thing to point out to people when walking into Hala Kahiki is the pineapple-shaped sign that says "Hala Kahiki Rules." Well, this sign can be taken two ways. Hala Kahiki does, indeed, rule! But the purpose of the remainder of the sign is not to brag, but rather to remind people that there is a dress code enforced, and that beer is not served. That's right, Hala Kahiki serves *only* tropical drinks. Cool! Hala

HALA KAHIKI, River Grove, IL

HALA KAHIKI, River Grove, IL

Kahiki also does not serve any food (except for that classic Polynesian delicacy – pretzels – and fortune cookies).

Hala Kahiki is a place for intimate encounters. Lone barflies are impossible to locate, and if you are trying to meet a new prospective romance, look somewhere else. Every one at Hala Kahiki is already with someone! Speculation that more people have proposed marriage in Hala Kahiki than in any other bar or restaurant in the

HALA KAHIKI, River Grove, IL

Chicago area is not unwarranted. The best time to visit Hala Kahiki is on a weeknight. Lines outside to get in are a phenomenon new to the millennium at Hala Kahiki, but you will have to deal with them on Fridays or Saturdays.

People seldom raise their voices, the music (typically traditional Hawaiian music) is kept at a low level, and there isn't a TV in sight. Occasionally, the Hawaiian music will vanish to be replaced by more contemporary hits; fortunately this doesn't happen often.

The actual bar is in the first room. It is quite long, and is full of appropriate clutter. Across from the bar are four private booths. A waitress clad in a muumuu will ask for your ID and direct you to a table of her choice in one of three main seating rooms. You may also chose to sit in a large enclosed patio area (open seasonally).

The decor of Hala Kahiki is largely beyond reproach and without equal for a place of its size. The low ceiling and dim lights provide a cozy atmosphere. The only windows in the entire building are the ones that look out onto the patio. Hala Kahiki has one of the highest TiPSY Factors imaginable, and not one of the many Tiki objects on display has been defaced with the bright colors seen on "Disney Tikis." There are many, many pieces from Witco at Hala Kahiki; some authorities claim that they have the best surviving Witco collection anywhere. Some of the other classic Tiki bar decor providers (such as Orchids of Hawaii) are represented as well. All of the usual accouterments are present – blowfish, floats, nets, and bamboo for miles. There is a Witco fountain in the third (rear) room, and a larger concrete fountain on the patio.

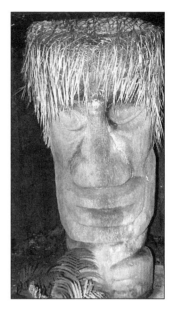

HALA KAHIKI, River Grove, IL

HALA KAHIKI, River Grove, IL

HALA KAHIKI, River Grove, IL

One can spend hours perusing Hala Kahiki and still find interesting details in the decor: the leopard skin trim in the entranceway, the turtle shell lights in the rearmost room, the *Pearl of Wisdom* in the bar area... you'll keep noticing things all night long.

There are 95 drinks on the menu. The drinks are reasonable in price, particularly compared to the brilliant but pricey Trader Vic's menu or the sawbuck-per-drink at Ft. Lauderdale's Mai Kai. Most of the bevvies at Hala Kahiki range from $4 to $6. However, you might want to stick to the few drinks marked "strong" when ordering. This is because Hala Kahiki prefers to keep their potables on the less potent side. The "strong" drinks are, by most Tiki bar aficionado standards, about average in strength.

Unfortunately, the most popular of these drinks are not made fresh, but are poured pre-mixed from plastic jugs. Until recently, many of the drinks were served in Tiki mugs, mostly modern repros of vintage Orchids of Hawaii designs (original OoH Mugs were used in the more distant past). A few drinks are still served this way, but for the most part, you will get your drink in a clear glass with a garnish of fruit skewered with a plastic palm tree. Of the drinks that do come in a Tiki mug, none of the mugs are to keep, but you can buy a decent selection of them in the gift shop (usually $8-$10). At one point Hala Kahiki had a very unique custom souvenir mug (see photo). These are tough to find now.

The gift shop in the back of the building offers a wide range of Hawaiiana. There is plenty to see, including an extensive selection of muumuus and Aloha shirts.

A block down the street is the Tonga Trader, a much smaller bar also owned by the Sacharski family. It is currently closed, and although the exterior has the same "beach shack" architecture as Hala Kahiki, Rose Sacharski says that it never had any Tiki on the inside. In fact, it was more of a shot 'n' beer type place for the local blue collar workers.

MALAHiNi TERRACE • 321-25 W. 75TH ST., WiLLOWBROOK, IL

A weather beaten turquoise awning hidden among dollar stores in an old strip mall is the only indicator that one has reached Malahini Terrace. Although it looks a bit grubby, stick your noggin inside and have a gander.

(630) 325-0520

Category III
**CHINESE
RESTAURANT**

TiPSY Factor

Malahini Terrace sports some etched glass panels dividing the booths, one of which contains both a Tiki and a hula girl. There are the requisite Tiki god poles and masks, a thatched roof, a few passable oil paintings of tropical scenes, the usual array of hanging lamps, and a nice diorama by the door containing a tall Tiki and an assortment of cactus(!). They even have a small rock wall, but there doesn't appear to be a fountain installed.

One Tiki looked like it had been painted in Native American war paint – that and the cactus inspire debate as to whether someone has confused Polynesia with New Mexico.

The drinks (at $4.95) are worth noting (of course!). All are served in modern repro Fu Manchu mugs; the Fog Cutter, Mai Tai, and Scorpion are reasonably strong. Garnished with a paper umbrella, a chunk of pineapple, and a cherry, all three drinks are pretty much the same thing, but not worthy of complaint – worse drinks for more money are easy to find.

MALAHINI TERRACE, Willowbrook, IL

For $11.95 per person, the Island Dinner gets you soup, cho-cho, a big egg roll, fried shrimp, ice cream, tea, a fortune cookie, and a generous entree. The portions are large, so come hungry.

TONG'S TiKi HUT • 130 ARMY TRAiL RD., GLENDALE HEiGHTS, IL

(630) 893-4666

Category III
**CHINESE
RESTAURANT**

TiPSY Factor

Tong's Tiki Hut, 100 E. Roosevelt Rd. (1 mile west of RT. 83), Villa Park, IL (630) 834-7464

Tong's Polynesian Village, 1239 E Ogden, Naperville, IL (630) 357-7120

Considering Tong's location in a part of the Chicago suburbs where interest in Tiki — or in any sort of middle-20th century culture for that matter — is pretty near zero, one should be amazed that the Tong Dynasty has survived and thrived as long as it has.

Tong's Tiki Hut in Villa Park is the quintessential Type III Tiki bar, a Chinese restaurant that happens to have Tikis mingling with red dragons and golden Buddhas. The food is more than passable, and the drinks are on the good side of adequate. The owners are enthusiastic and friendly. The decor consists of a great leopard-skin covered bar, a fountain with a large Tiki in it, a big photographic mural of a Hawaiian beach scene, and a few fierce looking Tiki masks.

An additional room is full of bamboo and more Tiki artifacts, and contains one single big table. Sitting there is like

TONG'S TIKI HUT, Glendale Heights, IL

TONG'S TIKI HUT, Glendale Heights, IL

being in the knights of the round table... except that it is a square table, made of bamboo, and you'll all be wearing Aloha shirts rather than armor. So, in actuality, it isn't like Camelot at all. Never mind. The service is great.

Have a look at the accompanying photos, and tell us that a night at Tong's wouldn't be better than a poke in the eye with a bamboo spear.

Tong's Polynesian Village used to have hula dancers. They were replaced a few years ago by a big screen TV. The interior is also very Tiki, but a bit run down.

We'll leave the third remaining Tong's (on Army Trail Road) a mystery for you urban archaeologists on a mission. Get there quick: as of December 2002, it is for sale.

Finally, we have **Tong's Garden,** which was on Route 20 just west of downtown Marengo (between Belvadere and Marengo). This fourth location in the Tong Dynasty of Chicago's western suburbs is shrouded in mystery. Mr. Tong closed this spot in the mid-1990s, but the bridge over the river Koi remains, as do Tikis and hula girls in the windows. In the 1960s, the place was said to have been busy enough to warrant two bartenders at all times. The actual bar is in the hands of a collector.

AKU-TiKi ROOM • ANDRiS' WANEE FARM, 2314 HWY 34, KEWANEE, IL

(309) 852-2481

Category II
CASUAL DINING

TiPSY Factor

Located among 80 acres of farmland land on route 78/34 (about 15 miles south of I-80 and a bit south of Kewanee) is a large restaurant built in 1932 by the name of Andris' Wanee Farm. Tikiphiles cruising through the farmlands of Illinois would doubtlessly drive right by it without a second glance. Those of you in the know will want to stop in, however, for the 700-seat restaurant has a little secret, invisible from the road: the 160-seat Aku-Tiki Room. Owned by Glen Andris and managed by his charming wife Carol, the Aku-Tiki Room was added to Wanee Farm in 1967, and expanded in 1984.

AKU-TIKI ROOM, Kewanee, IL

AKU-TIKI ROOM, Kewanee, IL

Divided into a restaurant and a bar (both completely separate from main restaurant on the other side of the building), the establishment is decorated with Orchids of Hawaii lanterns, a dozen Witco pieces, fishing float lamps, and a bunch of airbrushed murals depicting tropical scenes. Black lava rock covers the walls in the bar area, and the table tops are decorated with unique tapa-patterned formica. Some Tiki poles on the railings in the bar area are beautifully carved, and are of a sort we've never seen before. Also original among Tiki bars is the Aku-Tiki's pair of Hula-Teddy Bears in an alcove near the restrooms.

Bartender Tom mixes up a serviceable Bacardi and Meyers Mai Tai in a *vintage* Otagiri "Aztec" mug. Excellent!

Field collecting, we remind you, is uncool – leave those vintage mugs where they are!

Food is of the "rural comfort" variety, meaning lots of beef and fried chicken. The closest thing we saw to a traditional Polynesian dish was the Polynesian pork chops – another Aku Tiki Room original. The owners take pride in their cooking however, and grow many of their own ingredients, including the apples and veggies from the farm. Apparently the buffet on the other side of the building (the larger non-Tiki side) is quite famous locally.

Three types of bread show up on the table, and the Aku-Tiki also has a longer wine list than one would expect. The broiled catfish comes with tail and fins intact, and is a good sized piece of fish. The sautéed mushrooms are a tasty appetizer, and the mashed potatoes are apparently smooshed fresh on the premises. The salad bar ingredients are a little lacking, with not enough veggies and too much emphasis on cheese chunks and Jello. But the apple salad is amazing, and made on site, of course.

The Aku-Tiki Room is comfortable, clean, and well-maintained. Their dinner show is gone, but the management is looking into adding hula performances. Given its location, it is a miracle that it has survived for 35 years. Carol Andris is as friendly as they come, and loves to meet people who are into Tiki. If you're driving down I-80, make the detour and check out the Aku-Tiki Room! Waunee Farm Restaurant is open Wednesday through Saturday, but the Aku-Tiki Room is open Fridays and Saturdays only.

AKU-TIKI ROOM, Kewanee, IL

AKU-TIKI ROOM, Kewanee, IL

AKU-TIKI ROOM, Kewanee, IL

TiKi TRUCK STOP/TiKi MOTEL • RTS 80 AND 51ST (I-80, NEAR EXIT 75), LA SALLE, IL

(815) 224-1109

Category 0
DON'T BOTHER!

TiPSY Factor
0

Don't get too excited by the impressive sign here. The Tiki Truck Stop has no Tikiness about it whatsoever; not a stick o' bamboo anywhere on the premises. There is a $19.95 per night trucker's flophouse motel, a small restaurant, and a gas station, but you won't even locate a tropical plant here, let alone a tropical drink.

THE CHICAGO SUBURBAN TIKI GLAMOUR CONSPIRACY

House of Tiki, 8209 N. 2nd St. Machesney Park, IL (815) 633-0355

This is a hair salon. Tiki decor has been removed, save for a stone sign outside.

Mr Singletary's Tiki Beauty, 26 Chicago Ave., Oak Park, IL (708) 386-9563

Aside from the palm tree logo on the door, you won't find anything exotic here. In fact, you may get shot if you poke around the neighborhood too much.

Neenee's Tiki Hut, 6170 Grand Ave # 893, Gurnee, IL (847) 855-9160

This is a beauty salon with no Tiki. Neenee is not related to Mr. Singletary, by the way.

TIKI TRUCK STOP, La Salle, IL

MORE ILLINOIS TIKI SITES TO EXPLORE

Aloha, 3025 N. Kandy Lane Decatur, IL (217) 875-5540

Black Pearl, 28 W. Golf Road, Schaumburg, IL (847) 843-1555

There is a very small bar that is almost Tiki. One glass float, one bamboo lamp, and the bar has a grass skirt lining. There is a Tiki mask hanging on the wall right before you walk into the bar.

ILLINOIS SITES PERMANENTLY CLOSED

Ciral's House of Tiki , Chicago, IL

"The Tiki" joined the Tiki Bar Death Race 2000 when Ted Ciral closed its doors for good on September 30, 2000.

Unlike the sadly missed Kahiki (Columbus, OH) which closed a few weeks earlier, Ciral's shut down with virtually no hype, no press, and no warning. The following night, throngs of Tikiphiles and local regulars held a vigil on the doorstep, lighting candles, and leaving notes, drawings, and photos for Ted, his wife Bea, and the Tiki gods themselves. The Chicago *Reader* ran a brief article on House of Tiki the following week.

CIRAL'S HOUSE OF TIKI , Chicago, IL

Mr. Ciral and his wife had run House of Tiki for nearly 40 years. They offered the business to their sons; none of them wanted to take it over.

It is true that Ciral's House of Tiki was far from the highest rated Tiki bar, but as authentic vintage Tiki bars continue to become extinct at a rapid pace, any and all losses are tragic ones.

The dingy single room was divided into bar and seating areas. Bar food (burgers, wings, etc.) was served at the tables. The menu was colorful and amazing. Tropical drinks were available, though most of the dozen drinks on the menu consisted of room temperature Hawaiian Punch poured over ridiculously large quantities of cheap rum in a flute glass. A few ice cubes may or may not have cooled the concoction off sometime before they melted.

Their amazing neon sign still hangs in front of the building; rumor has it that a steak house will be there soon. Look for House of Tiki in the Gene Hackman movie *The Package*.

Diamondhead, Southwest Highway, Chicago, IL
Just south of 79th Street on Chicago's south side was

KONA KAI, Des Plaines, IL

Diamondhead, a Hawaiian/Asian restaurant and lounge. Tropical drinks were served in Tiki mugs by a staff of Asian waitresses. Diamondhead closed sometime in the 1980s, and became Beyond the Reef, which maintained the Tiki format until it closed around 1996.

Don the Beachcomber, 101 East Walton Pl., Chicago, IL
This was Don's third franchise (built in 1940 on Chicago's touristy Magnificent Mile). The first was in Los Angeles, and the second was in Palm Springs. The Tikis were created by Ely Hedley. Now fashion shops.

Honolulu Harry's Waikiki, Wilson at Outer Drive, Chicago, IL

Jimmy Wong's, 426 S. Wabash, Chicago, IL
Souvenir mug was in a quasi-Marquesian style. Site is now a parking lot.

Kola Terrace, on Dundee road, Northbrook, IL

Kona Kai, O'Hare Mariott Hotel, 6155 North River Road, Des Plaines, IL
The Kona Kai closed to the public during the last week of December 1998. The Mariott has removed the three huge Tiki poles from the garden in the parking lot (all three have made it into the hands of collectors), but the rest of the Kona Kai remains intact. It is available as a rental hall for private events.

The Kona Kai is a pretty large place. When open to the public, they served a complete menu of food in a vast dining room complete with rattan thrones and floral carpeting. Many of the Kona Kai Tikis are of the "Disney" sort (painted with white or bright colored highlights), but there are plenty of traditional ones too (giving the Kona Kai a more than adequate TiPSY Factor). Against one wall is a mammoth stone waterfall, trickling water into a little stream that runs right through the center of the restaurant. The little bridge over the stream leads to some of a half-dozen cozy little "cabins" where your private party can sit; these hold about 20 people.

In the center of the Kona Kai are dual octagonal gazebos, which served as the stage for the floor show (by Barefoot Hawaiian) every Friday and Saturday night. Just behind the gazebo is a small band-

KONA KAI, Des Plaines, IL

stand. The show started off with two girls doing traditional Hawaiian hulas. A fella joined them after a few numbers and a couple of costume changes. Eventually, some audience participation came into play. After that, the show built to a rousing finale as the band mutated into an all-percussion ensemble while the male dancer busted out the flames and heated things up with the nifo'afi.

Tiki Puk Puk might have been the most popular drink on the menu; it also happened to be the most expensive. It was pink, tasty, and seemed to have had about 20 shots of rum in it. Their Suffering Bastard and Kiss of the Tiki god were favorites too. At one point the Kona Kai offered a custom Otagiri mug to keep. It featured a Maori-like design in relief on a sloped mug.

One can only hope that the Mariott will realize that they closed the Kona Kai just as Tiki was mounting a major come-back; with everything but the outside statues still intact, it is always possible that we will see a resurrection.

Kon Tiki Ports (Stephen Crane's), Hotel Continental, 505 N. Michigan, Chicago, IL

The original incarnations of Stephen Crane's Kon Tiki chain were simply called Kon Tiki. Later locations were opened as Kon Tiki Ports, and his final restaurants were created under the name Ports of Call. Chicago's Kon Tiki sign is now on display in the front room of the Barefoot Hawaiian store in Des Plaines, IL.

Shanghai Lil's, 5400 block of Milwaukee Ave., Chicago, IL

SHANGRI-LA, Chicago, IL

This huge Polynesian paradise is said to have been so dark inside that you couldn't see your food. It featured a full Polynesian revue; some of the band members are now part of the Barefoot Hawaiian group. Fondly remembered by native Samoans in Chicago, who say that Shanghai Lil's was *always* packed to capacity. Closed about 1981, razed no later than 1990, the property is now new-construction condos.

Shangri-La, 222 N. State, Chicago, IL

Artifacts recovered from this legendary Chicago spot include a swizzle stick with a detailed wahine atop it. This entire block is now home to a single modern glass-n-steel office building. The chief chef moved to the suburbs and opened Chef Shangri-La (still open) around 1976.

Tropical Hut, Stoney Island and 91st, Chicago, IL

This barbecue joint was said to be outstanding. Decor included palm plants and a Tiki theme.

INDIANA

INDIANA TIKI SITES TO EXPLORE

Tiki Bob's, 231 South Meridian St., Indianapolis, IN (317) 974-0954

IOWA

BRUCEMORE • 2160 LINDEN DR. SE, CEDAR RAPIDS, IA

Brucemore is a nineteenth century mansion, built by the Sinclair family in Cedar Rapids, Iowa. It was later maintained by the Douglas family. Two theme rooms, located in the basement of the mansion, were created in 1937 by Howard Hall – who married into the Douglas family – to entertain his business associates. These are The Tahitian Room and the Pacific Northwest-themed Grizzly Bar.

(319) 362-7375

Category VI
OTHER

TiPSY Factor

The Tahitian Room is decorated with a painted map of Tahiti and Moorea on the floor (which still looks brand-new after 65 years), plus Deco-era hula girl sculptures, dioramas of exotic themes within small alcoves cut into the walls, perfectly maintained bamboo furniture, and hand painted maps and murals. A slanted tin roof hangs below the "real" ceiling, onto which "rain" falls from a sprinkler system hung above it. The water trickles down the sloping tin roof, falls along the side walls of the room, and is then recirculated.

Of course, Mr. Hall is no longer entertaining guests, so no food or drink is being served, but the Tahitian Room is an interesting spot to scope out. It will definitely appeal to all Tikiphiles, if for no other reason than because it might be the first – and is certainly the oldest surviving – home Tiki bar!

BRUCEMORE, Cedar Rapids, IA

Of course, to see the Tahitian Room, you'll have to take the entire tour of Brucemore (which occurs daily – except Mondays – every hour starting at noon). The mansion is definitely worth a look; there are some fascinating things to see including a huge vintage pipe organ and a mural depicting Wagner's *Ring Cycle*. Brucemore also hosts a blues festival every summer.

MORE IOWA TIKI SITES TO EXPLORE

Seven Seas Lounge, 1312 Commanche Blvd. (Rt.30/Rt.67), Davenport, IA (563) 242-7209
There is a tavern and a pizza restaurant in this quintessential 1960's building, but we couldn't confirm Tikiness inside.

KANSAS
KANSAS TIKI SITES TO EXPLORE

Aloha Kai, 7329 Quivira Rd., Shawnee, KS (913) 962-8828

KENTUCKY
KENTUCKY TIKI SITES TO EXPLORE

Joe's Palm Room, 1821 West Jefferson St., Louisville, KY (502) 581-1251

Polynesian Palace, 2239 West Oak Street, Louisville, KY (502) 778-7391

LOUISIANA

LOUISIANA TIKI SITES TO EXPLORE

Kon Tiki Restaurant & Lounge, 5815 Youree Drive (at Southfield plaza), Shreveport, LA (318) 869-2316
The sinister Moai on their advertising is another of many clear appropriations of Kahiki's (Columbus, OH) iconic fireplace.

Mai Tai Restaurant 5796 Crowder Blvd., New Orleans, LA (504) 246-9998
Chinese restaurant with no Tiki.

LOUISIANA SITES PERMANENTLY CLOSED

Bali Hai at the Beach, New Orleans, LA
This bar had an interesting souvenir Tiki mug in that it was a knock-off of the distinctive Tiki Bob mug from San Francisco.

Huki Lau, Metairie, LA
Souvenir mug was a green quasi-Moai reminiscent of both PMP designs, and certain Dynasty mugs.

Tiki Club, Thibodaux, LA
Advertising graphics show a sleepy-looking Moai.

MAINE
MAINE TIKI SITES TO EXPLORE

Polynesian Village, 152 Main St., Westbrook, ME
(207) 854-9188

MARYLAND

TIKI BAR • ISLAND MANOR HOTEL, 77 CHARLES STREET, SOLOMONS ISLAND, MD

The Tiki bar in Solomons Island is not a huge tropical paradise, and probably falls pretty firmly into the category of "Florida Tiki Bars." However, it has a certain charm that suggests a higher rating than its Sunshine State contemporaries down south.

(410) 326-4075

Category I
CLASSIC TIKI BAR

TiPSY Factor

Solomons Island is actually a small boating town on the peninsula in southern Maryland, on the west side of the bay. The Tiki bar is part of the Island Manor Hotel in Solomons Island, right on Route 2. It is easy to miss the dwelling altogether, because The Tiki bar dominates the entire front of the property. Driving by, all you see is the open and friendly looking Tiki bar, just a few feet from the road. Pull into a space, walk up, and you're ready for a Mai Tai (the house specialty).

The Tiki bar is smallish, with only about 20 seats, plus a half dozen tables off to the side. It is open to the air on three sides, so a fresh breeze from the water and warm sunshine are allowed to enhance the atmosphere. The view of boats on the bay as you sip your Orange Blossom (not bad; tastes like alcoholic Tang) is pleasing.

The TiPSY Factor is rather low; there are only a half dozen Tikis in evidence. Additionally, the drinks are not made fresh. Rather, they are poured out of big plastic jugs into plastic cups. They only have about six different recipes, and the rum used in them is very cheap. Although the Mai Tai is potable, avoid the Blue Hawaiian at all costs; it looks and tastes like window cleaner. In fact, the bartender may try to talk you out of ordering it! Speaking of the bartenders, they are extremely friendly, and will happily recommend a nearby place to eat, providing both casual and more elegant dining options, both within walking distance.

Aside from the name, a few token Tikis, and some obligatory pre-mixed sub-tropical drinks, you'd be hard pressed to call this place a true Tiki bar. However, all the bare-bones criteria are filled, even if some of the oh-so-enchanting details are missing. Okay, *all* of the oh-so-enchanting details are missing, like blowfish and Arthur Lyman, and Tiki mugs and hula shows and stuff. But that's okay. This place is fun.

TiKi STEAK AND SUB • BALTiMORE, MD

Category 0
DON'T BOTHER!

TiPSY Factor
0

One doesn't head out to a place with a name like Tiki Steak and Sub prepared to discover the next Hala Kahiki. At the very worst, however, it might be a sandwich shop with some Tikis nailed up on the walls.

If only it were that...

Put shortly, Tiki Steak and Sub is in a condemned building in a condemned neighborhood.

Don't go there.

VERA'S WHiTE SANDS RESTAURANT • LUSBY (NEAR SOLOMON'S ISLAND), MD

(410) 586-1182

Category II
CASUAL DINING

TiPSY Factor

On the way to Solomon's Island, you will pass Calvert County's greatest contribution to the Tiki lifestyle. The venerable Vera Freeman – whose entrance is always announced with the ringing of a gong – presides over her bar in a muumuu, a seashell necklace (from Rapa Nui), rings on every finger, a hibiscus in her hair, and a champagne cocktail in hand. Look for the giant Tikis and Moai scattered around the grounds, along with Vera's prized banana trees (brought from Florida in 1965).

Inside, Vera's waterfront bar is filled with room after room of authentic Polynesian kitsch. The leopard skin bar is home to live piano music, and artifacts collected during Vera's extensive travels with her late husband, Dr. Freeman. Vera's was captured on film for the Calvert County episode of the BBC's popular *Mystery!* program.

Chef Mary Gross, a 40-year veteran of Vera's, provides guests with a mixture of Polynesian favorites and New England seafood dishes. Tiki fans will want to try the ruma-ki ($5.95) or a Javanese satés ($5.95). For salads, go for the outrigger ($5.95) or shrimp Oahu ($6.95). The barbecue pork with Chinese spices ($18.95) makes a good entree, and the tropical trifle ($4.95) is a great dessert for those not already in a sugar coma from the tropical drinks. Vera's offers all of the classic Tiki drinks plus a few of Vera's own creations.

Located on the Patuxent river in the town of White Sands, Vera's is about 10 miles north of Solomon's Island. It is only open during the summer (remaining open for week-end dining through mid-September). Take Solomon's Island Rd. to Solomon's Island, and just before Calvert Cliffs you will pass a small sign stating "Vera's White Sands" with an arrow pointing to the right.

MORE MARYLAND TIKI SITES TO EXPLORE

Aloha Inn, 608 Quince Orchard Plaza, Gaithersburg, MD (near DC) (301) 840-9434
Formerly Tiki, now just a Chinese food joint.

Duffy's Love Shack, Worcester St., Ocean City, MD
They serve all the classic Polynesian drinks in Orchids' mugs. Volcanoes too!

Magothy Seafood Restaurant & Tiki Bar, 700 Mill Creek Rd., Arnold, MD (410) 647-5793

Surfside 7, 48 South River Rd., Edgewater, MD (410) 956-8075
No affiliation with the Surfside 7 in Colorado; this bar appears to be of the "Florida Style."

MARYLAND SITES PERMANENTLY CLOSED

Hawaiian Room, Emerson Hotel, Baltimore, MD

Their reputation for serving minors might have contributed to their closing. The floor show featured the expected hulas and nifo'afi. Drinks came in coconut, skull, Moai, and "Aztec" mugs. The hotel has been demolished.

Luau Hut, Silver Spring, MD

Offered a unique square-ish, souvenir Tiki mug.

MASSACHUSETTS

ALOHA • ROUTE 53, HiNGHAM (SOUTH OF BOSTON OFF OF RT. 3), MA

(781) 749-6957

Category II
CASUAL DINING

TiPSY Factor

Open since the early 1970s. The food is good, the bar is sunken and moody (though the TVs kind of ruin it), and the music is often Hawaiian guitar. Tiki masks, PuPu platters, and Dr. Fong mugs abound.

BALi HAi • 93 MOULTON DR., LYNFiELD/SAUGUSS, MA

(781) 593-8600

Category II
CASUAL DINING

TiPSY Factor

Bali Hai was updated somewhat in the '70s, although you can find many remnants of its past, beginning with the classic A-frame entranceway. Tribal drums decorate the lobby, along with some crazy bamboo and seashells. The restaurant has large windows, along which are red vinyl booths and a variety of aquariums. The wallpaper is a hoot; backlit scenes of Hawaiians gathered for a hukilau. The mugs and dinnerware are worth checking out; the dinner plates are imprinted with a sunburst pattern along the edge, and include the Bali Hai name and outrigger canoes sailing to a volcanic island.

Drinks are served in Moai-shaped mugs, emblazoned with raised Polynesian scenes and the Bali Hai logo, or you can get drinks in coconuts and pineapples. There is a huge cocktail menu entitled "Exotic Potions," and the potions offered therein are pretty "potent!" They offer the usual Sufferin' Bastard, Fog Cutter, and Dr. Funk. For the wonderfully ridiculous amount of alcohol they put in these things, the drinks are very reasonably priced, running from $3.00 to $4.75.

The food includes typical Chinese/American fare, as well as Shrimp Pago-Pago, the Bali Hai Volcano, Chicken Kailualu, the PuPu Platter, and the Happy Talk Platter. The dinner menu itself is great: created around 1973, it depicts islanders along a shore serving up a suckling pig. You can buy a souvenir menu for $3.00.

There is entertainment at the restaurant's "Happy Talk" lounge on Friday and Saturday, although the lounge has been renovated into a dark sports bar.

BALI HAI, Lynfield/Sauguss, MA

HUKE LAU • 705 MEMORIAL DRIVE, CHICOPEE, MA

Featuring a working volcano, the inside is like the islands at night. Huke Lau also has a Polynesian show. Drinks are still served in a square-ish, Aztec-looking Tiki mug, although the mold currently in use has lost all detail.

(413) 593-5222

Category II
CASUAL DINING

TiPSY Factor

TiKi PALACE • 1177 WASHiNGTON ST. (RTE. 37), BRAiNTREE, MA

(781) 380-3808

Category III
**CHINESE
RESTAURANT**

TiPSY Factor

Tiki Palace makes a strong Mai Tai ($5) prepared with fresh lime, shaken and poured over ice. It is a very good yellowish/brownish in color, with a sweet taste. Tiki Palace has an impressive collection of spirits. Their glasses are decorated with an image of hula girls and a Hawaiian sunset.

As a Tiki bar, however, Tiki Palace leaves a bit to be desired. A brown atmosphere prevails, with cafeteria style tables and chairs. Various Tiki masks can be seen on the walls, but a Japanese mural seems very out of place.

KOWLOON • 948 BROADWAY (ROUTE 1), SAUGUS, MA

(781) 233-0077

Category III
**CHINESE
RESTAURANT**

TiPSY Factor

Kowloon Restaurant, with a capacity of 1,200 seats (4th largest in the U.S.), was established by the Wong Family in 1950. Located on Route 1, among the legendary strip of googie weirdness north of Boston, Kowloon's Tiki paradise fits in well with its neighbors.

Kowloon was expanded in the early 1960s, and partially remodeled in the 1980s. The present-day building looks like a huge pagoda, with a 15-foot replica of the Hawaiian temple image Kukailimoku towering over the front door. The inside decor (by Oceanic Arts) contains several rooms: the Tiki Lagoon is just that, a lagoon surrounded by booths, with a large Tiki watching over it. Palm trees line the booths, which are built to look like Tiki huts. The Luau Room has a stage and hosts entertainment. Tiki masks adorn the bamboo walls every eight feet or so. Off to the left is Volcano Bay, a room comprised entirely of half of a real schooner. A moving volcano mural on the

KOWLOON, Saugus, MA

KOWLOON, Saugus, MA

wall is surrounded by very realistic palm trees. The Thai Grille is a more modern addition.

The tropical drink menu is quite extensive. The Fog Cutter comes in an Orchids of Hawaii Moai mug, the Pi Yi in a well-detailed pineapple cup. They use Island Oasis brand Daiquiri mix, and Bacardi in their rum drinks. The Mai Tai, Scorpion, and Planters Punch are all served in the Orchids of Hawaii Ku R-74 style mug. At one point, Kowloon had a custom mug to keep, which vaguely resembled a Marquesian Tiki. Another design made for the Kowloon (and bearing their logo) was a hula girl mug, which appears to be a knock-off of the one previously seen at the Luau Hut. These are long gone, however.

The chow is good too, try Volcano Lychee Duck ("Sweet and Sour roast duck sautéed in fresh lychees"), or Flaming Ambrosia ("fried chicken in a pungent sauce with fruit served in a flaming shell of fresh pineapple").

Route 1, beginning about 10 miles north of Boston, is a treasure trove for urban archaeologists, kitsch lovers, and mid-century enthusiasts. Look for a huge T-Rex in a mini golf course, plenty of 1950's motels with elaborate neon signs, the Leaning Tower of Pizza, The Ship (a restaurant in a schooner), The Hilltop Restaurant (with its 70-foot tall neon cactus – the biggest neon sign *anywhere*), The Golden Banana (a strip club!), and an exact replica of Beijing's Weylu's Imperial Palace. Twelve miles of tacky bliss.

LUAU HALE • 569 PiTTSFiELD RD., LENOX, MA

(413) 443-4745

Category II
CASUAL DINING

TiPSY Factor

The atmosphere is slightly dark with murals of Polynesian island shores and mountains and, of course, Tikis covering every wall. There is a little stage in one corner; they may have had Polynesian dance shows in the past.

MORE MASSACHUSETTS TIKI SITES TO EXPLORE

**Aku Aku, 11 E. Central St., Worcester, MA
(508) 792-1124**

**Aku Aku, 81 Nardell Rd., Newton Center, MA
(617) 491-8646**

**Hawaiian Village, 689 Cochituate Rd., Framingham, MA
(508) 872-0344**

**Hawaii Garden, 300 Plymouth St. (intersection Rt. 58
and Rt. 106), Halifax MA (781) 283-5779**

Kahula, Rt. 131, Sturbridge, MA (508) 347-7121
Opened October 25, 1977. No Tiki. Tropical drinks. Chinese food.

Kailua, 964 Saratoga St., Boston, MA (617) 567-1162
Opened around 1979, moved in 1987. No Tiki. Tropical drinks. Chinese food.

**Kailua, 153 E. Washington St., North Attleboro, MA
(508) 699-4467**
Opened around 1982. No Tiki. Tropical drinks. Chinese food.

**Ming Jade Polynesian Restaurant, MA 113, West
Newbury, Newburyport, MA (978) 462-8941**
Exit 57 from I-80.

**Orchid of Hawaii, 201 Bedford St., Lakeville, MA
(508) 946-0088**
Chinese food, no Tiki, no tropical drinks.

Pago Pago, 396 E. Main St., Milford, MA (508) 478-0710
Opened with Tiki galore in 1972, Tiki decor has since been removed. Still serves Polynesian food, and tropical drinks in Tiki mugs.

Royal Hawaiian, 34 Cambridge St., Burlington, MA
(781) 273-0220

South Pacific, 1152 Beacon St., Newton, MA
(617) 332-7250
Open for at least 50 years, still serving Cantonese food and tropical drinks.

Tahiti Restaurant, Three locations: 22 Dwight St., Dedham, MA (617) 329-2575; 22 Jade Lane, Dedham, MA (617) 329-0145; 101-103 Wahconah St., Pittsfield, MA (413) 499-4711.

Tiki Hawaii, 331 Cotuit Rd., Sandwich, MA
(508) 888-3543

Tiki Kye, 2 Montello St., Carver, MA (508) 866-7733
Chinese food, tropical drinks.

Tiki Palace, 1177 Washington St. (Rt. 37), Braintree, MA
(781) 380-3808

Tiki Port, 712 Route 132, Hyannis, MA (508) 771-5220
No Tiki. Tropical drinks. Chinese food.

Wind Tiki, 154 Thompson Rd., Webster, MA
(508) 943-6996
Opened 1974. No Tiki. Tropical drinks.
Chinese/Polynesian/American food.

MASSACHUSETTS SITES PERMANENTLY CLOSED

Aku Aku, 149 Alewife Brook Pkwy, Cambridge, MA
Closed in late April, 2000

Life-sized Moai greeted the visitor to Aku Aku. Inside, a great TiPSY Factor awaited, with huge Tikis, plenty of masks, Orchids of Hawaii lamps, and murals reminiscent of Les Baxter album covers. This is now Jasper's Summer Shack, who supposedly have allowed a few Tikis to remain, in spite of painting the Moai outside to look like fishermen(!).

Honolulu Restaurant, 160 Turnpike Rd. (Rt. 9), Westboro MA

Honolulu Restaurant, Rt. 1, Norwood, MA
Honolulu had a great custom Tiki mug with their distinctive logo on it, and an amazing color menu with the same characteristic design. This logo seems to be a stylized Tiki with a pineapple atop its head, and strange horns or antlers branching out from the sides, making it look like some sort of water buffalo.

Hula Hula, 864 Main St., Waltham, MA

Islander (Bob Lee's), Boston, MA

Kona Islander Restaurant, 108 Washington St., Foxboro, MA

Kon Tiki Ports, Sheraton Boston Hotel, 39 Dalton St., Boston, MA
The Chicago, Cleveland, and Boston locations (and possibly others) had a nice souvenir mug reminiscent of the classic PMP design.

Lanai Island, 455 Totten Pond Rd., Waltham, MA

Ocean Kai, 300 Lincoln St., Hingham, MA

Sing's Polynesian, 41 Washington St., Bangor, MA

South Seas Restaurant and Lounge, 21 Harrison Ave., Boston, MA

Tiki Garden, 201 N. Quincy St., Abington, MA

Tiki House, 569 Moody St., Waltham, MA

Tiki-In, 165 Massachusetts Ave., Arlington, MA

Tiki Island, 269 Middlesex Ave., Medford, MA

Tiki Luau Restaurant, 355 Littleton Rd., Westford, MA

Trader Vic's, Statler Hilton, Park Square, Boston, MA

Waikiki House, 682 Bedford St., Whitman, MA

MICHIGAN

CHiN'S • 28205 PLYMOUTH RD., LiVONiA, MI

Not to be confused with the notorious Chin's in Detroit (closed for decades but still intact), this Chin's (opened in 1955) is somewhat less spectacular, but still worth a visit. Look for stone Tikis outside, wooden ones inside, and the usual Orchids of Hawaii-supplied lamps, blowfish, and rattan. The sub-tropical drinks are present, but are made too sweet with syrupy mix and cheap booze. As expected, the chow includes Cantonese-Szechwan and American dishes with few surprises. Chin's is certainly Tiki, but it is also yet another "Type III" being indifferently run by a family who seem bored of the restaurant business after 47 years.

(734) 525-CHIN

Category III
**CHINESE
RESTAURANT**

TiPSY Factor

CHIN'S, Livonia, MI

MORE MICHIGAN TIKI SITES TO EXPLORE

Hut, The 15 South Saginaw St., Pontiac, MI
Don't let their Tikified advertising fool you, this lame dance club is about as un-Tiki as things get.

Island Outpost, 806 South Huron Ave. ("in the Straits area"), Mackinaw City, MI (231) 436-8757
The outside of the building is painted coral.

Jimmy Lums Aloha Lounge, 429 S. Dort Hwy., Flint, MI (810) 233-7081

Tiki Lounge, 212 E. Ludington Ave. (inside Stearns Motor Inn), Ludington, MI (231) 843-3407

Press reads: "Wednesday is teen nite (during the summer), college nite on Thursday (18+), and Friday and Saturday nights (21+) have 25 cent drafts from 9:00 to 10:00 pm, and domestic longnecks for $1 all night, all year. There are 4 video screens and a loud DJ."

A great place... to avoid.

Tiki Motel, 14111 Telegraph Rd., Taylor MI (734) 287-3680

No Tiki action here; just the name.

MICHIGAN SITES PERMANENTLY CLOSED

Boom Boom Room (Ziegler's Charcoal House), Lansing, MI

Advertising graphics show a crude Tiki and a drum.

Chin Tiki, Chinatown, Detroit, MI

Built in 1965 and closed in the early 1980's, Chin Tiki remains completely intact behind locked doors. The 500 seat restaurant was decorated by Oceanic Arts, and sported 2 floors, 2 bars, and 2 waterfalls. They had a souvenir mug in a Hawaiian deity style. Photos taken as recently as 2001 show two stone Kukailimoku statues outside, and plenty of Polynesian decor inside (including some Orchids of Hawaii pieces). Featured in the 2002 movie *8 Mile*.

CHIN TIKI, Detroit, MI

Hawaiian Gardens, Holly (north Detroit), MI
A restaurant, supper club, and small motel. Built in 1962, closed around 1970. It was immensely popular with the crowds from nearby Detroit. Built by a man who made his money in the auto industry and always wanted to own a Polynesian-style club. Plates had a nice image of a Maori Tiki on them.

Mauna Loa, 3077 W. Grand (at Cass), Detroit, MI
The whole block where the Mauna Loa once stood was bulldozed sometime in the late-1980s to make a shopping mall/office complex. The Mauna Loa was built in 1967 (at great expense) by some sports fans who didn't realize the Tiki fad was on its way out; it closed by 1968. The result of this short-lived experiment in Tiki is that Mauna Loa's custom Tiki mugs are hard to find. The elaborate venture was designed by the same team who put together Ft. Lauderdale's incredible Mai Kai.

Trader Vic's, Detroit, MI

Tur Mai Kai, 5640 S. Westnedge, Kalamzoo, MI

MINNESOTA
MINNESOTA TIKI SITES TO EXPLORE

Nye's Polonaise Room, 112 Hennepin Ave., Minneapolis, MN (612) 379-2021
While not completely Tiki-centric, this place is amazing. It's got the lounge feel left over straight from the mid-1960s. It simply hasn't changed in all that time.

MINNESOTA SITES PERMANENTLY CLOSED

Bali Hai Supper Club, 2305 White Bear Ave., Maplewood (St. Paul), MN (651) 777-5500
One of the greats, closed in 2000.

Don the Beachcomber, St. Paul Hilton, MN

Tropic Bowl/Outrigger Lounge, Fifth Ave. SE and 4th St., Rochester, MN

MAINLANDER, Louis, MO

MISSISSIPPI

MISSISSIPPI TIKI SITES TO EXPLORE

Tiki Restaurant Lounge and Marina, 3212 Mary Walker Dr., Gautier, MS (228) 497-1591

Appears to be a live music venue.

MISSISSIPPI SITES PERMANENTLY CLOSED

Trader John's, West Beach, Biloxi, MS

MISSOURI

MISSOURI TIKI SITES TO EXPLORE

Terry's Polynesian Room, 3930 N. Kingshighway Blvd., St. Louis, MO (314) 389-2206

MISSOURI SITES PERMANENTLY CLOSED

Kona Kai, Hilton Hotel Plaza Inn, 45th and Main, Kansas City, MO
A fierce Tiki face with Maori-like facial patterns decorates their advertising.

Mainlander, Clayton/St. Louis, MO
A nice looking matchbook can still be unearthed by the intrepid urban archaeologist. Circa 1968, prom night dates and other VIPs were seated at a private table, set off from the rest of the room by palm fronds. The food was excellent, particularly the rumaki – a liver dish.

Mai-Tai Resort Motel, Osaga Beach, Lake of the Ozarks, MO
"Authentic Polynesian decor... Where the guest reigns supreme" The Mai-Tai also included the Sky-Line Tiki Lounge.

MONTANA

MONTANA TIKI SITES TO EXPLORE

Kon Tiki Resort, Camdenton, MT (573) 873 5320
Their graphics seem to be inspired by the fireplace Moai at the legendary Kahiki in Columbus, Ohio.

Sip and Dip, Great Falls, MT

NEBRASKA

MAi TAi LOUNGE (MT. FUJi INN) • 7215 BLONDO ST., OMAHA, NE

The Mai Tai Lounge is in the basement of Omaha's Mt. Fuji Inn restaurant. With an ornate red gate over the driveway, and a nice neon sign, you can't miss it from Blondo Street. This Nebraskan Tiki spot is no Hala Kahiki, but you won't find another Tiki bar within 500 miles, so if you're chillin' in the breadbasket, this is your best and only bet.

(402) 397-5049

Category III
**CHINESE
RESTAURANT**

TiPSY Factor

The interior of the restaurant is not decorated with much Tiki; it is more interesting for its history: the original location burned down in the 1960s, and soon reopened in the present spot. It was once a nightclub featuring a swimming pool in the center of the main room. The pool was home to a dolphin and a young lady who would swim and frolic with the dolphin. Patrons in the basement bar had a sub-aquatic view of the marine life via a series of glass panels behind the bar. In the early 1970s, the pool was drained and covered by a slightly raised platform, which is now a part of the main seating area of the restaurant.

MAI TAI LOUNGE, Omaha, NE

Mt. Fuji Inn is still owned and operated by the Japanese widow of the original American owner, who died about 20 years ago. The family's service is friendly and attentive, with some staff having been on hand for decades. The food is on the good side of serviceable, but the sweet and sour chicken is far too sweet; it is like sucking on candy. The sesame chicken is far more enjoyable.

The Mai Tai Lounge stays open a little later than the restaurant. A tiny section of the pool was left intact and turned into an aquarium (still viewed behind the bar), but there isn't much to see these days. This goes for both dolphins and Tikis. One will spot exactly two Tikis in the Mai Tai Lounge, both are wooden poles about four feet high. There are also three black velvet nudes on the walls, and while not Leetegs, they're fairly good renderings. A few Orchids of Hawaii lanterns hang from the ceiling. Typical juke box fare includes ambient remixes by The Cure. Not exactly Martin Denny, but the slow tempo and dreamy quality of the tunes make them not entirely unwelcome. The place has that musty sort of basement smell, the result of decades of booze mixed with cigarette smoke that has nowhere to go.

MAI TAI LOUNGE, Omaha, NE

The Mai Tai at the Mai Tai Lounge and their Scorpion are indistinguishable, both are far too sweet (a running theme here?), and are almost undrinkable.

South of Blondo on 72nd, look for a fun neon sign on an authentic retro diner – Bronco's Hamburgers – "Serve Yourself and $ave!" (Blondo and Pacific). On Dodge Street, just east of 72nd, look for more classic neon on Wolf Brothers Western Store.

NEBRASKA SITES PERMANENTLY CLOSED

Aku Tiki Lounge (in the Villager), Lincoln, NE

NEVADA

CALIFORNIA HOTEL & CASINO • 12 OGDEN AVE., LAS VEGAS, NV

The hotel of choice for Pacific Islanders in Las Vegas, the Cal is host to over 100,000 visiting islanders per year (the resident Pacific Islander population in Las Vegas is estimated at 80,000 – some Hawaiians refer to Las Vegas as "The Ninth Island"). Look for video poker machines with Hawaiian-themed names such as Shaka Five Way, Diamond Head, and No ka 'oi (The Very Best); dealers in Aloha shirts; a stand selling Lappert's Hawaiian ice cream: and a coffee shop serving traditional Hawaiian favorites like saimin noodles, oxtail soup, and mahi-mahi sandwiches. Guests can buy Honolulu newspapers, dried mango, beef jerky, and T-shirts emblazoned with frogs (a symbol of good fortune in Hawaii). Asian Pacific alumni of high schools on Maui and the Big Island attend class reunions in the hotel's O'hana and Maile rooms. The hotel co-sponsors a two-day Lei Day festival adjacent to the hotel every May. The room and meals package for Pacific Islanders is $110.

(800) 360-8038

Category IV
OTHER

TiPSY Factor

JINX FALKENBURG

CHEESEBURGER AT THE OASIS • DESSERT PASSAGE, ALADDIN HOTEL, 3663 SOUTH LAS VEGAS BLVD., LAS VEGAS, NV

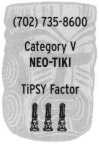

(702) 735-8600

Category V
NEO-TIKI

TiPSY Factor

Would you expect much Tiki from a place called Cheeseburger at the Oasis? You should! This medium-sized restaurant (located in the mall within the Aladdin casino/hotel) is filled with a huge collection of mostly vintage Hawaiiana and Tiki. They have several rooms full of masks, Tiki mugs, wigglers, hula lamps, postcards, and more. Most importantly, they have a well-stocked bar under a thatched roof, featuring their personal mutations of the Mai Tai, Planters Punch, Blue Hawaii, and a few others. After perusing their Hawaiiana collection for a while, *do not* try one of their namesake burgers (which their menu brags are the best in Las Vegas) – they taste like dirt. Do stop in to admire the amazing Hawaiiana collection, the waitresses in grass skirts, and to try a drink or three. Maybe the food will then taste more palatable. They also have a gift shop with an array of modern Tiki and Hawaiiana stuff.

CHEESEBURGER AT THE OASIS, Las Vegas, NV

CHEESEBURGER AT THE OASIS, Las Vegas, NV

IMPERiAL PALACE HOTEL • LAS VEGAS, NV

Since 1991, the Imperial Palace Hotel has hosted a poolside luau and Polynesian revue twice a week (from late April through mid-October). The festivities kick off at 6:30 p.m. every Tuesday and Thursday, and include a dinner buffet and unlimited free Mai Tais (don't expect much from these however). Admission is $29.95; make a reservation. The requisite hula girls, fireknife dancers, and exotic drummers are in full force, but the experience can be diminished by the occasional (and inexplicable) appearance of a Celine Dion impersonator.

(888) 777-7664

Category IV
OTHER

TiPSY Factor

PAPYRUS RESTAURANT AND TUT'S HUT BAR • LUXOR HOTEL, 3900 LAS VEGAS BLVD. SOUTH, LAS VEGAS, NV

(702) 262-4161

Category: ex-l
FORMER CLASSIC TIKI BAR

TiPSY Factor

Papyrus was once replete with Polynesian Drinks served up in good ol' fashioned Tiki mugs, lots of foliage, huge Oceanic Arts Tikis (installed in 1992), cute waitresses in sarongs, big aquariums, bigger blowfish (not in the aquariums, however), and just about everything else you might want out of a Tiki bar. The coffee shop was Tiki too, and in the early 1990s was staffed by some real Tiki princesses.

Someone finally woke up to the fact that a Tiki bar in an Egyptian themed hotel just didn't fit, so Papyrus, once perched on the second floor of the hotel atop a glorious red carpeted staircase, was de-Tikified in early 1997.

Four Tiki poles, each about five feet tall, can still be viewed near the entrance to the bar, but the theme is now purely Egyptian, in keeping with the rest of the Luxor.

VENUS LOUNGE AND TABOO COVE TiKI BAR • 3377 LAS VEGAS BLVD. SOUTH, LAS VEGAS, NV

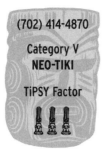

(702) 414-4870

Category V
NEO-TIKI

TiPSY Factor

Opened in 2001, and located in an out of the way alcove in the hotel complex, you'll be immediately excited by the "Venus" signs outside, with their big googie letters and a six-foot Moai guarding the door. Venus is a jetsetter's dream. Fabulous 1950s/1960s-style furniture and lamps, wall murals of the golden days of the Vegas strip, and a stage with gold lamé curtains and a leopard-print floor.

Taboo Cove is the Tiki lounge half of the business. Decor includes a Mark Ryden print, a number of Exotica LPs, and the "Green Lady" by Tretchikoff. Tiki carvings by Bosko are *everywhere*. Behind the bar are a stage and two walls of Tiki mugs that were made especially for the Taboo Cove. Every wall is marvelously bambooed, and glass fishing floats hang from the ceiling. But, in trying to make it upscale-modern Vegas, the designers failed to capture the kitschy feel of most other Tiki bars that we know and love.

TABOO COVE/VENUS NIGHT CLUB, Las Vegas, NV

The menu is fair in terms of food selection; fabulous in terms of drink selection; and glorious in terms of artwork: it is all by Shag. A lot of preparation went into designing the drinks. The staff apparently spent some time tracking down old Tiki geezers and getting them to give up their secrets. They have a number of standards (e.g. martini variations) and then a few specialties. There are about two dozen tropical drinks on the menu (including non-alcoholic ones). They lack some key standard drinks: the menu does not have a Mai Tai or a Scorpion. The unfortunately named "Tie Me To The Tiki Pole" is served in a massive bowl, specially designed for Taboo Cove. Drink prices are in the $8-$10 range.

TABOO COVE/VENUS NIGHT CLUB, Las Vegas, NV

Word has it that the club is in trouble already. Apparently the Las Vegas crowds of 2003 have forgotten the Aku Aku already, and can't handle this new dose of neo-Tiki. Let's hope it survives.

157

TRADER DiCK'S • JOHN ASCUAGA'S NUGGET CASiNO, 1100 NUGGET AVE., SPARKS (RENO), NV

(775) 356-3300

Category II
FINE DINING

TiPSY Factor

Trader Dick's was designed by Ely Hedley in 1958, and originally opened across the street from John Ascuaga's Nugget Casino in Sparks, Nevada (about three miles from Reno). Dick's moved into the casino proper in February of 1973. Further remodeling and expansion occurred in the 1980s.

The entrance is dominated by a 42-foot long bar (Douglas Adams fans rejoice), with an equally impressive aquarium behind it. Seating is available on both sides of the aquarium, so that's a grand total of 84 feet of whole-some Tiki goodness. More festive visitors may choose to drink on the side of the bar facing the casino, while those desiring some quiet may prefer the restaurant side. Little wooden signs hang above the bar, spaced a few feet apart. Each of them has the name of a drink on the left side, and a different Tiki mug imbedded in the wood on the right. These mugs are supposedly available for purchase, but don't set your heart on the famous ebony Aku Aku mug: they are sold out more often than not. Authentic Orchids of Hawaii R-86 Scorpion Bowls occasionally make an appearance, however.

The Fog Cutter is light yellow in color, and has a very fruity-citrus taste. It is garnished with a pineapple and a cherry on a sword skewer — no umbrella. Not a bad drink, but without the Tiki mug or the umbrella, it just seems to be missing something. Navy Grog is traditionally a strong drink, and Dick's version is no exception. It includes three shots of Rum (Bacardi Light, Bacardi Dark, and Meyers), 1 oz. of Rock Candy syrup, and 1.5 oz. of grapefruit juice over crushed ice for a very reasonable five bucks. This is a good one. The Scorpion is served in the aforementioned Orchids R-86 bowl. It is mixed fresh — no prefab ingredients. The Volcano is more for show; this red drink in a tall glass has only one ounce of hootch in it, but the dry ice eruption is a lot of fun. The Aku Aku (no longer in the ebony Moai mug as noted above) is $7 and has the distinction of being served with a flaming sugar cube floating on top of a lime wedge. It is awful.

Bar snacks are Pepperidge Farm Goldfish, cruelly served up in full view of their breathing brethren in the nearby aquatic prison. PuPus are available at the bar. The Easter Island Wantons are expensive and we can state with some certainty that they don't serve anything like these so-called wantons on Rapa Nui. They're essentially deep fried things that look more or less like crab rangoon, but they are stuffed with pork instead of crab and served with hot mustard, sweet and sour sauce, and cocktail sauce. Goldfish dipped in hot mustard are quite tasty, but Easter Island Wantons dipped in hot mustard are just as vile as Easter Island Wantons not dipped in hot mustard. Fortunately, the meals in the restaurant are far better than the PuPus at the bar. Let's go inside...

Moving beyond the bar into the restaurant is like walking into a black hole. The casino mayhem evaporates, and is replaced with a world of almost complete darkness. Deep blue and green lights, placed strategically at waist level, provide the only real illumination. The restaurant is labyrinthine. It is easy to get lost as you make your way through the jungle of plastic plants towards the back of a room that just seems to keep going and going.

Each "U-shaped" booth is completely surrounded by fake foliage, and when combined with the dim blue and green light, this makes it pretty tough to see the booth next to you, let alone anything farther away than that. This scheme makes things feel private and cozy. The TiPSY Factor at Trader Dick's is moderate. Look for the wooden Moai-like Tiki by the hostess booth. This bad-ass misrepresentation of some long dead Rapa Nui chieftain is a pillar reaching from ceiling to floor, and his red-lit eyes are the only light of that color in the room.

The spinach salad with red wine vinaigrette dressing is fresh, and the dressing is (thankfully) applied in moderation. The prawns and swordfish entree comes served in a plum wine butter sauce that is a little syrupy but very good overall. The three prawns are typically huge; the swordfish portion could be a little bigger. This is served with grilled vegetables and a steamer of white rice.

The waitresses are clad in Polynesian-influenced casino wear – floral bikini tops with matching floor-length sarongs. Cute, tasteful, and eye-catching. Catching the ear is the band, who entertains the guests during the early part of the night. They are (appropriately enough) a typical casino lounge act, and are more annoying than entertaining. A DJ takes over later, but don't think for a moment that he will spin any Exotica.

If you're in Reno, take a cruise through the downtown area – it is a gold mine for fans of cool coffee shop/cheap motel/retro/googie architecture and signage. Bring a camera! Document it before it goes away! There is also a mini golf course with a big Moai visible from I-395 near Reno.

NEVADA SITES PERMANENTLY CLOSED

AKU AKU ROOM, Las Vegas, NV

Aku Aku Room, Stardust Hotel, Las Vegas, NV

In southeast Las Vegas, beyond the airport, look for the island in the Sunset Park duck pond (2601 E. Sunset Rd); you will find the Moai (about 15 feet tall) that was carved by Ely Hedley for the Aku Aku. No Tiki remains in the hotel, however. Their souvenir Tiki mug shows up from time to time in collections, it is a style not unlike the classic PMP mugs. Look for a brief scene in the film *Casino* featuring Robert DeNiro in a re-created Aku Aku Room.

HARVEY'S WAGON WHEEL HOTEL AND CASINO, Lake Tahoe, NV

Bali Hai, 336-338 Desert Inn Rd., Las Vegas, NV
"Complete Resort Motel, One Block from the Fabulous Las Vegas Strip"

Don the Beachcomber, Hotel Sahara, Las Vegas, NV

Kona Lanes, bowling alley, Reno NV,
Promo photos exist.

Polynesian Room, Harvey's Wagon Wheel Hotel and Casino, Lake Tahoe, NV
Opened in 1960, designed by Ely Hedley and architect Frank Green.

Tiki Hunan, 5560 S. Virginia St., Reno, NV

Trader Nick's, Reno NV
Not to be confused with the still-open Trader Dick's in Reno. Closed in 1999.

AKU AKU ROOM, Las Vegas, NV

NEW HAMPSHIRE

KiNG TiKi • 2 BOW ST., PORTSMOUTH, NH

(603) 430-5227

Category VI
NEO-TIKI

TiPSY Factor

King Tiki is chock full of some really amazing Tiki collectibles; owners Robert and Melissa Jasper opened the bar because their house was so full of Tiki stuff that they needed somewhere to show it off and/or store it. Although the couple are genuinely friendly and seriously into Tiki (and all things retro), their client base doesn't seem to be very appreciative. Pabst Blue Ribbon and heavy metal Karaoke on Thursdays just don't say "Tiki."

MORE NEW HAMPSHIRE TIKI SITES TO EXPLORE

**Aloha, 901 Hanover St., Manchester, NH
(603) 647-2100**
Chinese restaurant with tropical drinks opened in 1988.

**China House, 52 Church St., Kingston, NH
(603) 642-6836**
Features an A-frame entranceway and wooden Tiki masks adorning the outside walls. The inside contains a very small amount of Tiki.

**Grand China, 7 Veteran's M. Parkway
(across from Rockingham Park) Salem, NH**
A dingy atmosphere with a small amount of Tiki and mediocre food.

NEW HAMPSHIRE SITES PERMANENTLY CLOSED

Mai Kai, Dover NH and Manchester NH
Vintage postcards show a spacious A-frame building with plenty of Tikis.

Waikiki, 914 Central Ave., Dover, NH

NEW JERSEY

CHAN'S DRAGON INN • 630 BROAD AVE. (NEAR THE iNTERSECTiON OF RT. 5 AND RT. 1&9), RiDGEFiELD, NJ

Chan's Dragon Inn has been at the same location since 1962, and has never been remodeled (that's a good thing!). It is a smallish establishment, with seating for less than 100 people. Outside, the only indication that it is a Tiki haven are two Tiki pillars holding up the entrance canopy.

(201) 943-1276

Category: III
CHINESE RESTAURANT

TiPSY Factor

Inside, a small waterfall made of conch and a carved Tiki (with red-lit eyes) greet the hungry visitor upon entering. Classic Hawaiian music plays softly in the background. The bar is to the right, and is divided from the main dining room by a wall of bamboo and statuary. The main dining room has a half dozen booths on the right side, completely framed in classic Tiki hut style: bamboo, thatch, and tapa. Pufferfish lamps hanging from the ceiling add a final touch of authenticity.

About 10 tables are scattered across the dining room floor. Above them are an assortment of classic lamps and two outriggers. Just to the left of the entrance is one of two smaller dining rooms. This is contains about eight tables, and is nice for couples wanting to be alone. To the rear is a large octagonal party booth, with two Tikis guarding its inside walls; it seats six. A third small room appears not to have been used for quite some time, but a little Tiki on the inside wall, and a classic Hawaii tourism poster make it worth a peek. All three sections of the dining room are framed in bamboo, tapa, and thatch. Several Tiki masks and shields hang on the walls throughout the place.

The classic cocktail menu features the Flaming Virgin (which comes on fire, natch) in a nice repro Scorpion bowl with a hollowed-out lime floating in the center. The beverages are made with Bacardi 151 and Meyer's Rum and with Trader Vic's mixers including Mai Tai, Scorpion, and Orgeat. The drinks are served with noodles and tea. At one point, Chan's offered a nifty ebony souvenir mug, but these are long gone, as are all traces of any other original Orchids of Hawaii mugs.

Entrees include the Hawaii 4-0 and other assorted Polynesian dishes. The presentation is excellent. Seafood dishes are served in a bowl of chow mein noodles surrounded by orange slices on a pedestal platter. The Hawaii 4-0 is ignited with a brandy sauce and put before the customer on fire. Portions are large, and prices on food and drinks are very reasonable. The good news is that Chan's Dragon Inn remains a busy restaurant in an urban/suburban New Jersey setting.

LUN WAH • 587 RARITAN ROAD, ROSELLE, NJ

(908) 245-0656

**Category: III
CHINESE
RESTAURANT**

TiPSY Factor

Lun Wah has been in this location for about 30 years. The building has two rooms, both decorated with bamboo tables and booths. In each booth, a Tiki mask backlit by a colored bulb watches over your meal. Overhead seashell lamps still provide illumination (they used to have puffer fish lamps, but they discarded most of these about five years ago). There is a small waterfall in the corner, but you have to request for it to be turned on due to splashing. On the way to the restrooms there is another small waterfall that falls into a goldfish pond.

MORE NEW JERSEY TIKI SITES TO EXPLORE

**Aloha Bay, 306 Cedarbrook Rd., Sicklerville, NJ
(609) 262-0608**

**Canton Casino, 920 Bergen Ave., Jersey City, NJ
(201) 653-4728**
Canton Casino dates to the the early-1930s with decor that has remained the same since day one: a multi-tiered dining room with lots of dimly lit red leather booths and lanterns. The bar serves traditional tropical drinks in Tiki mugs, and there's a little gift nook by the door where you can buy the mugs. Still run by the same family that opened it back in the Depression, the restaurant has also been used as a movie location (*To Wong Fu... Julie Newmar*). Also in Journal Square is the wonderful restoration-in-progress Loew's Jersey movie palace, so there's a time-capsule evening waiting to happen.

LEE'S HAWAIIAN ISLANDER, Lyndhurst, NJ

China Paradise, 82 Hamburg Tpk., Wayne NJ (973) 696-6464

They have remodeled, yet Tikis still leer at you from the walls. The drinks are amazing, as is the menu. All drinks served in surfer girl mugs or Tiki mugs.

Jade Garden, 229 North Avenue West, Westfield, NJ (908) 232-3309

Wonderful Polynesian bar/restaurant. Pools of goldfish everywhere; very serious Tiki.

Lee's Hawaiian Islander, 768 Stuyuesant Ave., Lyndhurst, NJ (210) 939-3777

Lee's Hawaiian Islander, 635 Lexington Ave. (corner of Piaget), Clifton, NJ (973) 478-1977.

On Saturdays, the Clifton location has a Hula show at 7:30 p.m. and 9:15 p.m. The location in Lyndhurst doesn't do this. The scene is low light bamboo huts, gold tablecloths, and black seats. The waterfall "sort of" works. The mixologist is adequate, but the drinks start tasting the same after a while.

Paradise East Polynesian Restaurant, Route 440 & Danforth Ave., Jersey City, NJ (201) 333-0072

Wildwood New Jersey: Tikiland USA!

Wildwood, New Jersey is an Atlantic resort area that has plenty to offer (in addition to a gang of Tiki-themed motels) for enthusiasts of atomic or googie architecture. The city council has dedicated themselves to preserving Wildwood's mid-century feel. Tiki abounds, mainly in the long and colorful strip of motels (check out the Starlux hotel too!).

Ala Kai Motel, 8301 Atlantic Ave., Wildwood Crest, NJ (609) 522-2159

Ala Moana Motel, 5300 Atlantic Ave., Wildwood, NJ (800) 633-7666

Casa Bahama Motel, Orchid Rd. and Atlantic, Wildwood, NJ (609) 522-5500

In spite of the Caribbean name, photos indicate that the Casa Bahama is Polynesian in design.

Hawaiian Rumble Pancake House and Mini Golf, Surf Ave., between 24th and 25th, Wildwood, NJ

The Mini Golf course is certainly Tikified, but the ice cream parlor has nothing Tiki about it at all. The pancake house contains an adequate amount of bamboo.

Kona Kai Motel, 7300 Ocean Ave., Wildwood Crest, NJ (609) 522-7778

Opened in 1962, the most recent owners (Ralph and Jo Ann, since 1999) have taken steps to restore (not remodel) the Kona Kai. The Tiki garden and rock wall are intact, and the gas torches have been repaired. Tiki masks still hang on the walls of each room. Ralph also plans to replace some stolen Tiki poles.

Royal Hawaiian Resort Motel, Orchid Rd. and Beach, Wildwood, NJ (609) 522-3414

Tahiti Inn, 12th and Ocean Ave., Ocean City, NJ, (609) 399-0130

Tahiti Motel, 7411 Atlantic Ave., Wildwood, NJ (609) 522-2984

Tiki Motel, E16th & Beach, North Wildwood, NJ (609) 522-5310

Waikiki Oceanfront Inn, 6211 Ocean Ave., Wildwood Crest, NJ (800) 62-Aloha

Waikiki's rooftop restaurant overlooks the beach.

NEW JERSEY SITES PERMANENTLY CLOSED

Chan's Waikiki, 147 Broadview Terrace., Paramus, NJ

Hawaiian Cottage, Rt. 38, Merchantville, NJ
One mile from garden state race track. "Unexcelled food in an enchanting atmosphere of the paradise isles of the Pacific."

South Pacific, Fords, NJ
South Pacific, Edison, NJ
Opened circa 1975, closed in 2001 when owner Yee Lau retired.

NEW MEXICO

BURT'S TiKi LOUNGE • 313 GOLD AVE. SW, ALBUQUERQUE , NM

This downtown live music club is decorated in surf-boards, sombreros, life jackets, taxidermy fish, and a few small Tikis. Cheap beer seems to be the drink of choice, and punk rock music is the musical fare. Might be a fun place to hang out, but Burt's (like the Burt's in Salt Lake City) is Tiki in name only.

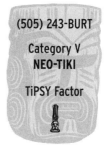

(505) 243-BURT

Category V
NEO-TIKI

TiPSY Factor

HAWAIiAN RESTAURANT • 102 LOUiSiANA BLVD. SE, ALBUQUERQUE, NM

(505) 266-8160

Category III
**CHINESE
RESTAURANT**

TiPSY Factor
0

Just off of Central Ave. (Route 66), a few miles east of the New Chinatown Restaurant, you will find this old Chinese restaurant with nothing to recommend it. It is a large, ugly, square concrete building, musty and dilapidated inside. Typical Cantonese and Thai food is served up at what seems like an hefty price for the location and the quality. Look for the Mei Cafe across the street, a Vietnamese restaurant with a giant statue of a lumber-jack(!) atop the building. Continuing east, look for a long chain of googie motels, and a great sign in front of Caravan East Western Dancing.

POLYNESIAN LOUNGE • NEW CHiNATOWN RESTAURANT, 5001 CENTRAL AVE. NE , ALBUQUERQUE, NM

(505) 265-8859

Category III
**CHINESE
RESTAURANT**

TiPSY Factor

Opened in the mid 1980s, this mid-sized lounge (with the requisite wooden Moai outside and an outrigger hanging from the ceiling) is part of a larger building which contains three other sizable and elaborately decorated rooms (The Lantern Room, The Peacock Room, and the Golden Pavilion). Dinner in the Chinese-themed rooms runs about $10 average for entrees; tropical drinks in the Tiki Lounge (about a dozen of the usual classic recipes are on the menu) average $6.

Owner Freddie "Kekaulike" Baker and his Kamaainas perform Hawaiian music Thursdays through Sundays from 7:00 p.m. to closing. Freddie was born in Honolulu in 1921, and was playing music professionally by the age of 13. He was a member of the house band at legendary Waikiki hotels such as Queen's Surf and the Royal Hawaiian, joining such notable performers as Monte Beamer, Hilo Hattie, and Gabbie Pahinui. Moving to Hollywood in the 1950s he became a champion surfer and appeared in *Road to Bali* with Bing Crosby, *Thunder Bay* with Jimmy Stewart, and others. By the 1960s, Baker was a regular musician Aku Aku Room in the Stardust Hotel in Las Vegas. He first performed

FREDDIE "KEKAULIKE" BAKER

POLYNESIAN LOUNGE, Albuquerque, NM

at the enormous Tiki Kai in Albuquerque around 1958, and after it closed (in 1976) he remained in Albuquerque.

Central Ave., east of downtown Albuquerque, happens to be one of the remnants of Route 66, and there are many great mid-century buildings in the immediate vicinity of New Chinatown Restaurant: look for the Desert Sands Motel (across the street), the Highland Theatre, the Octopus Car Wash, and a few antique malls. Further down the street to the west are more motels (some as cheap as $19.95) like the Deanza, the Premeire, the Aztec, the American Indian... and a creepy taxidermists' shop. Beyond that is the University of New Mexico, and the wide array of hipster stores that come with the territory. Should be easy to get some neo-Tiki stuff there.

NEW MEXICO SITES PERMANENTLY CLOSED

Tiki Kai, Central Ave., Albuquerque, NM
Opened in 1965 by Jane Ong and her brother-in-law, Harry. Seated 300 and featured a full Polynesian Revue. Closed in 1976, but reopened as Polynesian Lounge and New China Restaurant in 1990 (see above). The huge sign was in the shape of a palm tree. Next to it sat an enormous Tiki, at least 20 feet tall, carved in a Melanesian style.

NEW YORK

JADE ISLAND • 2845 RICHMOND AVE., STATEN ISLAND, NY

(718) 761-8080

Category III
**CHINESE
RESTAURANT**

TiPSY Factor
NR

Jade Island has pretty good decor (blowfish lamps, etc.), drinks are elaborately garnished, and some of the food arrives on fire. Staten Island has some very groovy 1960's architecture; take a drive around the neighborhood.

KAHiKi LOUNGE • 354 BOWERY, NEW YORK, NY

(212) 475-7621

Category V
NEO-TIKI

TiPSY Factor
NR

Every summer, Marion's Continental Restaurant and Lounge transforms itself into the Kahiki Lounge. From mid-July through Mid-August, the Kahiki is New York's only Polynesian Supper Club. It is a tribute to the original Kahiki in Ohio, and a salute to all things Polynesian. They serve PuPu platters, flaming cocktails, and feature live entertainment.

KAHIKI LOUNGE, New York, NY

LEi • AVENUE A AT THE CORNER OF 7TH STREET, NEW YORK (EAST ViLLAGE), NY

Opened in January 1998, Lei is the name given to one of the downstairs bars in Niagara, a retro-looking cocktail lounge. Unfortunately, it draws a fratboy crowd on the weekends, but for the most part it is populated with East Village rockers, cocktail scenesters, rockabilly aficionados, and locals.

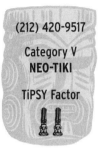

(212) 420-9517

Category V
NEO-TIKI

TiPSY Factor

Downstairs features the Tiki bar. It is has matting on the walls, a tiny thatched roof bar, a brightly colored aquarium, and some bamboo framing. There is one three-foot Tiki on the bar, and a dozen or two very small ones (six to twelve inches high) in glass cases and shelves throughout. DJs and theme nights change daily; unfortunately they never seem to have any Exotica/Tiki music. For the most part it is rock n' roll. No real tropical drinks either. Get there early to avoid the crowd; it gets really smoky.

OTTO'S SHRUNKEN HEAD • 538 E. 14TH ST. (BETWEEN AVENUES A AND B), NEW YORK, NY

Another of the handful of Tiki bars that suddenly invaded NYC in 2001 and 2002, Otto's (owned by Steve Pang) is a live rock club with a Tiki theme. Tikis carved by Wayne Coombs (one of which emits smoke from its nose) abound. A photo booth features a Tiki scene as a backdrop. Other decor includes vintage Tiki mugs, puffer fish, leopard-print bar stools, and a decidedly non-Tiki vintage Playboy pinball machine. Classic drinks (served in Tiki mugs) include Missionary's Downfall, Drunken Bastard, Patty's Passions, Pang's Punch (which come recommended), and a Zombie which is unfortunately made with Hawaiian Punch.

(212) 228-2240

Category V
NEO-TIKI

TiPSY Factor

TiKi ROOM • 4 WEST 22ND STREET OFF 5TH AVE., NEW YORK, NY

(646) 230-1444

Category V
NEO-TIKI

TiPSY Factor
0

The bar looks good from the outside, with a neon "Tiki Room" sign, and big windows covered with bamboo curtains. Once inside the magic fades fast: no Tikis, no tropical decor. Tiki Room *is* decorated with a potentially appealing retro jet set/space age decor, but internet access(!) and several flat screen TVs playing sporting events undo any TiPSY Factor that might have been present in this clubby Flatiron hangout. There are a few Tiki mugs in a display case and a few paintings of Tahitian wahines. There are no tropical drinks unless you count the Honolulu Hangover. Expect to be annoyed by ostentatious patrons on cell phones figuring out where to go next. Look for a 1960's-style Go-Go show on Fridays during the summer months.

WAiKiKi WALLY'S • 101 E. 2ND ST., NEW YORK, NY

(212) 673-8908

Category V
NEO-TIKI

TiPSY Factor

Youri Benoiston opened Waikiki Wally's in September 2002 on the former site of the notorious bondage club La Nouvelle Justine. Decor is by Oceanic Arts and Crazy Al Evans with Tiki Farm mugs. Benoiston refers to his decor style as "early Don the Beachcomber." A running fountain, plenty of foliage, exotica music, wall-length murals, and a Lucite bar with Hawaiiana objects embedded in it make this one a winner. Reports indicate that Wally's, of all of the neo-Tiki bars popping up in NYC, is the most old-skool and authentic. Live steel guitar and dancing on Monday nights is provided by Malakina, who used to perform at Hawaii Kai.

WAIKIKI WALLY'S, New York, NY

For Tiki shopping in Manhattan, try **Dullsville** (13th street between 3rd and Lafayette). The couple who own it may have a few vintage mugs for you. **Exit 9 Gift Emporium** (64 Ave. A) also has quite a selection of neo-Tiki stuff to spend a few clams on.

ZOMBiE HUT • 261 SMiTH ST. (BETWEEN DOUGLASS AND DEGRAW), BROOKLYN, NY

Possibly named after either the club seen in the 1945 Bela Lugosi movie *Zombies on Broadway* or the now-defunct Zombie Hut in Sacramento (the city from which owner Tod Bullen hails), this diminutive bar has been gaining positive acclaim among Tikiphiles since opening in 2002. The drinks (served in Tiki mugs) are said to be quite strong (up to 3 oz. of liquor). One drink's recipe requires the bartender to actually set the bar on fire.

(718) 855-2736

Category V
NEO-TIKI

TiPSY Factor
NR

MORE NEW YORK TIKI SITES TO EXPLORE

**Hawaii Fountain 403 Rt. 211 E. Middletown, NY
(845) 343-8773**
Polynesian-Cantonese fare with tropical drinks and some Tiki decor.

**Hawaii Sea, 1477 Williamsbridge Rd., Bronx, NY
(718) 863-7900**
No Tiki or tropical drinks.

Howard Johnson's Tiki Resort and Waikiki Supper Club, Lake George, NY, (888) THE-TIKI
Great 1950's-1960's architecture and interior design. Take Adirondack Northway I-87 to Exit 21. Follow signs towards Lake George Village. At the end of the ramp turn left at the stoplight. The Tiki Resort is 1/2 mile north on Rt. 9.

King Yum Restaurant, 181-08 Union Turnpike, Flushing, NY (718) 380-1918
"For a Truly Outstanding Dining Experience." King Yum is a vintage Chinese restaurant, dating to 1953. The decor is retro-Chinese, but they have a Tiki-ish bar, and advertise Polynesian food and tropical drinks.

ALOHA, THE, Rochester, NY

**Ronjo Resort Motel, South Elmwood, Montauk, NY
(631) 668-2112**
Look for at least one giant Tiki Mask (12 feet tall) on the outside of the building, and two Moai holding up their sign.

**Tiki Bar, 832 West Beech St., Long Beach, NY
(516) 897-9801**

NEW YORK SITES PERMANENTLY CLOSED

Aloha, The, Rochester, NY
Opened in the mid-1960s, and closed around the late-1980s. It had a lagoon, and the band (in crushed purple tuxes) took requests. Although the building is still standing, it has been transformed into a "China Buffet." It was the perfect Tiki bar, although small in size. The Aloha motel still exists a few buildings away. Bamboo thrones from the restaurant are now in the lobby of the motel.

Bali Hai, Northport, Long Beach, NY
Souvenir Tiki mug was a light, tan-colored Moai design.

East Islander, Route 17M, Monroe, NY

Hawaii Kai, Broadway at 50th. St., Times Square, New York, NY
Closed in the 1980s. One of their souvenir mugs was a Moai design. Another was unique in that the glaze was green on the outside, but a mustard color in the inside. Look for the words "New York City" on the back.

HAWAIIAN ROOM, New York, NY

HAWAIIAN ROOM, New York, NY

Hawaiian Room, Lexington Hotel, New York, NY
Early Hawaiian-themed nightclub (as far back as the early 1940s); hula and song by Haleloke.

Hurricane Tahitian Room, 49th and Broadway, New York, NY

Kona Kai, on Broadway, New York, NY
Featured a full floor show as recently as 1972 with hula dancers, and plenty of fire.

Luau 400, New York, NY

South Pacific, Pittsford Plaza, Rochester, NY
Advertising graphics show an unusual, almost Chinese-looking Tiki.

Trader Vic's, NYC, NY, New York Plaza.
Built 1965, the restaurant closed in 1989; the bar remained until 1993.

Trader Vic's, NYC, NY, Savoy Hilton.
Built 1958, on current site of General Motors building. Peter Seeley, grandson of Victor Bergeron, announced late in 2002 that a new New York Trader Vics was planned as one of at least five new North American Trader Vic's locations.

HURRICANE TAHITIAN ROOM, New York, NY

NORTH CAROLINA

MAMA KWAN'S • MiLE POST 9 1/2 ON U.S. 158, OUTER BANKS, NC

(252) 441-7889

Category II/V
**CASUAL DINING/
NEO-TIKI**

TiPSY Factor

The decor is a mix of Polynesian and Caribbean, with quite a few Tikis both at the bar and as part of the general decor. Tropical drinks are offered in Tiki mugs. They make a good Mai Tai. The cuisine includes dishes such as pad Thai and fish tacos. It is a nice establishment and is the closest that anyone in North Carolina is going to get to the Tiki experience.

Mama Kwan's Grill & Tiki Bar wants you to know that...

"We built the place with our own hands and credit cards. About once every 3 months, we add something new to the place. We have just replaced the old tables with ones that were painted by local artist and then fiberglassed. Next we hope to thatch out the entire roof. We hope you will come by and visit us. By then we may have our 'work in progress' about done."

NORTH DAKOTA

We have no evidence of any Tiki bars, past or present, in North Dakota

OHIO

CLEVELAND

There ain't no Tiki in Cleveland! We have *scoured* the greater Cleveland area, and there is *nothing* Tiki *anywhere*.

Tiki-hunting disasters in Cleveland:

The Bamboo Palace at 16610 Lorain is just a really dirty Chinese restaurant.

Tradewinds at 319 E. 200th St. in Euclid is a local pub. No Tiki.

The Bali Ha'i restaurant on Euclid Avenue is another Chinese restaurant, but there is a small lounge. Behind the bar, you may spot one or two Tiki mugs. Aside from the cool signage though, there is no real reason to stop by.

The Beachcomber in Grand River, Ohio (about 45 minutes east of Cleveland) used to be a Tiki bar, but like the Kon Tiki (in the Sheraton Hotel) in downtown Cleveland, it is now gone.

The Islander Grille is at 7581 Pearl Rd. in Middleburg Heights. A few doors down is the **Islander Cleaners**(!) (7563 Pearl), and around the corner is **The Islander Apartments** (7711 Normandie). Clearly there was a **Polynesian Dynasty** in Middleburg Heights at some point, but there isn't so much as a stick of bamboo left in any of the three locations. Nothing Tiki whatsoever. Reports indicate that there was once a mighty Tiki Temple on the spot, however.

If you drive east on Pearl road from these spots, you *will* find a googie ice cream stand, an equally cool bowling alley, another googie car-wash, and a few other semi-retro buildings. There is also a great old-skool drive-in on Miles Road in North Randall. The **Sea World** that was located in nearby Geauga had a Hawaiian-themed area with Tikis, but that has long since been dismantled.

All hope is not lost, however. Those desperate for a Mai Tai can find some satisfaction:

Bamboo House Chinese Restaurant, 640 Dover Center Rd., Bay Village, OH (440) 871-1966
Bamboo House still has its original 1960's decor, and some of the best Chinese food in town. Try their gingery, homemade sweet-sour sauce and homemade egg rolls, the honey chicken, and the pork egg fu yung. Suffering Bastards are served in Tiki mugs, while other tropical drinks are served in pana mugs.

Dragon Gate Chinese Restaurant, 8701 Brookpark Rd., Parma, OH (216) 661-0800
Dragon Gate is an old-fashioned Cantonese restaurant has been a Parma institution for decades. Sample the sizzling Hawaiian dishes, pupus served in native style with flaming

hibachi, Tiki-patterned menus, and exotic drinks. Also of interest is the golf driving range behind it with the neat super-sized golfball and their own retro vending machines that dispense beer.

TiKi LANES • 1521 TiKi LANE ROAD, LANCASTER, OH

(740) 654-4513

Category VI
OTHER

TiPSY Factor

The building's facade is a lovely 1950's tiled mosaic of Tiki masks, torches, and spears, and electric lit faux torches on the columns.

The interior is as bland as a Kenny G record. Just inside is the door to the "Tiki Restaurant," a reminder of what once was: frosted glass with the words etched in an Ameri-Polynesian-style font. The staff all have name tags with the same font, and the walls on the far ends of the alley are covered with murals of a sunset-hued beach and sailboats. Other than that, there is nothing left of Tiki. Tiki Lanes used to have full-on Tiki decor, but it was removed around 1990.

The bartenders will need to consult their bartender's recipe book if you order a Mai Tai; however the resulting drink is typically strong, and inexpensive.

OHIO SITES PERMANENTLY CLOSED

Kahiki, 3583 East Broad St., Columbus, OH

Opened in 1961, and meticulously maintained for 39 years, there are few Tikiphiles or urban archaeologists who would fail to place Kahiki on a list of top five Tiki bars of all-time. The Kahiki was originally conceived by Lee Henry and Bill Sapp, and designed by Coburn Morgan. The architects were Ned Eller and Ralph Sounik.

To the dismay of Tiki aficionados, fans of mid-century culture, and even historical societies and architectural foundations, Kahiki closed in August of 2000. The owners cited a decline both in business and in the neighborhood as factors, as well as deterioration of the building.

KAHIKI, Columbus, OH

The owners made numerous statements in 2000 about re-opening Kahiki in a new location; these comments have since been retracted. The owners currently have no plans to rebuild. The major artifacts from the Kahiki are said to be in storage.

What was it that made the Kahiki so great? For a start there was the menu, which contained an extensive selection of dishes from all around the Pacific Rim (categorized into Island, Asian, and American). A favorite was the Samoian Flaming Chicken, which was a full-sized sabre impaling an array of chicken and vegetable kabob, set alight at the table by a waiter. Malagasy Chicken was also a staple, although Madagascar (indeed the island said to have inspired this meal), is hardly Polynesian. The Tahitian Mermaid was a great dish as well, although it has come under suspicion as to whether Kahiki used real mermaid meat in this dish.

KAHIKI, Columbus, OH

The *important* menu – a separate document entirely – included the world famous Mystery Drink. Upon placing an order for this classic libation, a gong would sound in some far off corner of

KAHIKI, Columbus, OH

the vast Kahiki. Eventually, an attractive gal in a sarong – The Mystery Girl – would wordlessly bring the large Volcano Bowl out to the table, flaming and ready to drink. Speaking of the Mystery Girl, vintage press from the Kahiki indicates that "most of the cocktail waitresses are wives of service-men, and all are from Japan or Korea."

With the Headhunter, Kahiki maintained the tradition of allowing patrons to keep the Tiki mug from which they had quaffed their rum and fruit juice. This Moai mug with a "Kahiki" inscription on the bottom is still not uncommon. The Kahiki's take on the Zombie was also in a mug to keep; this one was in the shape of a skull. The Smoking Eruption was filled with dry ice that would soon create a layer of fog across the entire table. Who cares how it tasted?

A three-piece band set up near the Outrigger Bar on week-ends, and the mallet player lent an authentic Arthur Lyman feel to the night's entertainment (the original 1961 band – the Beachcombers – consisted of Henry Burch on vibes, flute, French horn and congas; Bob Chalfant on piano and claves; and Marsh Padillo on guitar, flute, and percussion. All three members played conch shell, too).

The architecture was without peer; the building was extremely tall for a stand-alone restaurant, with a long, sloping roof similar to an inverted outrigger. The general design was inspired by a New Guinea male meeting house. Two large black Moai, heads aflame, guarded the door, which was accessible by a bridge over a moat. Painted motifs in bright colors detailed the edges of the facade and the sides.

Inside, Kahiki was set up like a Polynesian village, with a half dozen little side rooms (Molokai Hut, Kauai Garden Booths, Niihau Hut, and Rain Forest Booths) set back from the center of the restaurant (palm-lined Kalakaua Street). The iconic Moai fireplace, red eyes blazing and fire always lit in its mouth has been variously described as being anywhere from 30- to 80-feet tall; the former estimate is probably most accurate, although it *seemed* like the latter at times.

KAHIKI, Columbus, OH

KAHIKI, Columbus, OH

A careful examination of the Kahiki revealed little touches of craftsmanship in every corner that might go unnoticed to the casual visitor. One could see vintage tapa cloth covering the walls next to some of the booths. It was also interesting to note the beautiful mosaic work which was an intrinsic part of the structure. These details are what made the Kahiki the architectural masterpiece that it was. It wasn't the big, in your face Oceanic Arts Tiki gods that set the Kahiki apart, but rather it was the little Maori motifs painted along the edges of a doorway, or the detail on a painted turtle shell. It was the quality of the black velvet paintings in the Molokai Hut. It was that huge mess of a sculpture above the Outrigger Bar, or the hand painted tropical murals surrounding it. Effective lighting and even thunderstorm sound effects (in the lobby) added further touches.

In short, when the Kahiki closed its doors, we lost one of the finest remaining Tiki treasures. It is missed.

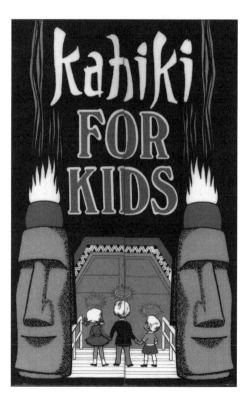

KON TIKI PORTS, Cleveland, OH

**Kon Tiki Ports (Stephen Crane's),
Sheraton-Clevleand Hotel, Cleveland, OH**

**Kon Tiki Ports (Stephen Crane's),
Sheraton-Gibson Hotel, Cincinatti, OH**

The original incarnations of Stephen Crane's Kon Tiki chain
were simply called Kon Tiki. Later stores were opened as
Kon Tiki Ports, and his final restaurants were created under
the name Ports of Call. The Chicago, Cleveland, and Boston
locations (and possibly others) had a nice souvenir mug
reminiscent of the classic PMP design.

KON TIKI PORTS, Cleveland, OH

The frighteningly named Terminal Tower in the center of
downtown Cleveland was once the home of Cleveland's
Kon-Tiki Ports location. A complete renovation of the property in the 1980s utterly decimated any trace of the Kon
Tiki's existence that might have remained.

Kon Tiki movie theatre, Dayton, OH

Rattan Room, Warren, OH

Tropics, Dayton, OH

OKLAHOMA
OKLAHOMA TIKI SITES TO EXPLORE

**Aloha Taste Of Hawaii, 7133A S. Yale, Tulsa, OK
(918) 488-9990**
Authentic poi and hula dancing with your Luau For Two.

OKLAHOMA SITES PERMANENTLY CLOSED

**Jade East Restaurant/Shanghai Lounge,
corner of 41st and Memorial, Tulsa, OK**
Owned by Henry Jin (no relation to Qui Gon) who moved to
Tulsa in 1959. Featured a fountain, plenty of rattan, and at
least two large Tikis in the entranceway. These 10-footers in
a Hawaiian style may have been carved by Saint Clare
Homma, and are now owned by a collector. Now the Tokyo
Garden.

**Kon Tiki Koni, 4418 Admiral Pl., between Pittsburgh
and Yale, Tulsa, OK**
Featured a big Tiki head statue with lit-up eyes, which
stood in front of a thatched Tiki Hut and a bar. Opened in
1961 by James and Tom Lester, and Morse Purkey. By 1968, it
had become "Kon-Tiki Motors," a used car lot.

**Tiki Nook Club, Trade Winds West Motor Hotel,
1120 E. Skelly Drive, Tulsa, OK**
Evidence suggests it was opened between 1961 and 1963 by
Morse Purkey.

**Trade Winds East/West (1120 E. Skelly Drive.)/Central
hotels, Tulsa, OK**
The West building is still there, but no evidence of Tiki
exists. The cool neon sign is gone. The Tiki Nook was located at the Trade Winds West, Trade Winds East, and was
home to the Trader's Cove Club, Trade Winds Central had
the Showboat.

OREGON

KOKO MO'S ISLAND GRiLL AND BAR • 707 WiLLAMETTE STREET, EUGENE, OR

KoKoMo's is one of those bar and grille type places that tries its best to be "lots of fun for the whole family" (although this one turns into a dance club for the local college kids later in the evening). The menus are slick and colorful, the decor is festive, the staff is almost too energetic, and the whole place screams of trying way to hard to insure that you "have a good time, all the time." If they were billing themselves as a Tiki bar, we might have to call in the Tiki cops in to dish out some violations for numerous offenses.

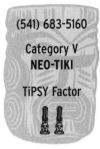

(541) 683-5160

Category V
NEO-TIKI

TiPSY Factor

However, they are making some effort to serve semi-old-skool tropical drinks. Their Three Legged Monkey is served in a coconut mug, their Rusty Anchor comes in a green Dynasty Tiki mug, and they have a mean looking Zombie. Better still, the Volcano comes in a Hula Girl bowl for $12, the Kokomo Smoothie is served in a clam shell ($9.95), and The Big Island is served in a huge glass clamshell, contains 84 ounces of fun, and is only served to parties of at least six (for $25).

The decor is pan-tropical, meaning that Polynesian stuff like Tikis and Moai are mixed with more Caribbean motifs like pirates, monkeys, bananas, and occasional Australian icons as well. The volcano by the front door is fun, a four-foot Tiki sits outside by the door, and several other mid-sized Tiki and Moai statues populate the room. A whimsical happy Moai guy appears ubiquitously on their menus and their other propaganda. The three large windows that face Willamette street are double-panes, with water bubbling up between them, and an array of brightly colored plastic sea creatures bob about in the festive flowing water.

The food is typical bar food – nachos, wings, burgers, tacos. They make a feeble effort at having it seem exotic by giving things names like Kokomo's Big Kahuna (burger) and Kauai Coconut Shrimp. The Venice Beach Club Wrap ($5.75) actually makes a pretty tasty lunch, as do the slightly less impressive fish tacos ($6.75).

Maybe the thing that recommends KoKo Mo's the most as a Tiki bar is that it might be used as a training ground for the kids, in order to get the Tiki into their subconscious, and to prepare them for an adult life of drooling on the bar at the Alibi, just 50 miles up the road. Also note that it is adjacent to a Honky Tonk accessible through a swinging door.

ALiBi LOUNGE • 4024 N. INTERSTATE AVE, PORTLAND, OR

(503) 287-5335

Category II
CASUAL DINING

TiPSY Factor

The Alibi was founded in the late-1800s as the "Chat 'n' Nibble," and was redone as a Tiki lounge in 1947. Located in a rather out of the way section of Portland, this Tiki bar is well worth a trip – even if you're in Georgia at the moment. The huge sign outside features backlit painted panels of Tiki masks and dancing natives from some unspecified far-off island. Neon torches and other details make the sign a wonder to behold. Looking at the rest of the building clues the intrepid Tiki trekker in to the fact that whoever redesigned this place when it became a Tiki bar had envisioned it to be a real swinger's mecca.

One comes into The Alibi through a barrel-shaped anteroom, and then enters the bar area. There are two platforms, each containing a half dozen booths and tables. Dig the swanky interior with the high-backed, plushly upholstered booths, some great etched mirrors next to the booths, and even a table surrounded by palm trees. Very cozy. A step down is the bar, and to the left is another seating area, containing a fountain guarded over by a big wooden Moai-type figure (not a Witco design, although it looks like one), and a day-glo mural of dancing hula girls (added in the 1970s). This area is festive and less private than the cozy booths in the prior room. Beyond that is a third room, with another dozen tables and an array of Oceanic Arts masks, spears, and shields on the walls.

As Tiki bars go, The Alibi is probably the most swank of them all. The booths are all red leather(ette?), the lights are dim, and the general aura of the place is one of extreme Sinatraness. This is the Tiki bar for the post-Rat Pack set.

The TiPSY Factor is moderate to high, with a dozen or so substantial wooden Tiki gods watching over the festivities. The obligatory lanterns, nets, floats, and blowfish are more carefully placed than in most Tiki bars, making The Alibi feel less cluttered, and giving the atmosphere a touch more refinement.

As is the case with so many vintage Tiki bars that have survived, the ownership has seen fit to add a few modern accouterments. Lottery machines, the ubiquitously hated TVs (one behind the bar and *three* in the hindmost dining room), and some other modern bar clutter ruin the behind-the-bar area. But, if you stick to one of the three aforementioned table-filled areas, The Alibi is reasonably untouched.

ALIBI LOUNGE, Portland, OR

ALIBI LOUNGE, Portland, OR

The bartenders tend to be friendly, efficient, and are sometimes decked out in cool Tiki bowling shirts. It is good to see the waitresses in sarongs.

The drinks are good overall. The Mai Tai is served in a pint glass with a cherry, a lemon wedge, and an umbrella. It strays pretty far from the classic Mai Tai recipe, but it is enjoyable and strong. The Missionary's Downfall is served with identical garnish and glassware, and while flavorful and tart, it can be too syrupy and sickly-sweet. The lack of Tiki mugs is disappointing, but to be fair, there are almost *no* Tiki bars left that serve their drinks in Tiki mugs anymore.

ALIBI LOUNGE, Portland, OR

Music oscillates between the dreaded Bob Seger spewing from the juke, and more appropriate Exotica and Rat Pack stuff piped in from a CD player behind the bar.

Try Alibi at lunch time, and you'll be suitably impressed with the size of the hangover-killing Royal Reuben ($7.50). Dinner can be like something straight out of a 1950 Betty Crocker cookbook photo; the sautéed beef (excellent cut of meat) is served with a few pepper strips and onions on a bed of rice, in a soy-based, cornstarch-thickened sauce, with sesame seeds sprinkled on it. The only speck of green on the plate is the lettuce leaf under the two spice apple rings. The Laulau combination ($16.95) sets you up with a six ounce steak, a chicken breast, and batter dipped halibut. Hearty!

Half a block from the Alibi is the incredible Palms Motel. Visitors to Portland might also want to check out the 24-hour **Church of Elvis** near Broadway (7th and Burnside). Two blocks away is a great (but expensive) vintage store called **Avalon** (on the corner of Burnside and

PALMS MOTEL, Portland, OR

9th). Around the corner from that is **Palookaville** (211 SW 9th Ave. (503) 241-4751) that has a lot of vintage stuff.

JASMINE TREE • 401 S.W. HARRISON, PORTLAND, OR

The Jasmine Tree opened in 1977, and has had the same owners ever since. It is impressive that someone got into the Tiki decor that late in the game – most of the classic Tikis were closing up for good by the time J-Tree opened. Look for a large building with three big Tiki masks hanging on the side, and the words "Tiki Bar" in big Chinese-style letters by an inviting red door.

(503) 223-7956

Category III
**CHINESE
RESTAURANT**

TiPSY Factor

Inside, the large restaurant will immediately impress, with a moderately high TiPSY Factor, featuring plenty of Oceanic Arts stuff. The menu has fun little drawings of Tikis in the margins.

The food is above average: their *huge* bowl o' won ton soup is filled with the largest won tons you're likely to see, plenty of veggies, and substantial slices of roasted chicken. This may be the best won ton soup on record!

JASMINE TREE, Portland, OR

The Combination Mushroom Dish with Chicken is filled with tons of huge mushrooms in three varieties. They are really fresh, and very good. Combo Platter #5 is a culinary joy as well.

JASMINE TREE, Portland, OR

The Tiki bar in the rear of the restaurant is often tended to by Joyce, an exceptionally nice bartender. Her Mai Tai is a classic recipe, yellow-brown in color, topped with Meyer's, and garnished with a cherry, an orange slice, and a pineapple ring. She serves it up in one of those clear chalices with the happy Tiki on one side and the angry Tiki on the other. Excellent!

JASMINE TREE, Portland, OR

Unfortunately this Mai Tai is somewhat lonely on the Tropical Drink list at the Jasmine Tree, the only others offered are ChiChi and a Margarita, which do not qualify as authentic Tiki drinks (they're thought of as Caribbean). If you ask nicely, Joyce may improvise a pineapple daiquiri, with a real hibiscus floating on top. Good stuff.

Look for the great pair of Marqesian cannibal Tikis by the bar. These guys stand about three feet tall. Unfortunately, as seems to always be the case in places like the Jasmine Tree, the ubiquitous TV and five gambling machines deface a large corner on the other side of the bar. The back wall of the bar area opens up to reveal another room, much larger than the main bar. This back room is open on the weekends, and one can hear live rock music. A big red-covered fireplace makes the space between the main bar and rock room, and can be a cozy little place to cuddle with your sweetie. Two outriggers hang above the festivities. There had once been five of them, but the owners sold them off. Bad news there; is a full Tiki-free remodeling job in the works?

Sweet River, 1126 Gateway Loop, Springfield, OR (541) 741-8676

They have a "Hoodoo Voodoo" retro theme and the glass Tiki mugs with the smiling Tiki on one side and the fierce Tiki on the other ($5). They also sell t-shirts with a Tiki and one of the mugs printed on the back.

**Sweet River Grill & Bar, 3000 Gateway St.,
Springfield, OR (541) 988-9558**

**Sweet River Grill & Bar, 285 Liberty Street Northeast,
Salem, OR (503) 585-7877**

TiKi LODGE MOTEL • 3705 MARKET STREET, SALEM, OR

(503) 581-4441

Category VI
OTHER

TiPSY Factor
0

Aside from the almost-cool A-frame over the driveway, the Tiki Lodge has nothing remotely Tiki about it whatsoever. There is no indication that in the past there may have been some Tikis guarding the pool, chillin' in the lobby, or decorating the rooms, and there is not so much as a stick of bamboo anywhere on the premises. The only thing tropical about this place are the dying plants in the lobby.

That said, rooms are as low as $35.97 per night (after tax), and it's only 40 miles from Portland, so if you're going to check out The Alibi, Jasmine Tree, or any of the other interesting things to do in Portland, this is as good a place to stay as any.

There is another location at 509 North Riverside Avenue, Medford, OR 97501, (541) 773-4579

MORE OREGON TIKI SITES TO EXPLORE

Hawaii Kai, 1165 Mill St., Waldport, OR (541) 563-5259

**Tahiti Restaurant/Burt Lee's Tahitian Lounge,
5850 State St., Salem, OR (503) 767-3333**
A whimsical Moai with his nose painted white (sun block?) watches over the very Tiki entrance to Tahiti Restaurant. Torches, Tiki masks, and dark wood enhance the ambiance. Inside, the TiPSY Factor diminishes considerably.

OREGON SITES PERMANENTLY CLOSED

Aloha Room, The Heathman Hotel at 731 SW Salmon, Portland, OR

Vintage press reads: "Sophisticated Polynesian-Hawaiian atmosphere. The room is bedecked with articles representing the best South Seas culture. Decor centers around a full-length mural, in resplendent tropical tones, depicting the arrival of King Kamehameha at the festival of the sea – 'The Hukilau.' Finer details (include) gracious, friendly waitresses dressed in black sarongs, translucent tabletops inlaid with gold ferns and shells, hurricane lamps on carved wooden bases, brilliant red Anthiriumand Ginger, flown in each week from the Islands, together with Vanda orchids which are presented to the ladies. What might be thought of as souvenir items are found across the hall in the Lanai Room, a combination gift shop and cocktail lounge. In the Aloha Room itself the South Seas atmosphere is deftly achieved by using accessories of museum-like quality. Exotic South Seas cocktails, served in equally exotic containers, are one of the many enjoyable features. The (food is) served on trays of carved monkey-pod wood... "

The Aloha Room is now a low income housing for the elderly.

Grotto, The, Portland, OR

Key Largo, Portland, OR
Closed in 1999.

Kon Tiki Ports (Stephen Crane's), Sheraton Motor Inn, Portland, OR

Stephen Crane's Kon Tiki chain went through several permutations. The original locations were simply called Kon Tiki, later stores were opened as Kon Tiki Ports, and his final restaurants were created under the name Ports of Call. This location was also called "Islands of Kon Tiki" at some point, and closed in the early 1980s. Look for their salt-and-pepper shakers, featuring funny little bald men giving a "thumbs up."

Pantley's Pagan Hut, OR

"Exotic island atmosphere"

Tiki Lodge, 509 North Riverside, Medford, OR

Trader Vic's, Benson Hotel, Portland, OR

Opened 1959, closed 1996 (now an "El Gaucho"). Originally an "Outriggers." Some early Trader Vic's franchises were opened as "The Traders," and others were opened as "The Outriggers." It seems that all of them eventually became simply Trader Vic's.

KON TIKI PORTS (STEPHEN CRANE'S), Portland, OR

PENNSYLVANIA

TiKi BAR • 2003 EAST CARSON STREET, PiTTSBURGH, PA

(412) 381-8454

Category V
NEO-TIKI

TiPSY Factor

Pittsburgh's only Tiki temple was opened in a trendy south side neighborhood in autumn 2002, and is said to be designed after Columbus's universally missed Kahiki (right down to the shell sinks in the washrooms). One enters the two-story building through a mammoth Tiki, to find a bar across from some booths. The rear of the room contains a dance floor, and the basement level is a non-smoking bar. The TiPSY Factor here is high, clearly a lot of thought went into Tiki Bar. Two waterfalls and plenty of Tikis exist among the dense foliage. Two glass display cases house a pair of cannibals. These mannequins appear to have been repatriated from some amusement park side show. Their patina makes them all the more interesting and adds further authenticity to Tiki Bar. A slate floor and thatched roofing complete the vibe.

Drinks are in the $11 range, but each is matched to a different Tiki mug, that is yours to keep. Outstanding! The owners also have a club called Volcano Lounge; this temptingly titled club is not Tiki, however.

MORE PENNSYLVANIA TIKI SITES TO EXPLORE

Briar's, Susquehanna PA (717) 853-4823
Appears to be a northeastern cousin to the "Florida Tiki Bar." About 10 minutes off of interstate 81 at exit 68.

Tiki Bar, 150 Manatawny Road, Boyertown, PA (610) 689-4707

Tiki Beachcomber Lounge, 222 S. Oak St., Mount Carmel, PA (570) 339-0443

Trader Vic's, Philadelphia, PA
Peter Seeley, grandson of Victor Bergeron, announced late in 2002 that a new Philadelphia Trader Vics is planned as one of at least five new North American Trader Vic's locations. Watch for an announcement in your local press soon.

Wildwood Heights Family Fun Center, 2330 Wildwood Rd., Wildwood Heights (near Pittsburgh), PA (412) 487-5517

Features a tropical-theme mini-golf course, built in 2000, that is home to almost two dozen Tikis... and mechanical monkeys.

PENNSYLVANIA SITES PERMANENTLY CLOSED

Chin's Polynesian Garden, Pittsburgh, PA

The owners retired in 2001, leaving the building, complete with brass Tikis(!), carved wooden masks, and seashell lamps, to their sons, who renovated the last remnant of vintage Tiki in Pittsburgh into "a normal restaurant." Notable for their Kahiki-inspired Moai outside, and their running streams (and turtles!) inside, Chin's offered 35 tropical drinks with unusual names such as Mermaid's Milk and Tiki Bouquet.

Kona Kai, Marriott Hotel, City Line Ave., Philadelphia, PA

Throughout the 1960s and '70s, this link in Marriott's Kona Kai chain featured an indoor waterfall which fed a brook that snaked through the room. PuPus were grilled on table-top hibachis, and their take on the Scorpion (served with a fresh gardenia) was said to be among the most potent aphrodisiacs in history.

Mauna Loa, Monroeville, PA (near Pittsburgh)

Sat 500 people; it was the largest restaurant in town.

Pub Tiki, Philadelphia, PA

Pub Tiki featured a Moai mug to keep. All of their mugs, swizzle sticks, cocktail napkins, and other ephemera contain a mysterious logo with the number "1 1/2" on it.

RHODE ISLAND
RHODE ISLAND TIKI SITES TO EXPLORE

Hawaiian Isle, 8 Hall St., Concord, RI (603) 228-0194 and Route 125, Plaistow, NH (603) 382-4746

Mai Tai Polynesian, 856 Tiogue Ave., Coventry, RI
(401) 828-4252

RHODE ISLAND SITES PERMANENTLY CLOSED

Luau Hut, (in Luke's Chinese restaurant), Providence, RI

A classic Tiki lounge, popular in the 1970s. Family owners sold the place in the mid-1980s and the place went downhill with the new owner. Closed for good sometime in the 1990s.

SOUTH CAROLINA
SOUTH CAROLINA TIKI SITES TO EXPLORE

Hawaiian Caverns, 42nd Ave. North Hwy. 17, Myrtle Beach, SC (843) 449-5555

Lush mini-golf course with tropical decor.

Hawaiian Rumble Mini Golf, 3210 Hwy. 17 South, North Myrtle Beach, SC (843) 272-7812

Look for the volcano and the Hawaiian Rumble sign at the intersection of Highway 17 and 33rd Ave.

Tiki Hut Bar, 1 South Forest Beach Dr. (on the beach), Hilton Head SC (843) 785-5126

"A great outdoor joint with live music."

SOUTH CAROLINA SITES PERMANENTLY CLOSED

Hawaiian Village, U.S. 17 (The Ocean Highway), at 39th Ave. N., Myrtle Beach, SC

"Myrtle Beach's most exciting new concept in resort motel leisure and comfort." They promoted themselves with a matchbook featuring a drawing of the slope-roofed building.

SOUTH DAKOTA

We have no evidence of any Tiki bars, past or present, in South Dakota

TENNESSEE

OMNi HUT • 618 SOUTH LOWRY STREET (U.S. 41, NEAR TN 102), SMYRNA, TN

Located about 16 miles southeast of Nashville, Omni Hut was opened by a USAF officer and his wife while they were stationed at the long-defunct Sewart AFB in the 1960s. The decor contains elements that have been part of the place since it opened, and they've gradually added more as years have gone by.

(615) 459-4870

Category II
CASUAL DINING

TiPSY Factor

The lobby will immediately impress, as it contains two large and unique Maori wall plaques. The usual Oceanic Arts accouterments are also present in quantity, as well as some of the best tapa cloth one is likely to see. This tapa was hand-made by a former employee who was born in the South Pacific.

There are two dining rooms, with the smaller of the two having an indoor waterfall, and the usual trappings of ceiling fishnets, glass ball floats, bamboo, clamshells, and of course, Tikis are in evidence at every turn. Especially amazing is a wall of artificial tropical flowers which have been painted in fluorescent colors to react with black light.

OMNI HUT, Smyrna, TN

The staff dress in muumuus, the music played is a mix of Martin Denny, Don Ho, and traditional Hawaiian slide guitar. The large aquarium is well maintained, and none of the decor looks old or run down. The artwork on the menu is very cool, the fountain still works... in short, this is one of the best and most lovingly preserved Type III vintage Polynesian restaurants you will see. Even the place mats – with their detailed Hawaiian vocabulary lesson – are worth keeping. The original (rare) Orchids of Hawaii silverware is also worthy of admiration.

OMNI HUT, Smyrna, TN

Of course, there is one thing missing – no Tiki mugs. You see, up until recently, liquor by the drink was illegal in Smyrna. However, it *is* legal to bring your own liquor into a restaurant. If you want a Mai Tai at Omni Hut, you'll have to bring the booze in yourself, and order a glass of juice to mix it with. For what it's worth, the colas (which you are welcome to enhance with the contents of your trusty flask o' rum) do come with paper umbrellas, once again showing the attention to detail present at the Omni Hut. It may feel a bit strange to whip out a bottle mid-meal, right in front of the waitress, and not have to be sneaky about it for fear of being forcibly ejected from the premises. Strange, but definitely liberating as well!

In November, 2000, new liquor laws were finally passed, but people seem to prefer the BYOB method, and getting the permits to allow Omni Hut to mix up a Scorpion Bowl would be very expensive. So they're maintaining the status quo for the time being. Our suggestion is that they add a "virgin" Mai Tai, Zombie, Scorpion, Blue Hawaiian, and Suffering Bastard to the menu. Kids will love the fruity and boozeless concoctions; adult Tikiphiles will love the fact that they can make them as strong or weak as they want to with their own favorite brand of rum.

The Tahitian Feast comes recommended (at $15.95 per person), but one may also opt for the Hawaiian Dinner, which is a similar idea with less food (at $12.25 per person). The dinner is essentially the same as what you can get in almost any Cantonese Restaurant: an array of soups and appetizers followed by an entree or two, and then dessert, tea, and fortune cookie.

As most Tikiphiles have consumed thousands of PuPu platters in Tiki bars across the globe, one may initially find themselves indifferent to the plate of egg rolls, fried shrimp, and Chinese Spare Ribs (aka Polynesian Pit Ribs) that are set before you after the Egg Flower Soup. But something new is afoot at Omni Hut! The tenderness of the large ribs is impressive, and with the amazing teriyaki sauce, of which just the right amount is applied, they become spectacular. This condiment is Omni Hut's own brand, and it is available for $2.99 a bottle. We suggest you stock up – it's a long drive back to Smyrna when you run out. The egg rolls are also surprising, and when you think about it, an egg roll has to be pretty darned good to be surprising! It is served with a bowl of sweet-n-sour sauce with a big dollop of *very* hot mustard in the center, looking like a big red and yellow fried egg.

Three bowls appear next: Beef Chop Suey, Chicken Chow Mein, and Sweet and Pungent Pork. The pork can be a little too sweet, but the beef and chicken dishes are both a notch above the fare you would get in most Chinese restaurants. Everything is fresh and tasty, reaffirming any doubts that this type of cooking can still impress. You'll regret resisting the temptation to order a chocolate volcano for desert, but if you manage, at least try a plate of Shaded Pit Pat (pineapple sherbet), served on a wooden pineapple-shaped platter with another paper umbrella.

Owner Polly Walls is friendly and likes the attention that the neo-Tiki craze is drawing to the Omni Hut. Eager to chat, she may tell you of the fire that nearly shut them down in 1999, or explain their ill-fated attempt to franchise, or orate – with refreshing enthusiasm – historical anecdotes about the Omni Hut's 42-year history. All of this, and you gotta

OMNI HUT, Smyrna, TN

love the picture by the door of the Russian Guard in Red Square wearing an Omni Hut baseball hat.

MORE TO DO IN TENNESSEE

Nashville: Mixed in among the Planet Hollywood-type franchises on Broadway is **Robert's** (not just a bar, but also a boot shop). There's no cover charge; tip the band. Check out the Ernest Tubb record shop across the street. **Rotier's** and **Brown's** are original 1930's diners, intact for all practical purposes. Brown's is still partly in a wooden trolley-car (Blair Blvd., just west of 21st Ave.). Rotier's (on Elliston Place just east of Centennial Park) burgers (served on toast, not buns) are a staple. **Dairy King** (Thompson Lane, at the Mill Creek bridge) is an original late-1940s drive-in. Only open during summer, it still features "bombers" that are made with actual beef. **The Arcade** (between 4th and 5th Ave., south of Union) dates from around the turn of the last century, and contains some original architecture. The city also abounds with loads more googie, 1950's Modern, and remnants from the deco periods plus a few still extant Tiki bits, scattered all over.

Leaving Nashville, heading north, find 31W, which snakes alongside I-65. From Nashville to Louisville, you get 180 miles of 1950's diners, motels with awesome vintage neon signs, plenty of small towns, and countless cheesy roadside attractions. Halfway between Louisville and Nashville you will find the intersection of SR 70. Turning left on SR 70 (heading west), drive about six miles (towards Mammoth Cave National Park. They have 10 different tours of the caverns that you can take for $8 each). You will find some of the most astounding examples of retro tourist traps ever. Look for a mini golf course with a Tiki-filled fountain. Haunted houses, water bumper cars, funiculars over the hills, and multiple zoos await; most of them have been there for 50 years. You will also see lots and lots of firecracker shacks. Check out the giant plaster Loch Ness Monster, too.

Back onto 31W, just north of SR70, exists the creme de la creme of all of this, **The Wigwam Village #2** (601 N. Dixie Hwy (31 W), in Cave City, KY (270) 773-3381), "Sleep in a Wigwam!" There used to be seven Wigwam Villages; two remain, the other is in Arizona.

Imagine 15 concrete Wigwams arranged in a semicircle around a sinkhole with a playground at the bottom. This is the sort of Mecca that fans of retro culture daydream about stumbling across. For the bargain price of $40 per night, you get your own concrete Wigwam, complete with private bathroom, cable TV, and air conditioner. The Wigwams are very clean, and carefully maintained. The furniture inside is all vintage. There is a park bench in front of each Wigwam so you can sit in front and relax with a view of the playground, the other Wigwams, and the trees and stars.

The gift shop is appropriately tacky, the owner is as nice as can be, and it is right on the road that you are driving on anyway. How can you *not* stop?

MORE TENNESSEE TIKI SITES TO EXPLORE

Tiki Beach Club, 124 Franklin St., Clarksville, TN (931) 542-0860

Tiki Lounge, Knoxville, TN
The race car posters on the walls and the mullet-clad clan at the bar make a quick getaway mandatory!

TENNESSEE SITES PERMANENTLY CLOSED

Mahi Mahi, Nashville, TN
Opened in 1971, Mahi Mahi had decor by Oceanic Arts, and was designed by Ely Hedley. The massive restaurant boasted a high ceiling, from which several outriggers and dozens of Orchids of Hawaii lanterns were suspended. An array of framed artwork and a high TiPSY Factor made the Mahi Mahi a real treat in its day.

TEXAS

HAWAiiAN BREEZE • 5825 RiCHMOND (BETWEEN CHiMNEY ROCK AND FOUNTAiN ViEW), HOUSTON, TX

(713) 782-6162

Category V
NEO-TIKI

TiPSY Factor

Opened late 2002. They serve tropical drinks in Tiki mugs and the food is truly in the Hawaiian style. The decor is still evolving, but look for small Tikis around the bar and some masks around the walls.

HULA HUT • 3826 LAKE AUSTiN BLVD., AUSTiN, TX

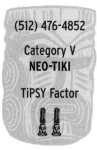

(512) 476-4852

Category V
NEO-TIKI

TiPSY Factor

A Hawaiian-themed restaurant with a bar, located on Town Lake. Their coconut-crusted shrimp is incredible. The drinks are great and the food is fabulous. The decor is like one of Don Ho's dreams after a night of too many Blue Hawaiians, and the wait staff is friendly and colorfully attired.

OCEAN'S 11 • 720 RED RiVER, AUSTiN, TX

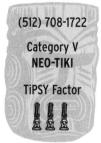

(512) 708-1722

Category V
NEO-TIKI

TiPSY Factor

Opened in 2000, Ocean's 11 has been getting some positive buzz. While their claim that they are "the first authentic Tiki bar built in North America in the last 40 years" is a bit arrogant (we can think of *dozens* built between 1960 and 2000), their atmosphere and drinks seem to have been crafted with quite a bit of attention to authenticity, and O-11 is worth checking out. We like the waiters in their red jackets, the karaoke machine, and the occasional live music.

MORE TEXAS TIKI SITES TO EXPLORE

Polynesian Gardens, 2910 Kemp St. Wichita Falls, TX (940) 692-0731

Tiki Island, TX
Tiki Island, Texas is a very small island immediately north of Galveston on IH45 (about 40 miles south of Houston). We haven't been able to determine if the whole town is one giant Tiki bar or not. Somehow we doubt it...

TEXAS SITES PERMANENTLY CLOSED

Club Bali Hai, Western Skies Motel, 7809 Katy Rd., Houston, TX

Don The Beachcomber, Houston, TX

Don The Beachcomber, Dallas, TX

Garza's Kon Tiki Club, 315 23rd, Galveston, TX
This appears to have been a Tiki gay bar; press reads "Located in the heart of old historical Galveston, Garza's Kon Tiki Club continues the fifty year tradition of bringing the best DJs, dancers, and female impersonators to Galveston."

KONA-KAI INN RESTAURANT, Dumas, TX

Kona-Kai Inn Restaurant Highways 87 and 287 S., Dumas, TX
Photos reveal a truly spectacular sign outside of a large but nondescript building.

Polynesian Village (Ren Clark's), Fort Worth, TX

Ports o' Call, (Stephen Crane's), Sheraton, Dallas, TX

Stephen Crane's original locations were simply called Kon Tiki, later versions were opened as Kon Tiki Ports, and his final restaurants were created under the name Ports o' Call. The Molokai Mule drink was served in its own distinctive tumbler with a decidedly un-Tiki – but very Texan – mule and horseshoe design. Crane also owned the Chapparal Club in Dallas's Southland Center.

Trader Vic's, Hilton Hotel, 5600 North Central Expressway (at Mockingbird), Dallas, TX

Rumor has it the room (like Chin's in Detroit and Mai Kai in Chicago) is intact behind locked doors...

UTAH

BURT'S TiKi BAR • 726 S. STATE ST., SALT LAKE CiTY, UT

(801) 521-0572

Category I
**CLASSIC TIKI BAR
(IN THEORY)**

TiPSY Factor

Because of some backward law, you have to be a member of a private club to drink in a bar in Salt Lake City, so explorers wishing to visit Burt's will have to find a resident to declare them guests. Burt's is home to enough random derelicts/club members that this should not be a problem; any ol' local will usually be cool with making some new pals.

The mullet-sporting bartenders are loathe to mix up anything resembling a Tropical Drink, and there is an almost complete lack of any Tikiness whatsoever in Bert's Tiki Bar – you'll find exactly one (almost) Tiki statue (see picture) upstairs in the billiard room. Burt's is a complete bust when it comes to Tiki bars.

But wait!

If you want a good punk dive, Burt's is probably the best place in SLC, if not the whole state of Utah. As Tiki bars go, it stinks, but as a trashy punk dive, it is every bit as good as Empty Bottle in Chicago, or the Grog Shop in Cleveland. They have cheap beer; crappy punk bands on a grimy corner stage; flyers, pictures, and posters all over the walls; a surly bartender; and free pool on Sundays.

BURT'S TIKI BAR, Salt Lake City, UT

MORE UTAH TIKI SITES TO EXPLORE

**Hawaiian Style Cafe, 4195 South 500 West,
Salt Lake City, UT (801) 281-4007**
Also has a fast food delivery service with Tiki Vans!

UTAH SITES PERMANENTLY CLOSED

Johnny Quong's Hawaiian, Salt Lake City, UT
Known during the 1960s as SLC's wildest bar. Their unique
Tiki mug was among the ugliest ever produced!

VERMONT

*We have no evidence of any Tiki bars, past or present
in Vermont.*

VIRGINIA

LUAU GARDEN • 1090 ELDEN ST. HERNDON, VA

Luau Garden is a neighborhood restaurant and lounge.
Their Chinese buffet (lunch) has improved vastly over the
years. Unlike most buffets, the items are hot, fresh, and frequently replenished. Several unusual items are featured,
such as mussels and shrimp toast.

(703) 471-1150

Category III
**CHINESE
RESTAURANT**

TiPSY Factor

The decor is certainly Polynesian, with lots of wicker
and bamboo, a few fake palm trees, and some incongruous
Chinese art. There is a huge art wood-block of pink flamin-
gos on the walls, and booths of deep-blue and pearled vinyl
upholstery (which is cracking).

The Mai Tai is smallish, but not bad for $4. Garnish is a
cherry, lime wedge, and orange slice. Color: light pink. Not
good. It is adequately strong and has a good flavor. The
color belies a drizzle of slow-acting cheap grenadine. The
drink is a bit too sweet, and leaves an alcoholic aftertaste.

HONOLULU RESTAURANT • 5634 TELEGRAPH RD, ALEXANDRiA, VA

(703) 960-3668

Category III
CHINESE
RESTAURANT

TiPSY Factor

Owner David Chan was a bartender at Trader Vic's in Washington D.C. from 1970 to 1976, and is reported to have been Richard Nixon's favorite bartender (Tricky Dick was a Navy Grog man). Chan bought the Honolulu from the previous owner in 1978, only 10 months after it opened. From the outside, Honolulu looks like a warehouse for rent, situated between a 7-11 and an Exxon station. The otherwise uninviting entrance is marked only by pair of Tiki totem pillars.

Inside, this family-run restaurant is definitely Tiki. Look for plenty of masks, bamboo, netting, Tikis, and huge tridacna clam shells with lights in them, all hanging from the black-painted ceiling. Silhouetted beach scenes glow in slowly changing primary colors on opposing walls. Palm matting covers the other walls. The booths feel semi-private due to the use of tied back bamboo curtains, and each table has its own little Tiki lamp in the center. Wicker chairs have plastic leis woven around the edges. A hula girl music box totters on the cluttered bar. A complete lack of windows is on oft-overlooked key architectural descision; Honolulu's windowless walls make it easy to completely forget that the freeway is almost directly outside.

The music is usually Hawaiian standards (although at lunch time things can be eerily silent), and there isn't a television in sight. Good deal.

Mr. Chan's experiences at Trader Vic's have not been forgotten. The friendly and personable owner of the Honolulu still mixes up a mean drink. The house drink is the Tiki Tumbler. For $6.50 you get to keep the mug. If you don't want the vessel, don't order the drink. It's from the same molecular group as the Mai Tai, but sweeter, probably from bombardment with high-energy grenadine atoms.

At $4.50 the Honolulu Mai Tai is a better drink; it is served in a large old-fashioned glass garnished with a pineapple cube, cherry, and a lime quarter on a plastic sword. The color of the drink is right – a foggy brown with no hint of grenadine. This is how a Mai Tai should taste.

Harmonious, refreshing, aging gracefully as the ice melts. The Puca Punch is also recommended. The multitalented Mr. Chan also personally drew the drink renderings depicted in the menu!

The food is westernized Cantonese, with Szechwan the specialty. Look for all the usual appetizers: Pupu platters, fried crab Rangoon, and shrimp toasts. As neighborhood Chinese restaurants go, it's above average. Try the banana flambe for dessert: the rum-fueled fire reaching to the ceiling is worth the price.

The Chans go on vacation every summer, so if you visit in July or August, call before heading over, or you may end up with nothing but a slurpee from the 7-11 next door.

HULA INN • 200 OLD OX ROAD, STERLING, VA

Hula Inn Restaurant and Lounge is at the edge of a Washington D.C. suburb in a light industrial area between a residential neighborhood and Dulles Airport. The "lounge" is a tiny barroom, which is stocked with local regulars on any given night. The restaurant has a moderate but tasteful TiPSY Factor, is slightly worn, but is otherwise pleasant if unremarkable. The staff is widely international. During the day the radio plays easy listening.

(703) 471-9000

Category III
CHINESE
RESTAURANT

TiPSY Factor

Hula Inn has good tropical drinks. The "House Special" drink is good, as are the Suffering Bastard and the Flaming Volcano. The Mai Tai is adorned with an orange slice, a pineapple cube, and a cherry. The cost is only $3.25, which is in line with the excellent values at Hula. This is a very pink Mai Tai, a bit sweet, but also complex. The complexity: the bite of licorice. It may also include a desperate dash of bitters, but the libation is still on the sweet side. There is no discernible fruit flavor (lime or pineapple).

The food is several cuts above the average neighborhood Chinese restaurant. It is consistently fresh, generous, and a bit different from the usual. Skip the meager buffet.

KYOTO • 1621 RiCHMOND RD., WiLLiAMSBURG, VA

(757) 220-8888

Category III
**CHINESE
RESTAURANT**

TiPSY Factor

Kyoto, located near Norfolk, on a strip of highway populated with some of the finest surviving examples of 1950s-
style ideographic architecture, is built in the shape of a
Japanese castle. The decor has a few scatterings of classic
Tiki elements – a mask here, a carved Pacific statue there,
bamboo, and straw. They serve more tropical drinks than
you can shake a swizzle stick at, each served in the appropriate Tiki mugs. The Bora-Bora Brew comes in a ceramic
pineapple, and many others are pictured on a wonderful
laminated drink menu that someone must have sent by
time machine from the spring of 1963.

TiKi-TiKi • 8917 PATTERSON, RiCHMOND, VA

(804) 704-7258

Category III
**CHINESE
RESTAURANT**

TiPSY Factor

This small, stand-alone building has a single, large and
colorful Tiki mask nailed to the outside wall. Inside, one will
find entrees like Tiki Tiki Chow Mein for $6.95, and Po-Po
Platter for $8.75. Tropical drinks are reasonable at
$3.25–$4.25.

TIKI-TIKI, Richmond, VA

MORE VIRGINIA TIKI SITES TO EXPLORE

DiamondHead Polynesian Restaurant, 4108 Meadowdale Boulevard, Richmond, VA (804) 275-2261
No Tiki, but interesting Japanese architecture. Chinese food.

Hula Inn, 200 Old Ox Road, Sterling, VA (703) 471-9000

Luau Garden, 1090 Elden St. Herndon, VA (703) 471-1150

Tiki Bob's Cantina, 110 North 18th St., Richmond, VA (804) 644-9091
Offers "Mexi-nesian" chow and a television in each of 20 booths. Next...

Tim's Rivershore Restaurant and Crab House, 1510 Cherry Hill Rd., Dumfries, VA (703) 441-1375
The Tiki bar on these premises appears to be of the so-called "Florida-style."

Waikiki, 11016 Midlothain Turnpike, Midlothian, VA (804) 794-4672
There's so much bamboo in the place, it is probably a fire hazard!

VIRGINIA SITES PERMANENTLY CLOSED

Pacific Inn, Alexandria, VA
Distributed an interesting matchbook die-cut into the shape of a hut with a Tiki mask on one side. This same design was actually used by a half-dozen D.C.-area Tiki bars.

WASHINGTON

SOUTH PACiFIC RESTAURANT • 3507 CAPiTOL BLVD. (NEXT TO THE MiLLER BREWERY), OLYMPiA, WA

(360) 352-0701

Category III
(barely...)
CHINESE RESTAURANT

TiPSY Factor

This large Chinese restaurant has some pan-Asian artifacts inside, and a large bar, but no sign of Tiki inside. Outside (right by the door), they do have a colorful painting of a happy Tiki mug sitting on the beach. You probably don't want to visit this one, unless you're really hard up to see the painting next to the door, or you happen to be in the neighborhood and hungry...

Near downtown Olympia, look for **The Spar**, a very cool 1920's diner. The Spar has 20-foot ceilings, amazing old woodwork, and a deco bar. Large vintage photos of the local industry at work in the 1910s-1930s cover the walls, and framed 1932 newspaper pages with articles about The Spar line a rear hallway. Olympia also has a Tiki-themed tattoo parlor.

LAVA LOUNGE • 2226 2ND AVE., SEATTLE, WA

(206) 441-5660

Category V
NEO-TIKI

TiPSY Factor

LAVA LOUNGE, Seattle, WA

LAVA LOUNGE, Seattle, WA

This is one of those hipster bars crammed full of whatever sort of ephemera the owners think is cool. There are definitely a few Tiki artifacts in the Lava Lounge. They don't serve any tropical drinks to speak of; this is micro brew territory (try the Mack and Jacks African Amber and the local fallback, Flat Tire). Not much Exotica in the house; the DJ spins 1970's rare groove funk and R+B.

Highlights: an old-looking "Hotel Krakatoa" sign, a movie poster for Coca Cabana that looks just like a certain Les Baxter LP cover, a sea shell lamp shade with little shells strung up in two spirals like a DNA double helix, a working 1950's shuffleboard penny arcade game, two enormous and very ugly Tikis behind the bar, a giant paper lantern from a very old Chinese restaurant, a paper mache octopus, a cool volcano mural, and money from all over the world pasted up behind the bar, including a Canadian dollar which had the portrait on it modified in ball-point pen to look like Mr. Spock. Oh, and something unreadable in our notes that looks like it says: "backlit '70's hula girls @ Dinner Table sign." Maybe you can go there and tell us what we thought we were writing about?

LAVA LOUNGE, Seattle, WA

LUAU • THE 2253 N. 56TH, SEATTLE, WA

(206) 633-5828

Category II
FINE DINING

TiPSY Factor

The Luau is decorated with surfboards (painted brightly with slightly cartoony modern day Tiki imagery), the suggestion of a woven leaf hut over part of the lounge, seafaring paraphernalia, and of course, the occasional Tiki statue. Polynesian-type music supports the theme. There is also an outdoor seating area, flanked with bamboo and dried grass skirting.

The coolest Tiki in the Luau (which isn't a real big place – it seats about 35, plus another 10 at the bar), is the hostess stand, which is a four-foot wooden Tiki with nooks carved in his back (ouch!) for telephones, menus, and other hostess tools. The area behind the bar is crammed full of artifacts. Favorites are two almost-flat Tiki carvings (above the collage of photos of people you don't know having a really good time). This pair of carvings will inspire the oft repeated question "where can I get some of those?" which has been uttered, or at least slowly cognated, in so many Tiki bars over so many years...

Although the Luau appears to be a rather casual and laid back little bistro at first, a look at the menu can easily fool you into thinking that you've been mysteriously transported into a fine dining establishment, and one with really good food, but without the snooty Maitre'D. Getting to eat something other than bad Chinese food while slurping a Mai Tai is always a treat. The wait staff is outstanding: super friendly, very knowledgeable, and ready to accommodate.

The Luau has an outstanding and original rethinking of the PuPu platter, consisting of eight wooden dishes and four bamboo skewers of meat, vegetables, and shrimp ring on a small, flaming, Tiki-esque grill. The PuPu offerings change frequently, but ones often seen are steamed mussels, fish cooked in a banana leaf pouch with coconut, and very hot homemade kim chee.

THE LUAU, Seattle, WA

THE LUAU, Seattle, WA

Oysters on the half shell, variously flavored, also appear regularly on the appetizer menu. The warm Hawaiian flat bread with sweet onion relish that comes automatically to your table before you order is a favorite starter. The salads are fresh and surprising in their choice of unusual ingredients.

The entrees also change occasionally; try the macadamia-crusted slice of pork loin on a bed of curried asuki beans, mussels in five-spice broth garnished with three duck-and-fig wontons, a beautifully presented vegetarian rice dish, chow mein with plum sauce and fried eggplant, sugarcane-smoked duck, and a pulled pork sandwich served with freshly made sweet potato chips and a papaya slaw. Other menu items include baby-back ribs with a dark, spicy glaze, and Shaggy's chicken, which seems to be a menu staple – an artistic stack of jerked chicken on a bed of spiced potatoes.

THE LUAU, Seattle, WA

Desserts include large, decadent offerings like coconut ice cream with macadamia brittle, and Bananas Foster (a flaming platter of ice cream, sugar, nuts, rum, and, of course, a couple of bananas). These are also a good value for the money.

THE LUAU, Seattle, WA

THE LUAU, Seattle, WA

Complimenting the Pacific Rim/Polynesian-inspired entrees are the excellent bar offerings. The Mai Tai is actually served up in a *Tiki mug*. Yessiree, how many other Tiki bars in the year 2003 can boast that they still serve their drinks in Tiki mugs? Not too many. The Zombie-for-Two is served in a large bowl with very long straws, and two garnishes that incorporate orange slices, maraschino cherries, and paper umbrellas to give the appearance of two people sitting in a big tub wearing rice paddy hats. There is also a Mai Tai variation made with guava juice also served in a Tiki mug, a coconut martini, Val's Blue Hawaii (lemonade spiked with Absolut Citron and blue curacao), and Pele's Revenge (Mount Gay rum and passion fruit juice are the main ingredients).

THE LUAU, Seattle, WA

OHANA • 2207 1ST AVE, BELLTOWN (SEATTLE), WA

(206) 956-9329

Category II
FINE DINING

TiPSY Factor

There is a pretty high TiPSY Factor here, including a number of booths in bamboo-framed huts topped with tapered Tikis, Tiki-esque masks, Oriental fans, glass floats in nets, puffer fish... the whole bit. Look for a textured wave mural, complete with a surfer and sharks, behind the large, grass-thatched bar trimmed with Tiki and palm tree lights. We can't really berate Ohana for their televisions, because they are draped with fishnets and seem to show only surfing programs with sound off, so it doesn't compete with the pseudo-Polynesian background music.

The food is predominantly Japanese, with occasional Polynesian touches. The vegetable-filled sushi rolls are good. The tempura prawns, yams, and peppers are well done too. Ohana's edame is livened up effectively with a bottled chili/sesame oil condiment. Another favorite is the poke ahi, an appetizer of chopped raw tuna, marinated lightly in citrus and sprinkled with toasted sesame seeds. This is served with taro chips for scooping up the fish. While we did not try the Spam Musubi (a slab of fried Spam on a cake of sushi rice, wrapped in dry seaweed), we did appreciate the panache it added to the appetizer menu.

The entrees are tasty and well presented. In addition, the sushi plate is a good value at about $15. The sushi pieces with raw fish are also of generous proportion, as the fish pieces were cut thicker than is the norm. The pork curry is delicious, and garnished with three interesting and brightly colored pickles, including pickled hibiscus blossoms.

Drinks ($6-$7) include some standards, such a well-made Singapore Sling and a Blue Hawaii. There is a Mai Tai variant flavored with Amaretto, and a couple of drinks served in Tiki mugs, which you can purchase for an additional $3. One of these is Mike's Cliffhanger, a house original. Quite good, frothy, not too sweet, and goes well with the food offerings. It was based on Cruzan banana rum, with cream of coconut, pineapple juice, and Kahlua playing a supporting role.

MORE WASHINGTON TIKI SITES TO EXPLORE

Dragonfish, 722 Pine St., Seattle, WA (206) 467-7777
Not a Tiki bar, but they do serve tropical drinks in Tiki mugs.

Tiki Bob's, Seattle, WA
Opened in 2001. Not connected to the classic Tiki Bob's in San Francisco.

Tiki apartments, 111 South Highland Ave., Tacoma, WA

Tiki Lodge, 1420 West 2nd Ave., Spokane, WA (800) 246-6835

Tradewinds Motel, 3033 North Division Street, Spokane, WA (800) 621-8593

Tradewinds Motel Downtown, 907 West 3rd Ave., Spokane, WA (509) 838-2094
Marked with a large, flat, plastic-type sign featuring a really neat graphic of a Tiki (flanked by Tiki torches on either side), which were once gas-lit.

Leilani Lanes bowling alley, 10201 Greenwood Ave., N., Seattle, WA (206) 783-8010
Another Tiki bowling alley.

Tiki Car Wash, 11909 Northeast 8th Street, Bellevue, WA (425) 455-4787

WASHINGTON SITES PERMANENTLY CLOSED

Clark's New Islander, corner of 11th and A St., Tacoma WA
Vintage press reads: "Clark's Islander, a charcoal broiler restaurant, is compounded of a starry tropical night... the whisper of the sands... the rustling of palms... From the foyer, luminous with its panel of laminated shells, you descend a series of sandstone steps to the main dining room. Here, all decorative details combine to produce the effect of a soft night in the tropics. Fronds and branches project into the room... the tiny glowing stars set in the dark ceiling are arranged in the patterns of the southern constellations... walls of tropical woods... island lanterns... banquettes of brown and tan native fabrics... even an authentic-looking

island hut shadowed by a Ming tree... Japanese screens... an extremely subtle use of lighting effects. There's a cocktail lounge too, with startling realistic tropical appearance... a back bar with a raffia roof from Madagascar... wood carvings of famous Balinese dancers... palm trees... an aquarium... banquettes of spotted hide... woven rush squares from the Philippines. The lighting is dim and restful. No effort has been spared to secure authentic appointments... table tops cut in Hawaii from Monkey Pod tree... Suva matting woven by natives of the Fiji Islands... rattan from Borneo... and reproductions of tribal masks from Java, Bali, Tahiti, and the Solomons."

Golden Door (near Pioneer Square), Seattle, WA
Had a live Polynesian dance show on weekends.

Hawaiian Village apartments, Tacoma, WA

Hula Hut, 7116 E. Green Lake Dr., Seattle, WA

Kau Kau, 1115 1/2 2nd, Seattle, WA
"Cocktails in the Polynesian Room."

Lapu Lapu, 3296 Aurora N., Seattle, WA
"Exotic Tropical Cuisine"

Luau Barbecue Restaurant, 314 Broadway E., Seattle, WA
"Cocktails in a tropical hut."

The Outrigger (later Trader Vic's), Benjamin Franklin Hotel, 5th and Virginia, Seattle, WA
Opened 1948, closed 1991. See Trader Vic's below.

Pantley's Pagan Room, 3201 156th S.E. Bellevue, WA

Polynesian Condominium Apartment/Motel, 291 Ocean Shores Blvd., Ocean Shores, WA
This deluxe resort by the ocean was home of the Pat Boone Celebrity Golf Classic. A new resort down the street (at 615 Ocean Shores Blvd. N.W.) seems to have taken over the name.

Polynesia Restaurant, Puget Sound, Seattle, WA
Built for half-a-million dollars in 1951, Pier 51's Polynesia featured a high peaked "long house" design, with interior walls of polished teakwood. Raymond H. Peck, the architect, borrowed the markings of ceremonial shields, canoe prows, and

the art of Tahiti, the Philippine Islands, and Pago Pago. Polynesia also sported lava rock from Hawaii, precious woods from the Far East, coral and tree ferns (hapu), art carvings, and sea shells. The heavy posts and beams were carved with designs created by Peck. The carving was done by Donald Keys and Donald Ingalls. The markings on the post and beams were repeated in the china. A ceremonial design, taken from a Marquesian shield, was used as the cover for the menu.

A spiral fireplace in the main dining room rose from a reflecting pool on the floor; the spiral was made of pipe, perforated to produce dozens of small open flames. The banquettes were carved by Witco. A huge Tiki was carved in Manilla of monkey pod. Transparencies with Tahitian emblems laminated in plastic by Fay Chong marked the front of the restaurant. Owner Dave Cohn hired Anita Moore, a former resident of Tahiti, to inform guests on the customs and art of the Polynesians.

The Polynesia Restaurant remained alive until the state condemned the Pier around 1981 in order to expand the Seattle ferry terminal. On the morning of January 25th, 1982, the entire Polynesia Restaurant was lifted in one piece off of Pier 51 by a large floating crane. The Polynesia was "placed on a barge and towed to a site on the Duwamish River while the owners searched for a new location." Sometime after the Polynesia's mothballing, Cohn gave up and let the Seattle Fire Department burn the structure for practice.

Reef Restaurant, 1001 E. Valley Hwy., Kent (near Seattle), WA
"Polynesian Atmosphere." "Cocktails in the Tiki Room."

Tapa Room, Hotel Windsor, Seattle, WA

Tiki Hut, 544 Elliot N., Seattle, WA
"Exotic cocktails in the Shell Room."

TRADER VIC'S, Seattle, WA

Tiki Lounge, Seattle, WA

Exquisitely kitschy haven for seamen off the freighters tied up in Elliot Bay. The dark, seedy bar was hosted by a wonderful and gracious Asian woman. The dining area was covered in fake fishnet, plastic crabs, and shellfish, and colored lights dangled everywhere. The drink of choice was beer: Pabst and Rainier. The hostess kept a map of the world behind the bar with thumbtacks representing where patrons called home: Singapore, Nigeria, Sri Lanka...

Trader Vic's, Benjamin Franklin Hotel, 5th and Virginia, Seattle, WA

Opened 1948 as an Outriggers, closed 1991. "A background as easy and comfortable as the South Seas itself. You have a selection of rooms that range from the Garden Room (plantings, corrugated tin roof and even Oriental newspapers pasted to the ceiling) to the Ship's Cabin, patterned after the main cabin of a Yankee Clipper... to the Tiki which is separated from two immense round Chinese ovens by floor-to-ceiling plate glass. The Outrigger has a (menu) of at least 200 items... ."

Tropics Restaurant 225 Aurora N., Seattle, WA

WASHINGTON, D.C.

POLiTiKi • 319 PENNSYLVANiA AVE. SE (BETWEEN 3RD ST. AND 4TH ST.), WASHiNGTON, DC

(202) 546-1001

Category: V
NEO-TIKI

TiPSY Factor

Between the early-1970s and the middle-1990s, there were few new Tiki bars built. One of the first to spearhead the neo-Tiki renaissance (as far back as 1993) was Politiki. They have had a difficult struggle, but they seem to be committed to hanging on for the long haul.

Located in Washington, D.C., just a few blocks down the street from the home of the President of the United States, Politiki was originally conceived as three floors of retro paradise. At that time, Politiki immediately distinguished itself with two giant Tikis on the front sign, bamboo window shades, and a string of plastic Moai-shaped lights across the sidewalk patio. Inside, there were strange plaster faces all over the walls, a collection of vintage Tiki mugs (that could only be the owner's private collection), and two giclee prints by the masterful Mark Ryden on the walls. The basement was more of a classic style Tiki bar (including three big wood Tikis carved by Bosko). The uppermost level was host to dancing and live swing music.

POLITIKI, Washington, D.C.

Unfortunately, by 1999, PoliTiki had become *the* Penn Ave. pub. Evidently, the frat boys and government wonks that frequent this neighborhood were more impressed with a new motif: Pittsburgh. Tikis apparently don't sell enough Bud Lite, but Pittsburgh-themed sports banners and the like do.

That said, as of 2001, the owner of Politiki had some encouraging news: "I am glad to tell you, that after a trying time (bad management, uncaring staff), we are re-organized and back, hopefully getting better and bigger. We have moved the PoliTiki permanently into the basement of our three-story bar. We have increased the size of the physical bar in the basement and added some great

POLITIKI, Washington, D.C.

booths. The cool lounge and Tiki music are back in the jukebox."

This seems to be as good a reason as any to give the PoliTiki a shot, and if you need another, the drinks there have always been good. The Suffering Bastard and Virgin's Downfall are made with decent rum, so you won't find yourself making the Lono-face that Castillo or other such cheap hootch inspires. They also have a short menu of food, consisting of your basic bar food (burgers and the like) and a few more traditional Tiki bar dishes (PuPus, basically).

POLITIKI, Washington, D.C.

POLITIKI, Washington, D.C.

MORE WASHINGTON, D.C. TIKI SITES TO EXPLORE

Smithsonian Institution, 1000 Jefferson Dr. SW, Washington, DC (202) 357-1300

There is a real Moai in the Smithsonian. It is one of the smaller Moai ever constructed, but it is there for those of you who can't make it to Rapa Nui to check out his brethren.

WASHINGTON, D.C. SITES PERMANENTLY CLOSED

Aloha Hut, Washington, D.C.

Their souvenir Tiki mug was green, and featured a unique Lono design that seemed the have "feathers" sprouting from its head. They also had a matchbook die-cut into the shape of a hut with a Tiki mask on one side. This same design was actually used by a half-dozen D.C.-area Tiki bars.

TRADER VIC'S, Washington, D.C.

Kona Kai, Mariott Hotel, Washington, D.C.
This was the world headquarters for the Mariott's Kona Kai chain. The spectacular carvings on the tympanum entrance were created by Oceanic Arts.

Trader Vic's, Capitol Hilton, Washington, D.C.
Closed 1995.

WEST VIRGINIA

We have no evidence of any Tiki bars, past or present in West Virginia.

WISCONSIN

MiLWAUKEE
There are no *true* Tiki bars in Milwaukee, (look for the Mai Kai in our "closed" section below), but here are a few places of definite interest if you're in beertown...

Foundation, 2718 N. Breman, Milwaukee, WI
(414) 374-2587
For many years Foundation has been an extremely cool punk rock bar with a few strings of Tiki lights and a weekly Exotica night (Tuesdays). The owners have become more committed to Tiki recently, and the bar is now covered with Bamboo, leopard skin, and Tiki masks. Check it out.

At Random, 2501 S. Delaware Ave, Milwaukee WI
(414) 481-8030
This post-atomic lounge sports a subfusc interior, a long curved bar, and excellent music selections. Randy Zeller, son of the original owners (who opened the place in 1964) still tends the bar. The drink menu is all "classic drinks" – there is no beer served. The Mai Tai ($9) is good, although it is not made with a traditional recipe. At $16, The Tiki Love Bowl is an amazing fruity concoction, and is probably too much for even the most amorous (and hard-livered) couple. Served in a huge crystal chalice, it'll do you some good. Their Missionary's Downfall ($9) is full of rum, brandy, and a hint of Galliano. Great stuff, if a hair pricey. Although they

aren't cheap, the drinks are great (fully up to Trader Vic standards) and quite strong. We suspect that part of the high price tag on all of the drinks (the cheapest is $7) is to keep the riff-raff out of this house of swank.

Great Northwest Haiawatha, on Stuart street, near Allyce street

Northwestern Haiawatha is an old 1940's train car, converted into a bar. The drinks and decor aren't that spectacular, but the eccentric two-man staff is entertaining.

Tip Top Atomic Shop, 2343 S. Kinnickinnic (414) 486-1951

Lots of true vintage items, plus neo-retro wares and Tiki stuff.

MORE WISCONSIN TIKI SITES TO EXPLORE

Leilani Motel, 18615 W. Bluemound Rd., Brookfield, WI (414) 786-7100

Polynesian Isle Hotel & Suites, 833 North Frontage Rd., Wisconsin Dells, WI (800) 254-4505
No Tiki whatsoever.

Tiki Bar, Water's Edge Restaurant (on Hwy 113, 4 miles north of Hwy 60) Lodi, WI (608) 592-OKEE (6533)
Open weekends, live rock music.

WISCONSIN SITES PERMANENTLY CLOSED

Fireside Restaurant and Playhouse, Fort Atkinson, WI
This one had a Moai Mug to keep with the restaurant name inscribed on the back.

Judge's Beyond the Reef, 16590 W. North Ave., (at Calhoun Rd.), Brookfield, WI

Leilani, 18615 Bluemound Rd., Brookfield, WI

Mai Kai, 5630 W Lincoln Ave, Milwaukee, WI
(414) 321-4401

As of June 2001, Mai Kai has been replaced by our dread
nemesis, a sports bar. Located too far out of the center of
town to attract whatever hipster scene Milwaukee might
have, the poor Mai Kai was lucky to last as long as it did.

The bar was de-Tikified in October 2000, when the old
owner (who had owned it since 1973) sold it to the new
owner, Michelle Manzella. She still pours a mean Mai Tai in a
brandy snifter (at $7), but has no interest in keeping any-
thing Tiki alive.

There are a few vague traces of Tiki left – the front
entrance is still a 15-foot-tall A-frame style with two big
torches sticking out of the sides like antennae on some
alien bug. Even more intriguing (or more pathetic) is that if
you look carefully, you can still see where a huge Tiki Mask
or shield and large wooden letters spelling "M A I K A I"
were removed from the front of the building. They had
hung on the side of the place for so long that the sun
bleached the paint all around them, leaving ghostly images.
And that's *all* that remains!

Tiki Bar, 6th and Rogers, Milwaukee, WI
Closed since approximately 1990.

WYOMING

We have no evidence of any Tiki bars, past or present,
in Wyoming.

CANADA

ALBERTA

ALBERTA SITES TO EXPLORE

Bamboo Tiki Room, 1201 1 Street SW, Calgary, AB
(403) 261-6674

Tiki II Restaurant, Calgary, AB (403) 264-0530

BRiTiSH COLUMBiA

TAHiTiAN LOUNGE/POLYNESiAN ROOM • WALDORF HOTEL, 1489 E. HASTiNGS ST., VANCOUVER, BRiTiSH COLUMBiA

(604) 253-7141

Category I/IV
**CLASSIC TIKI
BAR/TIKI MECCA**

TiPSY Factor

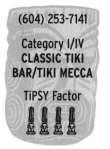

The Waldorf hotel is a two-story construct, with rooms on the second floor. The main floor is divided between a sports bar and the Tahitian Lounge, which is unfortunately only open during special events. The room is available for rental, and is also a popular spot for movie filming.

Entering the amazing Tahitian Lounge, there is a long, crescent-shaped bar on the left. The front of the bar is bamboo. The stools resemble bongo drums, with Tiki figures carved into the legs. These look just like the drums seen in the Leeteg painting on page 58 of *Leeteg of Tahiti*. A dozen frosted and etched mirrors make up the wall behind the bar, extending all the way to the 15-foot ceiling. Full-height (fake) palm trees are placed strategically around the room. In front of the bar is a stone parquet floor, with a series of small tables placed along a waist-high wall opposite the bar.

Two steps take you up to a second tier. This tier has two rows of larger tables, one along the other side of the waist-high wall, and another along the back wall of the room, farthest from the bar. The end effect of the semi-circular room is three concentric half-rings: the bar, then the stone-floored area in front of it with the smaller tables, and then the larger seating area two steps up.

TAHITIAN LOUNGE/POLYNESIAN ROOM, British Columbia

TAHITIAN LOUNGE/POLYNESIAN ROOM, British Columbia

The back wall of this largest ring is covered with woven thatch, and boasts four original Leetegs. Facing the wall, the painting second from the left is *Hina Rapa*, one of his most famous images. It is the painting featured on the cover of the aforementioned *Leeteg of Tahiti* book. That said, Leeteg was known to have repainted the exact same images many times, and *Hina Rapa* is the most notorious example of this; Leeteg is said to have painted her twenty-four times. The black velvet paintings are sunk into alcoves in the wall, and are shielded with Plexiglas panels.

This place is all class. Some favorite Tiki bars are kind of divey, or are trying to be elegant, but are being run cluelessly. The Polynesian Room seems to have been transported right out of 1955 (the year it opened), completely intact. There is nothing campy or kitschy about it. Even places like the Mai Kai (Ft. Lauderdale, Florida) pander to the tourists, and it isn't hard to imagine the owners winking at you, knowing that we know that they know that we know that kitsch is a big part of the appeal. But not here. This place is elegant and real. Picture white jackets on the waiters, cigarette girls in short dresses, and a maitre d' with a pencil thin mustache! Strip away the Tiki decor, and the place still serves as an amazing example of mid-century interior design.

TAHITIAN LOUNGE/POLYNESIAN ROOM, British Columbia

The Tahitian Lounge is only a quarter of the complex. The rest (the Polynesian Room and the Meneahune Banquet Room) is on the basement level, accessed via a wide spiral staircase. The walls of the stairwell are covered – from the downstairs floor to the tall, tall ceiling – with vertical bamboo. The handrails are bamboo too. Several (empty) picture frames on the way down are – you guessed it – bamboo. The only thing that isn't bamboo in this stair way are a *giant* map of Hawaii, a few Tiki masks, and a paper lantern. The floral carpet is tasteful, retaining a 1940's pattern, although it seems to have been replaced at some point.

A long and narrow hallway leads into the Meneahune Banquet Room. The doors to this room are especially cool. Etched and frosted glass in the center, with a border made of bamboo (of course) threaded through half-coconuts. Inside the room (used when bands perform) are further exotic artifacts, including a tall pole with carvings depicting mischievous characters, not unlike the Trader Vic's meneahune mascot.

Back down the hall, one passes an excellent little mini bar on the left. This tiny bar, with one stool in front of it, is shoved into an extra alcove, and is amazing in itself: simple, small, but great.

Moving down three more stairs, one enters the Polynesian Room, which is perhaps even larger than the Tahitian Lounge upstairs. The far wall contains a semicircular window, consisting of eight tall panes of glass, all tinted blue. The bright outdoor light coming through the aqua arch of glass gives the illusion of being in an environment we can only describe as "Pacific." A long bar, not dissimilar to the one upstairs, dominates the east side of the room, and the west wall contains an outstanding mural by Eugene

Savage depicting the discovery of Hawaii by King Kamehameha. For a sense of scale, keep in mind while viewing the picture on this page that most of the figures are life-sized, and that this picture only shows half of the mural.

Eight long and comfy looking benches fill out the room, which, while not as elegant as the one upstairs, looks like it could be host to a really swell shindig. A funny side note: we visited shortly after a minor flood had left six inches of water on the floor. They had several big industrial fans (wind machines, not Nine Inch Nails aficionados) drying out the floor. The fans were making the carpet ripple, and from a few feet away, it looked like the carpet was water, rippling in the tropical breeze...

Most of the other Tiki Meccas have some sort of showy architectural gimmick or giant "set-piece" as a central bragging point: the Tonga Room has its pond and rainstorm, the Kahiki had its Moai fireplace, the Mai Kai has its gardens and floor show. The Polynesian Room has none of these gimmicks, and it is still enthralling.

That it still stands, open or not, is a miracle. Far from the campy Tiki-kitsch palaces of the late-1950s and 1960s, the Polynesian Room was never intended to be a joke on any level. Hopefully, it will be open to the general public at some point, but for now, take advantage of any opportunity you may have to view it.

TAHITIAN LOUNGE/POLYNESIAN ROOM, British Columbia

MORE BRITISH COLUMBIA TIKI SITES TO EXPLORE

Courtyard Restaurant Tiki Village, Vernon, BC (250) 503-5566

Lum's Polynesian Restaurant, 914 Esquimalt, Victoria, BC (250) 385-2322

Tiki Shores Condominium Beach Resort, 914 Lakshore Dr., Penticton, BC (250) 492-8769
No Tiki here.

TRADER VIC'S, Vancouver, BC

BRITISH COLUMBIA SITES PERMANENTLY CLOSED

Hawaiian Village, New Westminster, BC
Once a fancy restaurant, it fell into decline and closed in the mid-1990s. Right until the end, waitresses handed out leis, and drinks were served in Tiki mugs.

Trader Vic's, Westin Bayshore, Vancouver, BC
The Vancouver Vic's was razed to make a park. The Westin hotel was expanding, and the developers could get more height if they added more green space. The Vancouver Tikis are in storage at Trader Vic's hidden warehouse in Emeryville, California, being readied to decorate the Trader Vic's in Beirut and Bahrain.

MANITOBA
MANITOBA TIKI SITES TO EXPLORE

New Hawaiian Restaurant, The Pas, MB (204) 623-2144

Tiki on the Waterfront, SE 16-9-17E, Falcon Lake, MB (204) 349-3190

ONTARIO

CAMELOT RESORT • RR#1 BOX 171, 506 ASTORVILLE ROAD, CORBEIL, ON

(705) 752-1119

Category IV
OTHER

TiPSY Factor

Located three hours north of Toronto, the Camelot Resort is the brainchild of Ken Agnew. Originally rental apartments on Lake Nosbonsing (just south of North Bay), it was converted into a bed and breakfast by Ken's widow Doris. This fantastic (if remote) find is definitely worth the trip.

Camelot is an Arthurian theme lodge with a poolside Tiki bar. The focal point of the premises is indeed the Tiki bar, because it seems that Mr. Agnew had a soft spot for Tiki. Tiki mugs, wooden Trader Vic's signs, and various other Polynesian goodies are displayed around the house, but this is just the tip of the iceberg – Agnew focused his energies exclusively on the indoor pool from the 1950s to the mid-1970s. Behind a nondescript door leading to the basement, lies an incredible, dimly-lit Polynesian grotto about three stories high.

A foot bridge leads over rivulets of trickling water that run downhill and into a small tidal pool filled with rubber sea creatures. This dribbles lazily into the main swimming pool. Beyond the bridge, past an amazing snake-entwined, African mask and a series of authentic African

CAMELOT RESORT, Corbeil, ON

CAMELOT RESORT, Corbeil, ON

spears – onto which phony skulls are impaled (non-paying guests?) – is the Tiki bar. The bar itself is a roofed, bamboo platform that hangs over the edge of the grotto overlooking the pool. It is decorated with fan-backed chairs, hanging basket lamps, lanterns, blowfish, nautical bric-a-brac, sea creatures, Tiki masks, and a 12-foot stuffed snake. Hawaiian music lends to the atmosphere. Behind the bar is a beaded doorway leading to a sauna, shower, bathroom, and steps down to the pool, hot-tub, and fireplace.

Standing on the edge of the pool is akin to being at the edge of a grotto in a quiet, underground cave. Along the edge of the far wall hang pink- and white-flowered vines. In the summer they turn the waterfall on, which cascades into the pool from the roof. The walkway runs behind this, and also leads to a dark corner with a scary surprise inside! Beside it stands a six-foot stone Moai. Right next to the fire-place, Mr. Agnew built a mountain, which can be climbed via stone slab steps, to the top of the pool slide. Underneath this mountain, a spiral staircase leads down to an underwater viewing deck, where one can watch people swimming. While the bar is pretty much self-serve, the ambiance alone and the obvious love that has gone into this amazing blast-from-the-past make it a very worthwhile stop.

CAMELOT RESORT, Corbeil, ON

MORE ONTARIO TIKI SITES TO EXPLORE

Aloha Room, 323 Banks Street, Ottawa, ON (613) 233-0307

Aside from being a good bar to have a drink, there is no Tikiness about it, except for its name and a few strings of Christmas lights.

Jack's Hawaiian Village Restaurant, 29 Gov't Rd. W. General Delivery, Kirkland Lake, ON (705) 567-4711

JJ Kapps Tiki Bar, Holiday Inn, Lake & Queen Elizabeth Hwy., St. Catherines, ON (905) 934-8000

They have a big sign in front of the hotel, complete with bamboo lettering and palm tree graphics advertising the Tiki bar. It looks like a Friendly's restaurant inside, complete with that horrid many-shades-of-green and brick-red floral design on all upholstery and drapes. There is not one iota of Tiki in the place.

ONTARIO SITES PERMANENTLY CLOSED

Naughty Native Tiki Bar, Port Dalhousie, St. Catharines, ON

Went belly-up circa 2000, now a drapy-pastel women's clothing store.

Kon Tiki Ports, SE corner of Yonge and Summerhill Toronto, ON

Closed in the 1980s. Gigantic supper club with live music and good food. Opened as Ports of Call. Stephen Crane's Kon Tiki chain went through several permutations. The original locations were simply called Kon Tiki, later stores were opened as Kon Tiki Ports, and his final restaurants were created under the name Ports of Call. Adding further confusion, some of the locations named the restaurant Bali Hai, and kept the club Kon Tiki Ports – or Ports of Call.

At this point the *only* Tiki in Toronto is at the head office of **Tilley Endurables** (Barber Greene Rd. at Don Mills and Eglinton): there's a giant Moai in front of the building!

Royal Tahitian, 2525 E. Riverside Dr., ON

Tiki Room, 50 Cedar Dr., Turkey Point, ON
A beach clothing store, closed in 2001.

Trader Vic's, Toronto, ON
Closed early/mid-1990s.

Trader Vince Tavern, Imperial Restaurant, 1845 Victoria Ave., Niagara Falls, ON

Volcano Room, Toronto, ON
A somewhat misguided attempt to turn an industrial/metal club into a Tiki bar. They threw together a mix of thatched roofs, zebra skins, African masks, and Tiki mugs with the concrete and metal that was leftover from the bar's previous incarnation. The music was all wrong – house music just doesn't say "Tiki."

QUEBEC

COCONUT INN • 7531 RUE NOTRE-DAME (NEAR ROUTE 138), TROIS-RIVIÈRES OUEST, MONTREAL, QC

(819) 377-3221

Category I/VI
**CLASSIC TIKI
BAR/OTHER**

TiPSY Factor

The Coconut Inn is a bar and a motel. It was built in 1958 and Tikified in 1963 when the owners came back from a honeymoon in Tahiti. The decor hasn't changed since the most recent update in 1973. Palm trees, bamboo chairs, blow fish lamp shades, blue lights under the bar, Tiki totem stools (solid wood at that), Hawaiian black velvet paintings. The music is great, and they serve a great Mai Tai and Aku Aku Coconut.

JARDiN TiKi • 5300 SHERBROOKE EAST, MONTREAL, QC

The Jardin Tiki experience is a must for any true fan of Polynesian Pop, cheap food, fruity drinks, and turtles.

Jardin Tiki (French for Tiki Garden) is located right near Montreal's Olympic Village, which includes a beautiful Japanese Garden, a bug museum, an arboretum, and a Chinese garden, all spread over a few hundred acres of foliage. Jardin Tiki opened in the late-1970s, around the time that a whole strip of restaurants near Montreal's Olympic village began to pop up.

Upon entering to the huge restaurant (it seats about 300), one is confronted with a 10-foot high Tiki. After passing the turtle pond (yes, they're real), a little bridge leads into the restaurant proper.

The seats are huge, high-backed bamboo thrones. Lanterns and plants of every description hang from the high-arched ceiling with hardly a foot of space between them. Grand, majestic Tikis of all shapes and sizes watch over your meal from carefully selected vantage points. A second floor balcony seats yet more people and accommodates all of your private party needs. Colored lights, running streams of water... we're talking about the complete package here!

The drinks come variously in classic Tiki mugs and standard glassware. The golden menu (decorated with a Cook Islands Tiki holding a drink almost as big as himself), showcases a dozen concoctions with exotic names and fruity flavors at $4.25 to $6 (Canadian). The Bolo is served in a real pineapple, and the menu says you can keep it (one has trouble imagining why they would want it back anyway). The all-you-can eat buffet will only set you back about 12 bucks (Canadian). The extensive, well-stocked buffet contains all you could possibly want from a Polynesian restaurant, with plenty of seafood on one side and Chinese fare on the other.

The food is of a quality you'd expect from an inexpensive buffet, but the sheer quantity of selections available means

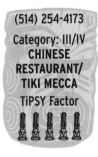

(514) 254-4173
Category: III/IV
CHINESE RESTAURANT/ TIKI MECCA
TiPSY Factor

JARDIN TIKI, Montreal, QC

that just about anybody can find something palatable. Several soups, a few different types of salad, many main courses, many, many side dishes, and even an array of desserts means that you will be well fed.

There isn't much action here after dinner time, so get there early and then move on: when in Montreal, Jardin Tiki is your mandatory first stop on any given night of revelry.

LUAU • 146, RUE MORIN, SAINTE-ADÈLE, QC

(450) 229-2911

Category II
CASUAL DINING

TiPSY Factor

Opened in 1973 ("cuisine chinoise et exotique depuis 1973"), Luau is reportedly far too bright inside, and has extremely bland food. On the upside, the TiPSY Factor is on the high end, and drinks are in coconuts and pineapples.

RESTAURANT ALOHA • 78 OUEST DE MARTIGNY, ST. JEROME, QC

(450) 432-3444

Sortie 43 de
Autoroute 15

Category II
CASUAL DINING

TiPSY Factor

Opened circa 1978, Aloha has been favorably compared to Montreal's Jardin Tiki, and some Quebecois claim that Aloha is actually a superior establishment. Cave-like walls, bridges over running streams, many grass shacks, palm trees, and the usual array of Tikiness await your discovery. Unique drink options include: the Bamboo, the Cocoboo, and the Flaming Tahitian. The Hibachi Platter and Aloha Beef come recommended from the kitchen.

MORE QUEBEC TIKI SITES TO EXPLORE

Restaurant Tiki, Montreal, QC
This is a hot dog stand in northern Montreal.

Tahiti, 88 St. Jean de Baptiste Blvd. (off of 138 southbound), Chateauguay, QC (450) 692-8112
Cantonese buffet, four-page Exotic Drinks menu, and plenty

of bamboo. Drinks are supposedly of high quality, and the owner is said to be friendly to Tikiphiles.

Tokyo Bar, 3709 St.-Laurent 842-6838, Montreal, QC (514) 842-6838
Recently remodeled from Asiatic decor to Tiki decor. Nice to see one going *to* Tiki *from* Asiatic, for a change!

QUEBEC SITES PERMANENTLY CLOSED

Hawaii Kai Bar (Beni Hanna's Restaurant), 7965 Decarie Blvd., Montreal, QC
Opened in the 1960s, it was a small, authentic Polynesian bar. Great dark atmosphere and decor, including a thatched roof over the bar, bamboo trim, fake rock walls with recessed lighting, and an amazing array of hanging lamps made out of everything from baskets to blowfish. The Yellow Bird (a good blend of rum, curacao, and juices), Mai Tais, and the Beni Hanna Special (you got to keep the glass, but it was nothing special) were favorite drinks. The Hawaii Kai is still open, but was stripped of its Tiki decor in 1999.

Kon Tiki Ports, Sheraton Mt.-Royal Hotel 1455 Peel St., Montreal, QC
The first of the Kon Tiki Ports restaurants, the Montreal location opened in 1958. It was completely windowless, giving it a great dark atmosphere. Kon Tiki also featured running water and lagoons; little bridges over the water; palms; dark walls; blue, green, and red lighting; and Tikis galore. It closed around 1981, and some of the decor may have made it to Jardin Tiki. Amazing menu graphics.

Tiki Dore, 6976 Sherbrooke East, Montreal, QC
Tiki Dore served the usual array of Cantonese and Polynesian food, and all of the classic tropical drinks. Reports state that it was small, and a bit of a dump towards the end of its days. In early 2000, Tiki Dore closed its doors for good. The support beams in the main dining room were Tiki totem poles. The decor was sold at auction.

Tiki Sun Polynesian, Lonqueuil, Montreal, QC
Bankrupt circa 1998.

AUSTRALIA

SMORGY'S • (299 BURWOOD HWY., EAST BURWOOD; 1091 PLENTY RD., BUNDOORA; 523 MAROODAH HWY., RINGWOOD; 415 WARRIGAL RD., BURWOOD; AND CUNNINGHAM PIER, CORIO BAY, GEELONG), VICINITY OF MELBOURNE, AUSTRALIA

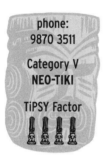

phone:
9870 3511

Category V
NEO-TIKI

TiPSY Factor

The Smorgy's chain was originally dubbed "The Island Trader," and has existed since the mid 1980s, when it was created by Eric Schwaiger. At that time, the five locations were decked out with A-frame entranceways, plenty of thatch, and a generally tropical atmosphere (with the exception of the Geelong store, which is a more straightforward nautical theme).

During the mid 1990s, the decor was expanded, with spectacular results. Several life-sized Moai were added to each location, detailed in a realistic manner that respects the original Rapa Nui Moai builders. A huge rock volcano now sits in front of the A-frame entrance; you must walk through the middle of it (via a bridge over a moat) to get into the restaurant.

The three-story tall interior of each location boasts an excellent TiPSY Factor with Tikis and other objects carved in the styles of New Guinea, Hawaii, and New Zealand. Every half hour, the volcano "erupts," and the Moai spew flames from their noses(!), as lights flash, and thunderstorm effects fill the room. This lasts for about five minutes.

The $12.95 all-you-can-eat buffet is nothing special, but you're not really going to care... Check out Smorgy's!

BELGIUM
BELGIUM TIKI SITES TO EXPLORE

Tiki's, Singel 17, 2275 Gierle, Belgium
Opened on December 1, 2000. Tiki gods, skulls, palm trees, masks, tropical decoration, leopard skin chairs. Lots of exotic tunes, plus rock 'n' roll, surf, and garage music.

CHILE

BALi HAi • RUT: 86.484.200-3, AV. C. COLON #5146, LAS CONDES, SANTiAGO, CHiLE

Bali Hai is an upscale supper club with a complete floor show, and is elaborate enough to compete with the best of the Polynesian restaurants in North America. A first impression of the Bali Hai might consist of being escorted from your cab by an urbane Chilean host, led across the circular driveway past a fearsome foursome of life-sized white plaster Moai, and through a pair of heavy glass doors, where an amazing wall of coral awaits. It gets better from there.

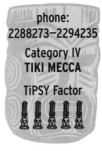

phone:
2288273–2294235
Category IV
TIKI MECCA
TiPSY Factor

Given that Rapa Nui is a territory of Chile, Bali Hai's designers have chosen to focus on Easter Island motifs for most of their decor. There are a few wooden Moai replicas about the place, and a lot of other Rapa Nui-influenced designs, suggesting Rongo Rongo tablets and the Orongo petroglyphs. The most famous Easter Island Petroglyph, the "Birdman," is the basis for the carvings on all of the wooden chairs in the restaurant. They are incredible.

There is a large grouping of 16 floats in all sizes and colors above one section of tables, looking like some weird school of fish. A big fountain dominates one corner. There are also lots of masks (that appear to be, of all things, Balinesian), and a plethora of expensive-looking statues of Polynesian kings. These are life-sized, and made of solid

BALI HAI, Santiago, Chile

wood. The ones in the bar area are in almost erotic poses; mounted on the wall is a life-sized wood carving of a Polynesian king reclining with two nude wahines.

You will want to make a reservation well in advance. Bali Hai usually has two seatings per night on the weekend, and one on weeknights. Cocktails are served before dinner to the recorded sounds of Martin Denny as people arrive for the 8:00 p.m. show. However, it is not unusual for the exotica to be cut off in mid-song and replaced with something like a bad version of *Theme to a Summer Place*. A request to "Bring back the Exotica, por favor" will only get you stared at by the waiter.

The drinks, speaking generally, are strong and cheap, but small. Many of them are served in sculpted mugs. Most of the drinking vessels actually placed on your table are inferior to the much more detailed mugs pictured on the menu, as is the case with more and more of the vintage Tiki bars. It seems that whomever was making these mugs back in the day has stopped, and it doesn't appear to be cost-effective for most establishments to continue to have them custom made.

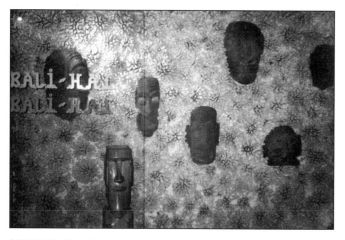

BALI HAI, Santiago, Chile

But it is the drinks in these cannikins that *really* matter: Captain's Cook is not bad, and comes in a small cylindrical mug with a face on it similar to the one on the classic Bali Hai-man mug. Iti-Iti is also tasty, and is served in a dark green "bamboo stalk" mug (smaller than the one made by Orchids of Hawaii). The Rhon Punch, the Rose Coral, the Tropical Daiquiri, and the Fantasia Bali Hai continue Bali Hai's selection of tropical drinks customized for South American tastes. Unfortunately, the Mai Tai is simply awful. It is orange in color, served in a clear glass, and garnished with an orange chunk and a cherry. Tastes like glue. The Zombie isn't much better, but it is at least served in a Chinaman's head mug (again, unique to South America and very different from the classic Fu Manchu mug).

All of the mugs mentioned above are of a style not seen in the U.S., so mug collectors now have a challenge ahead of them. But, most of these unique mugs seem to be made from fifth-generation molds, so more than anything else they look like blobs with no detail. A mug fashioned in the shape of a shrunken head, labeled "Bali Hai – Chile" on the bottom, might be obtainable to the crafty or generous among you. Upstairs by the restrooms, is a large display case containing a wide assortment of mugs that might be dubbed the "Chilean Tiki Mug Hall of Fame."

BALI HAI, Santiago, Chile

The food is great. The salads are tasty and fresh. The trout stuffed with crab meat au gratin is delicious – even though it is served with the fish head still attached. Ah well, if that's the way they do things in Chile, then who are we to complain? The turkey in champagne sauce is not quite as exciting, but how can you go wrong with champagne? Both meals are garnished with little sailboats made of fruit. The calamari appetizer is good too.

The floor show is unique, entertaining, sometimes campy, and sometimes beautiful. The house band warms things up, and features the world's oldest keyboard player, a bassist who really wants to be Mick Karn, and two pretty Chilean girls on backing vocals. The MC will then introduce the lead singer of the Platters (in Spanish, natch). This is the ultimate "where are they now" story: the lead singer of the Platters is spending his time singing with the house band in a Polynesian restaurant in Chile. Somebody alert *Behind the Music!*

After busting out "The Great Pretender," he moves into a few other Platters' hits, and then gets down with a Tony Orlando medley. A group of traditional Chilean musicians and dancers take over at this point for a show of traditional Chilean music and dancing. Cowboys dance around with hankies, as do their elaborately dressed paramours. Three other Chilean dances follow, each with different costumes and traditional music.

The house band returns, backing a new group of ethnic dancers, the long-awaited Polynesians. Log drums are unveiled, and the hula girls and nifo'afi do their thing. The entire show lasts for almost two hours while dinner is served. The MC is certainly aware that there are plenty of *touristas* present, and after interviewing audience members, he will instruct the band do a song from each of the tourist's home countries. The United States might be honored with "When the Saints Go Marching In," for example. Residents of the UK are honored in a somewhat less traditional manner with a sing-along rendition of "Yellow Submarine." Keep in mind that most of the crowd speak Spanish (with the expected accents), and hearing 150 Chileans singing "We all live in a Jello Submarine... " is worth the price of admission.

The Bali Hai is not a cheap place to dine, especially for Chile. Dinner for two, including the show, an included tip, tax, and a few drinks should set you back about U.S. $80. Worth every peso.

BALI HAI, Santiago, Chile

KOPAKAVANA • TE PiTO HENUA STREET, HANGA ROA, RAPA NUi (EASTER ISLAND), CHiLE

Located in Hanga Roa, the only village on Easter Island, this bar is marked with a big plaster Moai outside. Normally, this would be cause for excitement, right? Absolutely! But in Hanga Roa, *every business in town* is decorated with Moai images, as well as other traditional Rapa Nui carvings and petroglyphs. And don't forget – the *real* Moai are just outside of town! So seeing this Moai is no cause for any particular joy, except for the joy you will be feeling for actually being on Easter Island to start with.

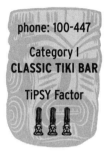

phone: 100-447

Category I
CLASSIC TIKI BAR

TiPSY Factor

In addition to the ersatz ancestor on the lawn, there are more Moai painted on the walls near the patio of this cozy tavern. Bamboo and thatch are primary construction elements, as are fishing floats, shell lampshades, and a high-arched roof, all of which create the sort of atmosphere that the North American Tiki bars have been trying to copy for 70 years.

Pisco Sour is the drink of choice, and local music by favorites Matato'a can be heard ubiquitously. Although rather nondescript compared to many of the wonderfully overdone behemoths here in the U.S., places like Kopakavana are where Victor Bergeron and Donn Beach got their ideas in the first place. This isn't any hipster bar left over from the 1950s – this is the real thing. Owner Jorge Tucki also owns a carving studio across the street.

KOPAKAVANA, Hanga Roa, Rapa Nui (Easter Island), Chile

CUBA

RESTAURANTE POLINESIO (FORMERLY TRADER VIC'S) • HAVANA LIBRE HOTEL (FORMERLY THE HAVANA HILTON), 23RD ST., HAVANA, CUBA

phone:
(53 7) 33-4011

Category II
FINE DINING

TiPSY Factor
NR

Both restaurant and hotel were completed in 1958, just a year before Castro took over. When the Soviet Union collapsed, Castro knew he had to do something to lure tourists. So he ordered that many of the old hotels and restaurants be restored. The old Havana Trader Vic's was meticulously reconditioned to its original state, using old photographs as reference. They didn't have any concept of "modernizing" it and ruining it, as so often happens. The restaurant still uses the same plates, the same glasses, and even the same menus (albeit with "Polinesio" stamped on top and the words "Ron Cubano" – Cuban Rum – on all the pictures of barrels). Bamboo wall coverings and two big Tikis (each about seven feet tall) remain intact. Pictures of the old Vic's hang on the walls to prove that it hasn't changed.

Drinks are strong, but not served in Tiki mugs, although they still have some of the original mugs (with hula girls on them) on display. The bartenders do not know a thing about tropical drinks, and they can't make a Navy Grog to save their lives. The closest you'll get is a Pina Colada made from a mix.

MORE CUBA TIKI SITES TO EXPLORE

Tikog Club, 23rd St., Havana, Cuba

ENGLAND

SOUTH LONDON PACIFIC • 340 KENNINGTON RD. (KENNINGTON TUBE), LONDON, UK

Opened in April 2002, and created by Josh Collins (who is next emigrating to Australia to build a Tiki theme park). South London Pacific looks a hundred years old, and the detailing is beautiful.

The room is quite large, and is comprised of different sections with varying degrees of intimacy, including a stage and small dance floor surrounding a central bar. Tikis, crocodile skins, and skeletons of all descriptions abound. The furniture and the bar are all bamboo. The "Trader Vic's Mai-Tai" and the Pago-Pago are both danger-ously good, reasonably priced, and are served in Tiki mugs (provided you can leave a £7.50 deposit, which will also buy you the mug if you desire). Hawaiian music is on the stereo, but a house band is planned.

phone:
020 7820 9189

Category V
NEO-TIKI

TiPSY Factor

TRADER VIC'S • LONDON HILTON, 22 PARK LANE, LONDON, ENGLAND

Like so many of the Trader Vic's locations, Vic's in London is located in the basement of a Hilton hotel. Several five-foot tall Tikis greet you at the door to the hotel. Vic's is accessed via an incredible spiral staircase. As you move down the wise helix into the darkened restaurant, you might notice a great quantity of very beautiful (and very rare) vintage tapa cloth covering every square inch of the walls and ceiling.

At the bottom is a reception area, with the lounge to the right and the main dining room to the left. The lounge is very cozy, and is two rooms' deep. It is rather subfusc, and is filled with a fairly dense array of the usual accouterments: a big outrigger, lamps, blowfish, and a bunch o' Tikis. Good TiPSY Factor here.

The drinks are from the standard classic Trader Vic's menu, and are more or less identical to the recipes used else-where. In other words — they are great. The Tiki Bowl comes

phone: (011) 020
7208 4113

Category II
FINE DINING

TiPSY Factor

TRADER VIC'S AT THE LONDON HILTON ON PARK LANE
22 PARK LANE, LONDON W1Y 4BE   TEL: 0171-208 4113   FAX: 0171-208 4050

TRADER VIC'S, London, England

in that big triangular Moai bowl, which are hard to get these days. No, they won't sell you one.

The waitresses are, for the most part, exotic beauties, all dressed in floor-length floral sarongs slit right up to next Thursday along one leg. Makes it a bit hard to focus on the Mai Tai...

Moving into the dining room, one may be reminded a bit more of the Chicago and Atlanta Trader Vic's locations, in that the decor is largely nautical in theme; most of the true Tiki action is in the lounge. The ceiling is rather low, so

TRADER VIC'S, London, England

don't expect to see any large Tikis like the towering giants seen in the Emeryville Trader Vic's; they just won't fit.

The dinner menu is, again, almost identical to the fare served up in the five United States Trader Vic's locations, and is complete with an enthusiastic mention of their antique ovens. However, as is typical in London, there is also an array of curry and other Indian dishes available. The prices are even higher than the prices in U.S. Vic's locations, but this is not to be unexpected: London is a very expensive place. The wait staff are attentive and professional, but be prepared for communication difficulties – it seems as though every member of the staff is from a different country, so accents and grasp of English vary wildly.

Absolutely worth a visit.

MORE ENGLAND TIKI SITES TO EXPLORE

Blue Hawaii, 2 Richmond Rd., Kingston Upon Thames, Surrey KT25EB (just outside of London), UK phone: 020 85496989
Hawaiian shirts and leis are commonly seen in this popular barbecue restaurant.

Blue Hawaii, The, 19 City Rd., Cardiff, South Glamorgan CF243BJ, UK, phone: 029 20493337

ENGLAND SITES PERMANENTLY CLOSED

Beachcomber Bar, Mayfair Hotel, London, UK
Opened 1960, closed 1985. Photos indicate an astounding TiPSY Factor!

FRANCE
FRANCE TIKI SITES TO EXPLORE

Le Paillote' (The Straw Hut), Paris, France
This is a jazz club, with a "tropical feel."

Maison de Tahiti & Des Isles, Paris, France
Essentially the Tahiti Tourist Board. Head upstairs to see some great wooden Tiki statues scattered around the Tahitian House. Also pick up brochures about Tahiti, which suggest Tahiti as being the true center of Tiki. Also, while is Paris, look for a shop selling ancient Pacific art, near the Pompidou Centre.

Tiki Cafeteria, Royan (south of France)
Three funny Tiki heads arranged in a pole on top of the building hold up the Cafeteria's sign; the Tiki offers "Tahitianized Drinks."

GERMANY

GERMANY TIKI SITES TO EXPLORE

Aloha Bar, Munich, Germany

They have a regular DJ on Sundays, which is the only evening supporting Exotica music. Usually the music in the bar is more rockabilly/surf-oriented and comes from a juke box. The cocktails at the Aloha Bar are strong.

Anthropology Museum, Hamburg, Germany

Hamburg has a complete Maori meeting house in its anthropology museum. Just after World War II, the occupying British troops used it as their officer's club, making it Germany's first Tiki bar.

Kon Tiki Restaurant, Untere Wörthstrasse 10-14, 90403 Nürnberg, Germany, phone: 0911/221139

Some Tikis, exclusive fine tapa wall covers, and original outriggers are on display. Lots of Lei and fine south seas food. It's usually hard to get a seat without a reservation, and during the summer and on weekends you must book at least three weeks ahead! Recently reopened after repairs from a fire.

Samoa, at the Baltic Seaside Spa town of Warnemuende, Germany

Big indoor spa with wave machines, big swimming areas, a great hula show, and tropical decor. Opened on February 15, 2001.

Waikiki Restaurant, Marktstr. 44, Boeblingen (a small town near Stuttgart), Germany, phone: (0 70 31) 22 61 02

The Hawaiian cook, Mr. Le, does a great job on the food. Nice decoration, and every first Friday of the month is a luau with a hula dancer and buffet. Seats about 30.

Waikiki Spa and restautants, Am Birkenwege 1, in 07937 Zeulenroda, Germany, phone: (03 66 28) 7370

Big indoor spa with wave machines, big swimming areas, and tropical decor (not to mention the original Lomi-Lomi Hawaii Temple Massage and the Kahi-Loa Massage of the elements). Cost U.S. $30 million to build. Includes three Polynesian restaurants: Sauna-Bar (seats 70), Tropical Beachbar (seats 140), and the Waikiki-Lounge (seats 50). Look for some small Tikis and other Hawaiiana, lots of leis, and some beautiful Tiki paintings. Two gigantic wooden Tikis are under contruction and will be ready at the entrance for the very first hula festival ever held in Europe (July 4–6 2003).

GERMANY SITES PERMANENTLY CLOSED

Polynesian Restaurant, Steinstr. 1, Kiel (60 miles north of Hamburg), Germany

Seated 70. Original Hawaiiana decor included two outrigger canoes, several Tikis inside, and one big one at the outside entrance. Opened circa 1976, closed in the fall of 2001 when the owner retired. The business was for sale at U.S. $170,000. Original owner Dieter Eggers was the chief cook trainer at the Hawaiian Hilton 30 years ago, and brought lots of original artifacts back from Hawaii, including paintings, shells, and kahilis. Tables had glass tops to dine on, with original black sand and shells from Hawaii under the glass. All of the walls were covered with original tapa. A reported 230,000 shells were used in the decor. Some of the pictures on the walls were obtained at an auction of decor from the Koings Palace at Honolulu, circa 1964.

YVONNE HEYERDAHL

GREECE

KONA KAi • LEDRA MARRiOTT HOTEL, 115 SYNGROU AVE., ATHENS, GREECE

phone: 934-7711

Category II
FINE DINING

TiPSY Factor

This Greek take on the Kona Kai is the last outpost in a once mighty chain of Tiki bars opened in Mariott's hotels world wide. The restaurant is large and spacious, with decor that is up to par with the closed-but-intact Chicago Kona Kai. A pair of waterfalls flank a Hawaiian-style Tiki, while wall-sized murals are guaranteed to impress. The large Tikis that populate the room are carved in a primitive style, as opposed to the overly-ornate specimens often seen in newer Tiki bars (this one opened 1984 – a rare thing that year indeed!).

Look for table lamps designed to look like the classic Kona Kai Tiki mugs; the original old mugs are long gone, but the bar does stock a good selection of neo-Tiki mugs. Drinks are garnished with fruit skewered on custom Kona Kai swizzles; munchies in bowls are on the house.

Kona Kai claims to be the first restaurant in Greece to offer Polynesian, Chinese, and Japanese cuisine, but it is hard to imagine that the ancient world's superpower never had chop suey until 1984.

MORE GREECE TIKI SITES TO EXPLORE

Blue Lagoon, Rhodes, Greece (in the new part of Rhodes City on the island of Rhode)
Not strictly a Tiki bar, although a few Tiki gods can be spotted here and there. It is billed as a "pirate bar," and the decor is truly spectacular, though the drinks are mediocre. The live parrots outside the establishment chattering at would-be customers is a nice touch.

ITALY
ITALY TIKI SITES TO EXPLORE

Mai Tiki, Naples, Italy

JAPAN

HAWAiiAN RESTAURANT • YOKOHAMA, JAPAN

Hawaiian Restaurant is hard to miss given the two big Tiki gods in front of the building, and the sound of slack key guitar piped through a speaker onto the street. The subfusc interior is decorated with bamboo, giant tridacna clamshells, floats, and plenty of Tikis.

Category II
CASUAL DINING

TiPSY Factor

The Mai Tai is served in a collins glass, contains plenty of good silver rum, triple sec, Orgeat, and a float of dark rum on top. It is garnished with a pineapple chunk and an orange slice.

Just like the Polynesian paradises in America, Hawaiian Restaurant features mostly Chinese cuisine, which is even less surprising given its proximity to Yokohama's Chinatown.

TiKi TiKi MOMONA • B1 SOUTETSU IWASAKi-GAKUEN, BLDG. 2-17-1 TSURUYACHO, KANAGAWA-KU YOKOHAMA, JAPAN

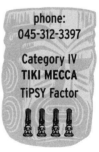

Built circa 1984 by the Suntory Corporation, Tiki Tiki has further locations in Shinjuku (Tiki Tiki Mahana), Saporo, and Okinawa. All feature decor by (you guessed it) the internationally ubiquitous Oceanic Arts.

phone:
045-312-3397

Category IV
TIKI MECCA

TiPSY Factor

Immediately upon entering (and crossing a bridge over halogen-lit water), one finds a large Tiki statue with moving eyes and mouth, who says (in recorded Japanese), "Hey, that's not the same girl you brought in last night!" and other similarly witty quips. The TiPSY Factor here is very high, with hundreds of pan-Oceanic carvings from New Zealand to Bali to Hawaii represented. Look for a concentration of western Melanesian-influenced artifacts in the bar area.

The faux alligator-volcano-clamshell orchestra pit may be occupied by the featured entertainers, some rock-on Japanese hipsters who are usually hell bent on mangling

TIKI TIKI MOMONA, Kanagawa-ku Yokohama, Japan

the oldies to the best of their abilities, whether they know the words or not. Some highlights are: "Rak Aranda Cat" ("Rock Around the Clock"), and (during the holidays) "Santa Cross Is Commie Two Tone" ("Santa Claus is Coming to Town").

The stage is soon occupied by Hawaiian dancers, complete with coconut bras and grass skirts. If you stay long enough you may see them come out for a couple of sets. Around the holidays, for their last set, they change from their traditional grass skirts to a sassy little miniskirt "Santas-Little-Red-Polyester-Clad-Helper" number.

Tiki Tiki's drinks are expensive at 900 yen; to keep the mugs is an extra 1,000 yen on top of the drink price. They are variously garnished with fruit, ice cream, and some funky Zulu swizzler sticks with googly eyes.

The food is "Izakaya style," which means you order a bunch of little appetizers and share it all. Kind of like a Japanese tapas. Vegetarians will find plenty to eat too. An entire meal with drinks for two is reasonable (for Japan) at about 9,000 yen.

The Shinjuku location is on the fourth floor of an office building surrounded by transvestites, brothels, and other theme restaurants. It is a little more run down than the Yokohama store, and the mugs are not for sale.

MEXICO
MEXICO SITES PERMANENTLY CLOSED

Aku Tiki, Acapulco, Mexico

NORWAY
NORWAY TIKI SITES TO EXPLORE

Kon Tiki Museum, Bygdoynesveien 36, Oslo, Norway, phone: 47-23-08-6767
As much a hero to Tiki culture as Donn and Vic, if not more so, a visit to Thor Heyerdahl's museum is a mandatory pilgrimage. See the actual famous Kon-Tiki raft as well as his reed boat RAII, and much more.

SPAIN

ALOHA • C/ PROVENZA, 159, BARCELONA, SPAIN

Aloha was designed by Antonio Romero and Jaime Pomares in 1976. Guests are served by Juan, Julio, and Miquel, who all used to work at the Kahala. The centerpiece of Aloha is a bar decorated with forests of bamboo. To the right is a display case with Tiki mugs and other souvenirs for sale. If you go deeper into the room you'll find inviting niches, ideal for an intimate rendezvous. The entrance area contains a billiard table, plus canaries and parrots, and an aquarium beside the bar. The live monkey, sadly, has been repatriated to parts unknown.

phone:
93 451 79 62

Category I
CLASSIC TIKI BAR

TiPSY Factor
NR

ALOHA, Barcelona, Spain

KAHALA (HAWAiiANO BAR KAHALA) • AVDA. DiAGONAL, 537, BARCELONA, SPAiN

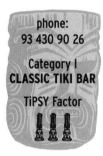

phone:
93 430 90 26

Category I
CLASSIC TIKI BAR

TiPSY Factor

Designed, built, and run by Joaquin Carreres, Kahala is Barcelona's oldest Polynesian bar. Old photographs show a more elaborate facade than what current visitors will see, but the bar is as impressive as it ever was. A stylized temple wall leads to a foyer with a bridge across a pond. A long bar extending into the depths of the room dominates the establishment. Beyond the bar, baby sharks can be seen swimming in aquariums, and facing it are intimate niches with bamboo seats, decorated with wooden masks and Tikis.

KAHALA, Barcelona, Spain

KAHiKi • GRAN ViA DE LAS CORTS CATALANES, 581, SPAiN

phone:
93 323 18 83

Category I
CLASSIC TIKI BAR

TiPSY Factor
NR

Designed by Esquinasi in 1977, the Kahiki is the least spectacular of Barcelona's three Tiki bars, but it is centrally located, right beside the university on the Gran Via. Kahiki is said to be rather quiet from Sunday to Thursday, and fills up with partying people on Friday and Saturday nights.

Metro: L1 and L2, Station Universitat, Bus: all lines to Plaça Universitat

MOANA BEACH • SiMÓN BOLÍVAR, 28, BiLBAO, SPAiN

phone:
34 94 422 2066

Category II
CASUAL DINING

TiPSY Factor
NR

The entrance to Moana Beach is home to a 15-foot-tall fiberglass Tiki. Moana Beach's additional use of fiberglass to create a "descent into a mysterious cavern" effect is impressive, especially with the green spotlights accenting ferns (both faux and live), the other foliage, and other Tikis. A recording of jungle noises playing in this foyer adds a nice touch. The bar itself is made to look like a giant tree with huge branches running along the ceiling, and with roots running along the floor. Rattan and bamboo are adequately incorporated as railing, tables, chairs, and barstools. Another cool aspect to the bar is its "twinkling star ceiling" – little fiber-optic lights were placed randomly throughout the deep-blue painted ceiling. The intensity of the lights varies, making for a "starry night" effect.

The back of the restaurant houses a banquet room where hula dinner shows are performed on weekend nights. Moana Beach's irritating neon elements are incongruous with the rest of the club's mostly dark and "mysterious" elements.

The drinks are good, and served in heavy coconut-shaped mugs. These are Moana Beach's only themed mugs. Also look for a three-foot-tall, deep-green, fiber-glass Tiki outside of a tattoo and piercing establishment in Bilbao's Casco Viejo.

MORE SPAIN TIKI SITES TO EXPLORE

Bora Bora, Madrid, Spain

Hula-Hula, Costa Brava, Spain

LeMartime Restaurant and Tiki Bar, Port 62 Bordeaux, Spain
Very elegant, very chic. A class act.

Mauna Loa "Bar Hawaiiano," Madrid, Spain

Moai Cafe, Spain
The mystery of the Moai: The owners have provided photos of several incredible and very authentically designed Moai being erected, but we haven't been able to track them down to get the address! On-line searches yield no clues.

Waikiki, Palamos, Spain
Eighty-five minutes north of Barcelona.

Waikiki Cafe Bar, Estanyol 11, Son Serveracala Millor Baleares 7560, Spain Phone: 34-97-1813479

SWEDEN

TiKi ROOM • BiRKAGATAN 10, STOCKHOLM, SWEDEN

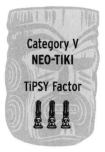

**Category V
NEO-TIKI**

TiPSY Factor

Tiki Room is situated in the basement of a bar called Mellow, but they're two separate bars with different personnel, menus, and prices. The bar has two rooms. The staircase from the upper bar descends directly into the first room, which holds the bar, a handful of tables, and one slightly elevated booth. The walls and ceiling are covered with bamboo, tapa cloth, and woven grass mats. There are quite a lot of Tikis.

TIKI ROOM, Stockholm,

Look for framed photos of various Easter Island and Hawaii-related things, as well as some Hula girl paintings. Naturally, the bar has a row of blowfish lamps and at least one glass float. Some of the furniture is bamboo and some is more of a 1950's diner-style (chrome and red vinyl). They have a beautiful printed drink menu, which also includes a small selection of coconut and pineapple-based Polynesian food. The staff wear Hawaiian shirts and are friendly. They run various compilation CDs of Hawaiian music, but the bar is equipped for DJs on livelier nights.

TIKI ROOM, Stockholm, Sweden

SWITZERLAND

KON TiKi BAR • NEiDERDORFSTRASSE, ZÜRiCH, SWiTZERLAND

The Kon Tiki Bar is marked from the outside by red neon letters in a primitive font, and a Tiki mask. The staff are friendly and multilingual, but the TiPSY Factor is low; Thor Heyerdahl's ghost is not to be found here. Tropical drinks and the sounds of Arthur Lyman have been replaced by pounding heavy metal, a TV, and cheap beer. For the thorough urban archaeologist and Tikiphile, we would recommend a visit in the early afternoon when the bar is still deserted.

Category I
CLASSIC TIKI BAR

TiPSY Factor

TAHITI
TAHITI TIKI SITES TO EXPLORE

Kon Tiki Pacific Hotel, Boulevard Pomare (near the Moorea Ferry docks), Papeete, Tahiti, French Polynesia

This is one of the less expensive hotels on Tahiti. The bar contains the usual array of Tiki bar decor, plus a pool table. Their drinks are good but pricey; the Mai Tai is made with Bacardi Silver and a commercial Mai Tai mix and is garnished with a pineapple chunk, a cherry, and a cocktail umbrella for U.S. $11.50.

Tiki Village, Moorea (Tahiti's sister island), phone: (689) 550-250

Developed in the late 1980s, Tiki Village seems to be the ultimate Polynesian tourist Tiki experience. "Polynesia's largest show spectacular with its great Tahitian party nights and performances of sixty dancers, artists, musicians, and the famous fire dancers." You can get married there while being towed out to sea and back on a raft decorated with wooden Tiki statues (accompanied by a guitar player).

VIRGIN ISLANDS
VIRGIN ISLANDS TIKI SITES TO EXPLORE

Duffy's Love Shack, Red Hook, St. Thomas, Virgin Islands

Duffy's Love Shack, Cruz Bay, St. John, Virgin Islands
Owned by the same people who own Duffy's in Ocean City, Maryland, they serve all the classic Polynesian drinks in Orchids' mugs. Volcanoes too!

INTERNATIONAL TRADER VIC'S LOCATIONS

Manama, Bahrain, Le Royal Meridian Bahrain, phone: 973-580000 or 973-589589

Havana, Cuba (see "Polinesio" above)

Cairo, Egypt, The Royal Gardens Hotel, phone: 202-575-9102

TRADER VIC'S, Munich, Germany,

Berlin, Germany
Peter Seeley, grandson of Victor Bergeron, announced late in 2002 that a new Berlin Trader Vic's is planned. Watch your local press for details.

Duesseldorf, Germany, Hotel Breidenbacher Hof (2nd oldest Euro-Vic's)

Hamburg, Germany, The Radisson SAS Hotel Hamburg, Marseiller Strasse 2, phone: 49-40-3502-3440

Munich, Germany, Hotel Bayerischer Hof, Promenadeplatz, 2-6, 80333 Munchen, phone: 49-89-212-0995
Their Tikis were carved by Barney West of Sausalito, California.

Fukuoka, Japan, Hakata Riverain, East Side, Hakataza-Nishigin Building B2F 2-1 Shimokawabata-Machi, Hakata-Ku, Fukuoka, phone: 81-92-263-1188

Osaka, Japan, Hotel New Otani, 4-1 Shiromi, 1-Chome, Chuo-Ku, phone: 81-6-949-3210
A little tough to find; 28,500 yen for a Tiki Bowl.

Tokyo, Japan, Hotel New Otani, 4-1, Kioi-Cho, Chiyoda-Ku, phone: 81-33-265-1111

Beirut, Lebanon, The Gefinor Rotana Hotel, Clemenceau Street adjacent to the Gefinor Center, phone: 961-1-371-888 or 371-999

Muscat, Oman, The Hotel Intercontinental, Muscat, Muttrah, Sultanate of Oman, phone: 968-698028

Singapore, Hotel New Otani Singapore, fifth floor, 177-A River Valley Rd., phone: 65-338-3333
Happy Hour specials include free spicy peanuts and half-price drinks. The Navy Grog at this location is said to be particularly potent.

Marbella, Spain, La Alcazaba Complex, Ctra de Cadiz 175, 29660 Marbella, phone: 34-9-5-281-6100
Set beside the pool in a massive resort complex. Out the window are real palm trees, a lit pool, and paths leading to the beach. There is seating available outside around the pool. There are big Tikis inside along with the usual floats and an outrigger canoe hanging from the ceiling. An eight-foot Moai stands guard over the entrance to the servicios.

Taipei, Taiwan, 7 FL, 135 Min Sheng E. Rd, SEC. 3, phone: 886-2-2545-9999

Bangkok, Thailand, Mariott Royal Garden Riverside Hotel, 257/1-3 Charoen Nakorn Rd., Bookalo, Thornburi, phone: 662-476-0021 or 476-0022

Abu Dhabi, U.A.E., The Beach International Hotel, phone: 971-2-6443000

Al Ain, U.A.E., Al Ain Rotana Hotel, phone: 971-3-515111

Dubai, U.A.E., The Holiday Inn Crown Plaza, phone: 971-4-3056399
Trader Vic's restaurants in Europe and Asia continue to be built to this day. A total of seven will exist in the Middle East by the end of 2003.

Drink Recipes

Sometimes it just isn't feasible to take a Tiki Road Trip. If you have to stay home (hey, we all do it one or two nights a year), here are a dozen ways to ease the pain.

MAi TAi

Mai Tai recipes used vary so widely that we couldn't narrow it down to just one version. First up is Trader Vic's "old way" Mai Tai, or more appropriately, the Mai Tai Roa Ae.

> 1 ounce Fine Jamaican Rum (15 or 8 year old Appleton) over shaved ice
>
> 1 ounce Martinique Rum (St. James)
>
> 1/2 ounce Orange Curacao
>
> 1/2 ounce Orgeat Syrup
>
> Juice from one fresh lime (about 3/4 ounce)
>
> Shake vigorously.
>
> Add a sprig of fresh mint

Mai Tai expert Kevin Crossman prefers this recipe:

> 2 ounces Mount Gay or your favorite rum
>
> 3 ounces Trader Vic's Mai Tai Mix
>
> 1/2 ounce orange curacao
>
> 1/2 ounce almond syrup
>
> 1/2 ounce vanilla syrup
>
> add lime juice to taste
>
> mix thoroughly

Here's a variant with juices other than lime (not technically a Mai Tai, but still pretty good):

1 ounce Fine Jamaican Rum over shaved ice

1 ounce Martinique Rum (St. James)

1/2 ounce Orange Curacao

1/2 ounce Orgeat Syrup

1/2 ounce lime juice

1/2 ounce orange juice

1/2 ounce pineapple juice

Shake vigorously.

Serve with a dark rum float.

Top with pineapple slice, cherry, and umbrella

"Not for the inexperienced"

"Let the drinker beware"

SCORPiON

The original 1946 Scorpion recipe was designed to serve 12, and included a bottle and a half of rum, a half bottle of wine, plus gin, brandy, Orgeat, lemon juice, and orange juice. Directions included letting the mixture sit for two hours. The recipe has been refined and simplified over the years:

> 3 ounces lemon juice
>
> 4 ounces orange juice
>
> 1 ounce Orgeat syrup
>
> 2 ounces brandy
>
> 4 ounces light rum

Add a scoop of ice, blenderize, and pour into a Scorpion Bowl (or Volcano Bowl) with more ice.

Add a gardenia and long straws. Ignite 151 Rum in the center of the bowl, if applicable, or float a 151-doused sugar cube on an orange slice. Serves two.

SUFFERiNG BASTARD

"Properly drunk through a straw while holding the nose so as to save the tender tissues of the lips and prevent premature insensibility." One of the newer – and one of the most memorably named – of the classic drinks, this one dates to 1968:

Juice of 1 lime

Dash rock candy (simple) syrup

Dash Orgeat syrup

Dash orange curacao

1 ounce light rum

2 ounces dark rum

Shake with shaved ice and serve in double old-fashioned glass with shaved ice. Decorate with lime shell and fresh mint.

"Served as an offering from the great god Tiki"

ZOMBiE

"A Real Dirty Stinker." This Zombie recipe dates to 1947:

1 ounce Jamaican rum

2 ounces Puerto Rican rum

1/2 ounce 151-proof Demarara rum

1 ounce orange curacao

1 ounce lemon juice

1 ounce orange juice

1/2 ounce grenadine

1 dash Pernod or Herbsaint

Mix with ice and pour over cracked ice in 14 ounce chimney glass.

"Persuasive ammunition for toppling giants"

MiSSiONARY'S DOWNFALL

This one was invented by Don the Beachcomber:

1/2 ounce lime juice

1/2 ounce honey

1/2 ounce peach liqueur

1 ounce light Puerto Rican rum

2 ounces fresh ripe pineapple juice

5 leaves fresh mint

6 ounces cracked ice

BLUE HAWAiiAN

A classic Tiki Drink that resembles window cleaner, and if mixed poorly, tastes like it as well:

1 ounce Light Rum

1 ounce pineapple juice

1 ounce sweet and sour Mix

dash of Cream

dash of Blue Curacao

Blend all ingredients with one cup of ice until smooth. Serve in a hurricane glass or Tiki mug

PLANTER'S PUNCH

"This punch made the planter potted ... "
As made shortly after WWII:

3 ounces Jamaica rum

1/2 ounce grenadine

Juice of 1 lime

1/2 ounce lemon juice

1/4 tsp. sugar

Stir with ice and strain into 12 ounce glass filled with crushed ice. Add seltzer to fill.

"One sip and you may see a Menehune"

SiNGAPORE SLiNG

The original 1947 recipe:

> 1 and 1/2 ounce dry gin
>
> 1/2 ounce cherry brandy
>
> 1/2 ounce lemon juice
>
> 1/2 lime
>
> 1 tsp. grenadine
>
> 1/4 ounce Sloe Gin
>
> 1/4 ounce Crème de Cassis

Squeeze 1/2 lime and drop into a 12-ounce glass with cracked ice. Add rest of ingredients and stir well. Fill with seltzer.

FOG CUTTER

Slight variations in the classic Fog Cutter recipe are noted:

> 2 ounces light rum
>
> 1 ounce brandy
>
> 1/2 ounce gin
>
> 1 ounce orange juice
>
> 1 1/2 ounces fresh lemon juice (or 1 ounce)
>
> 1/3 ounce Orgeat syrup (or 1/2 ounce)
>
> dash of sherry

Shake all ingredients except sherry with cracked ice. Pour into tall glass packed with crushed ice; float sherry on top.

NAVY GROG

  3/4 ounce lime juice

  3/4 ounce grapefruit juice

  3/4 ounce honey

  3/4 ounce dark Puerto Rican rum (Ron Rico)

  3/4 ounce Jamaican rum (Appleton Estate)

  3/4 ounce Navy rum (Pusser's or Lamb's)

  3/4 ounce soda

  2 dashes Angostura bitters

  1 ounce fresh guava juice

Shake and strain into 14 ounce glass with crushed ice.

"Neither weak nor lusty, it commands respect"

PISCO SOUR

This amalgamation of various recipes actually used on Easter Island and in Chile has been modified and tweaked by the author:

  5 ounces Pisco Capel

  4 ounces sour mix

  3 ounces orange juice

  1 ounce Triple Sec

  1 ounce rock candy syrup

After shaking, pour over crushed ice in a Moai-shaped Tiki mugs. Squeeze 1/4 lime into the Tiki mugs, and drop the rind in. Add umbrella skewering pineapple chunk. Serves two.

POLYNESiAN SPELL

This is the original 1961 recipe used at Kahiki in Columbus, Ohio:

> 1 ounce grape juice
>
> 1 1/2 ounces dry gin
>
> 1/4 ounce triple sec
>
> 1/4 ounce brandy
>
> 1/2 tsp. sugar
>
> juice of 1/2 lemon

Shake and strain into champagne glass.

"Be absolutely sure of immediate action"

TiKi BOWL

1/2 ounce orgeat

2 ounce orange juice

1 1/2 ounces lemon juice

1 ounce light rum

1 ounce dark rum

1 ounce brandy

Mix thoroughly and pour over ice in Volcano Bowl.

Glossary

Ahu – The platform on which a Moai stands.

Aloha Shirt – Any shirt with a brightly colored Hawaiian-style pattern on it, best exemplified by the collectible rayon shirts first popularized in the 1940s. Modern variations in various fabrics have been continually produced since. Also called a Hawaiian Shirt.

MOAI UPON AHU TONGARIKI

Art Deco – A design and architectural style prominent from 1925-1940. Adapted to mass production. Characterized by geometric designs, bold colors, stylized design, and the use of plastic and glass.

Bali Hai Man – Five-foot tall plaster statue of a whimsical headhunter (with a bone through his nose), seen in front of San Diego's Bali Hai restaurant. This image was made into a custom Tiki Mug for Bali Hai, but has also been appropriated for a wide array of iconographic uses in Tiki culture.

MR. BALI HAI MUG

Baumatay, Andreas – Carver of Tikis during the classic era.

Baxter, Les – One of the masterminds behind the creation of Exotica music; writer of perhaps the most famous Exotica tune, "Quiet Village."

LES BAXTER

Birdman – A famous petroglyph seen on Rapa Nui. Also, an annual ritual once held on Rapa Nui wherein young men would climb down a cliff to the sea, swim to a small islet, return with a tern egg, and present it to the chief. The winner of this race was outcast from the village – and yet treated like royalty, and had the honor of being the island's Bird Man for the following year.

COCO JOE KU STATUE

BOSKO MASK

Bosko – California-based carver of modern day Tiki objects.

Coco Joe's – Creator of Hawaiian Tiki souvenirs, largely made from either volcanic rock or a plastic resin called "Hapa Wood." Coco Joe's finally folded in the late 1990s; rumor has it their designs and inventory are now being produced by a Japanese firm.

Cook Islands – Group of 14 islands (population 14,000) located in central Polynesia, southwest of Tahiti. The capital island is Rarotonga. The Cook islands have their own language, government, and distinctive style of Tiki carving largely propagated by local fishermen.

DaGa – Originally founded by DAn Coscina and GAry Nelson (geddit?) as Polynesian Pottery in 1971, this Hawaii-based creator of Tiki Mugs has created at least 70 different designs. Some DaGa mugs are marked as such, others are completely unmarked, and still others carry the initials APO – a stamp of approval from Trader Vic's bartender Michael Apodovitch. Their most famous design is the "Tonga" (see photo).

DAGA MUG

Denny, Martin – One of the masterminds behind the creation of Exotica music, responsible for genre's first popular success with his recording of Les Baxter's "Quiet Village."

DISNEY TIKI

Disney Tiki – Any wooden Tiki statue that has been overpainted with bright colors.

Dynasty – New York restaurant goods supplier who continue to make a dozen or so styles of Tiki Mugs based on original Orchids of Hawaii designs.

Easter Island – Also called Rapa Nui, or Isla de Pascua, or Te Pito o te Henua. Easter is a tiny island (64 square miles) in the southeast Pacific, settled by Polynesians sometime after the fifth century AD, and found by the Dutch on Easter Sunday, 1722. Rapa Nui is most famous for the existence of their Moai statues, carved by the islanders out of volcanic rock to honor their ancestors. Most of the almost one thousand Moai built before the 17th century were toppled or destroyed, the last one went down in 1840. A few dozen have been restored to their Ahu in the past 50 years.

Exotica – Just as the decor of the classic Tiki Bars molded the gods of many far off lands into a fantastic mongrel called Tiki, a new hybrid music was called for too. It fell to Martin Denny, Arthur Lyman, Les Baxter, and a few others to take the mysterious music of many lands, run it through a blender full of rum and jazz, and emerge with a music that was equally as contrived and phony (but ultimately pleasing) as the decor and the drinks. It was dubbed Exotica, after the title of Denny's first LP, and with vibraphones, congas, and birdcalls, it was the perfect soundtrack for the Tiki Bar.

Field Collecting – *Strongly* discouraged practice of taking unauthorized souvenirs from classic Tiki sites. This sort of activity is taboo, kapu, bad karma, and often illegal. Don't make the gods angry – leave the stuff where it is, for all to enjoy.

Florida-style Tiki Bar – Commonly seen from Florida all the way north to Maryland (and elsewhere), the Florida-style Tiki Bar is any small shack by the water with a thatched roof. Tiki decor and Polynesian drinks are optional, and usually non-existent. Confusion may be fueled by fact that the first thatched roof structures in Florida were built by members of the Seminole or Miccosouki tribe. Their name for such a structure is "Chikee," and many Floridians call them Chikee Huts. One can see where people might then mutate "Chickee" into "Tiki." All of this said, there are also plenty of Chickee bars in Florida, but you wouldn't want to take your mom to them...

Fu Manchu – Style of Tiki Mug featuring an elongated Asian-looking face with a droopy mustache.

Googie – Douglas Haskell coined the term "Googie Architecture" in a 1952 *House and Home* article. Googie architecture was born of the post-WWII car-culture and thrived in the 1950s and 1960s. Bold angles, colorful signs, plate glass, sweeping cantilevered roofs and pop-culture imagery captured the attention of drivers. Bowling alleys looked like Tomorrowland. Coffee shops looked like something in a Jetsons cartoon. For decades, many "serious" architects decried Googie as frivolous or crass. Today we recognize how perfectly its form followed its function. Even as the best historic examples are bulldozed, architects are rediscovering the importance and utility of Googie and are adopting it for their own designs.

FU MANCHU MUG

Hawaiiana – Having to do with Hawaiian culture; ephemera or collectibles from Hawaii. The Islands: O'ahu, Maui, Kaua'i, Hawai'i, Moloka'i, Lana'i, Ni'ihau, and Kaho'olawe

Hedley, Eli – Possibly the "original Beachcomber," Eli sold his wares to Donn Beach and others from a shack on the Pacific coast. He eventually ended up as one of the primary designers of Tiki Bars during the original Tiki heyday, staying busy right through the 1970s. His grandson, known as Bamboo Ben, carries on the tradition.

Heyerdahl, Thor – Norwegian anthropologist (born 1914, died April 18, 2002). Traveled to Fatu Hiva (in the Marquesas) in 1936 to study flora, and soon became obsessed with discovering how Polynesia was originally populated. Famously sailed his raft, the Kon Tiki, across the South Pacific in 1947 to prove his theories about Polynesians being of South American descent. Studied Easter Island extensively beginning in the 1950s. Wrote books on his adventures which include: *Kon-Tiki, Aku Aku*, and *Fatu Hiva*.

THOR HEYERDAHL (RIGHT) AND MOAI

KU

EDWARD LEETEG PAINTING

LONO

Holland, August – Artist responsible for the two mass-produced paintings *The Pearl of Wisdom* and *Power Within*, which are both staples of Tiki Bar decor.

Kahili – Feathered standards used by Hawaiian royalty to show status, lineage, and family ties.

Karn, Mick – Bass player for the band Japan from 1975-1981. Has since recorded albums with Polytown, JBK, Rain Tree Crow, and solo.

KC Company – Modern wholesalers of Tiki Mugs and other Hawaiiana, based in Aiea, Hawaii.

King Kamehameha – A fierce but wise ruler (from 1795-1891), he united (some say conquered) the Hawaiian islands, forged bonds with the British, and brought Hawaii into the modern age.

Kona Kai – Mythical home and resting place of the original creator god Tiki. Polynesia's Shangri-La, Avalon, or Valhalla.

Kukailimoku (Ku) – One of the most iconic and widely recognized of the ancient Hawaiian Tiki gods, the "original" (or at least the oldest surviving) six-foot-five wooden Ku effigy is located in the Bishop Museum in Hawaii.

Leeteg, Edward – American artist who lived in Moorea (near Tahiti). Often called the American Gaugin (more for his lifestyle than his art), the painter was something of a bon vivant, cultivating an exaggerated reputation for excess drinking, fighting, and for bedding his exotic Tahitian models. He died in a motorcycle crash in 1953, but left behind a legacy of about 1,700 black velvet paintings.

Leilani – Extremely common Tiki Mug, based on the Orchids of Hawaii R-09 design.

Left Orbit Temple – Series of enhanced CD/CD-ROMs featuring original music and art by a revolving group of creative talents, focusing on themes of primitive cultures, dreams, and mysticism.

Long Pig – Cannibal term for human meat.

Lono – Hawaiian god.

Lounge – Broad definition for a variety of musical styles most prevalent in the 1960s. Exotica is often lumped into the lounge category.

TIKIS CARVED BY MAI TIKI

ARTHUR LYMAN GROUP

Lyman, Arthur – Master of the vibraphone, successfully went solo after years in Martin Denny's band.

Mai Tiki – Trade name used by modern day Tiki carver Wayne Coombs of Florida.

Makemake – Creator of the world, in Rapa Nui lore.

Maori – Indigenous peoples of New Zealand. Replicas (and occasionally original examples) of their excellent and distinctive carvings can be seen in many Tiki Bars.

Maori men's house – Central structure in a traditional Maori settlement where men gathered to conduct the affairs of the village. Similar structures can be found in other Oceanic cultures, such as in New Guinea.

Marquesas – Group of 10 islands (about 1,200 miles northeast of Tahiti), notable for a distinctive style of carving which influenced artists from New Zealand to Hawaii. Settled circa 200 B.C., possibly by Samoans. First European contact was in 1595, the second was almost 200 years later by Captain Cook in 1774. Annexed by France in 1842. Marquesian tattooing is among the most elaborate in the world. Any image of a human figure is called "Tiki" by the Marquesians.

MAORI CARVING

MENEHUNE FIGURE
FROM TRADER VIC'S

Meneahune – According to Hawaiian folklore, the meneahune were shy, tiny people who lived in the forest or the mountains of Pu'ukapele (Hills of Pele). They were excellent

MOAI

MAORI WITH MOKO

OCEANIC ARTS

builders, and (usually working at night) could complete major construction projects very quickly. The word may have come from "manahune," the term for the servant class on other Pacific islands.

Moai – A carving made of volcanic rock as found on Easter Island. Moai were built as effigies honoring the carver's ancestors. Each of the 996 Moai on Easter Island has a name. Many of them have been buried up to mid-chest over the centuries by erosion on the hillside of the Rano Raraku volcano/quarry, giving some people the impression that they are just heads, when in fact they are all full carvings from the waist up. All of the completed Moai were toppled in tribal wars, but a few dozen have been restored in the past 50 years.

Moko – Traditional facial tattoos of the Maori people. The word, literally, means "lizard."

Monkey Pod – A type of wood found in Hawaii. Once commonly used in carvings and furniture making, the tree is now protected.

New Guinea – Located in western Melanesia, this second-largest island in the world is home to several diverse and distinct cultures. Loosely divided into the western Irian Jaya and eastern Papua regions, many languages, social systems, and cultures freely cross this border. The art of the Sepik region is particularly distinctive, and is the style of the Massim, West New Britain, and the Papuan Gulf.

New Ireland – A province of New Guinea, this small island on the Bismarck Archipelago was settled 33,000 years ago, and is known for ornate carvings.

Nifo'afi – Traditional Hawaiian fire-knife dance.

Oceanic Arts – Company based in Whittier, California, who provide decor to Tiki Bars and Polynesian restaurants. Begun in 1956 by Bob van Oosting and Leroy Schmaltz, OA is still carving Tikis and may be the last surviving members of the original generation of mid-century Tiki carvers. If you have been in a Tiki Bar in your lifetime, it is a good bet you have seen Oceanic Arts' work. Also see Witco and Orchids of Hawaii.

Orchids of Hawaii – Best known as a primary maker of Tiki Mugs, Orchids also made dishes, silverware, Tiki carvings, lamps, and a wide variety of the decor we see in classic Tiki Bars. Over the years, Orchids created *dozens* of different Tiki Mugs, which can be identified by the style number (usually found on the bottom of the mug) in the format of the letter "R" followed by a number (i.e. "R-4," or "R-86").

ORCHIDS OF HAWAII

Orongo Petroglyphs – An awe-inspiring collection of primitive rock art/petroglyphs exist at the ceremonial village of Orongo on Easter Island. Located on the edge of the Rano Kau volcano, Orongo is where the Birdman rituals were held.

Otagiri Manufacturing Co. (OMC) – Early manufacturer of Tiki Mugs. Their history is shrouded in mystery; no one seems to be able to obtain any information about them.

BIRDMAN PETROGLYPH AT ORNONGO

Page, Betty – Famous pin up and fetish model. Photographed extensively by Bunny Yeager and Irving Klaw during the 1950s.

OTIGIRI TIKI MUG

Pele – Hawaiian volcano goddess.

Pisco Capel – Liqueur made from grapes in Chile, exported in a Moai-shaped bottle.

Pitcairn Island – First spotted in July of 1767 by the son of one Major Pitcairn; eventually settled by the crew of the *HMS Bounty* (after the famous mutiny of Fletcher Christian versus Captain William Bligh). The *Bounty* drifted about the Pacific, picking up 6 Tahitian men and 12 women, reaching Pitcairn in January 1790. The Tahitians were treated as slaves; their revolt against the Mutineers resulted in the

PISCO CAPEL BOTTLE

death of most of the English. By 1800, John Adams was the sole male survivor — with 10 women and their children. The *H.M.S. Briton and Tagus* rediscovered the settlement in September 1814. The British commanders were impressed by Adams and his flock, and thus began relations between Pitcairn and the British Navy which exist to this day.

Platters — Famous Motown recording artists from the 1960s. Not to be confused with PuPu Platters (see below).

PMP — Paul Marshall Products, makers of (among other things) Tiki Mugs in the classic era. The quintessential PMP mug is one of the most famous of all Tiki Mugs: a light brown matte finish Tiki, with a glossy dark brown band around both the top and bottom edges of the mug. This design has been continually appropriated, and has appeared as patio lights, a shirt, part of a Tiki font collection for designers, and elsewhere.

Polynesian Pop — Term coined by Sven Kirsten to easily describe the Tiki aesthetic as exemplified in mid-20th century popular culture.

PuPu Platter — Any collection of various appetizers served up together on a platter (usually over a Sterno flame) in a Polynesian or Asian restaurant.

Rapa Nui — Native name for Easter Island. Other names for this tiny island are Te Pito o Henua and Isla de Pascua.

Retro/Retro Culture — An appreciation for the specific aesthetics of mid-century America, covering the Art Deco era through the Kennedy years, and more specifically the late 1940s and the 1950s. Architecture, clothing, cars, films, fine art, illustration, pin-up calendars, music, and of course, Tiki.

Rongo Rongo — Still indecipherable, this mysterious and ancient form of writing is found on tablets of wood on Easter Island.

CLASSIC PMP MUG

RONGO RONGO

Royal Crown Revue – Seven member band (formed in 1989) who are largely credited with inspiring the neo-swing movement of the late 1990s.

Ryden, Mark – Modern surrealist artist who often uses Tiki themes in his work.

Savage, Eugene – Artist renowned for his historical murals of Hawaii, as seen in many classic Tiki Bars.

EUGENE SAVAGE MURAL

Shag – Phenomenally popular Los Angeles-based artist and graphic designer influenced by mid-century illustration and animation styles.

Slack key guitar – A Hawaiian guitar playing technique, named for the loosening the instrument's strings to create a unique tuning.

Tiki Bar – In the strict sense, a Tiki Bar is any establishment open to the public, containing wooden replicas of Tikis (carved Polynesian figures), selling an array of alcoholic drinks. For the context of this book, the definition is loosely used to describe *any* point of interest to the aficionado of Polynesian influence in popular culture.

SHAG

TIKI FARM MUG

Tiki Farm – Modern day makers of a large variety of Tiki mugs.

Tiki Mug – Ceramic vessel for holding a Tropical Drink. Usually in the shape of a Tiki. Most often seen *without* any sort of handle, making the term "mug" somewhat of an inaccuracy. Occasionally seen as large bowl meant for holding a drink to be shared by several people, sometimes called a Volcano Bowl in this configuration. Hundreds of styles exist, and up until the mid 1990s they could be found at thrift stores, garage sales, and flea markets for under a buck. Collectors have driven prices up during the past half decade; rare mugs are now fetching upwards of $30, while common specimens seem to have leveled off in the $5-$8 price range.

TREASURECRAFT ASHTRAY

TiPSY Factor – Acronym for "Tikis Per Square Yard." It is essentially a rather freely used shorthand reference referring to the density of the decor in any given Tiki Bar. A Tiki Bar with many Tikis and other appropriate artifacts is said to "have a high TiPSY Factor," while relatively sparse decor equals a "low TiPSY Factor." Speaking generally, a Tiki Bar with a high TiPSY Factor is more favorable.

Trader Luke – Yes, *another* "trader." Luke was a carver during the Tiki heyday.

TreasureCraft – Maker of ornate ceramic (and later plastic) Tiki Mugs and related products, mostly for the Hawaiian tourist trade.

Tretchikoff, Vladimir – Artist known in the Tiki community for his creepy mid-century portrait of a Chinese woman.

CHINESE GIRL BY TRETCHIKOFF

Tropical Drink – Beverage consisting of alcohol (usually rum) in a fruity base, often garnished with fruit and a paper umbrella, preferably served in a Tiki Mug. Don't be fooled by substitutes – anything that resembles a slushy is not the real thing. Accept no imitations. Some drinks that are often labeled as "tropical" and served up in Tiki bars, but which are not true examples of the genre, are: Margarita, Chi Chi, and Daiquiri. Demand the best: Mai Tai Roa Ae! Singapore Sling! Suffering Bastard! Zombie! Missonary's Downfall!

Tuvalu – Pacific island on which 8,000 year old human remains have puzzled archaeologists who generally agree that the South Pacific was settled no earlier than 6000 years ago. A key American outpost during World War II, the Tuvalu government has since become unique among Polynesian islands for their continuing zealous issuance of collectible postage stamps.

Vanuatu – A group of 83 Melanesian islands sporting 113 languages and a population of 170,000 (up from 40,000 in the 1920s, down from 600,000 in pre-colonial times).

Vintage Clothing – Strictly, any garment made before the 1980s. Used in the vernacular, the term refers more to clothing of a collectible, valuable, or quintessential nature created during or before the middle-20th century (i.e. pre-1966). Many classic Aloha Shirts are of a vintage dating back as far as the 1940s, and can often be acquired from vintage clothing dealers.

Volcano Bowl – Large, round variation of the ceramic Tiki mug used to serve drinks meant to be shared by two or more people. Frequently seen with a volcano in the center which may be filled with 151 rum and/or lighter fluid to create a flame. Also, Tiki Bowl.

VOLCANO BOWL

West, Barney – Well-known carver during the Tiki heyday.

Westwood – Another ex-creator of distinctive geometric Tiki mugs. A small but easily identifiable assortment of Westwood products are not hard to find.

WESTWOOD MUGS

Witco (Western International Trading Co.) – Company based in Mount Vernon, Washington, who provided decor to Tiki Bars and Polynesian Restaurants. Founded by William Westenhaver. Hala Kahiki

in River Grove, Illinois may own the best remaining collection of Witco artifacts, which are distinctive for their ubiquitous darkened cedar wood. Graceland's Jungle Room was done in Witco decor, not to mention parts of the Playboy Mansion, and Tiki Bars everywhere.

WITCO FOUNTAIN

HAWAIIAN VOCABULARY

Consonants are pronounced as they are in English, with the exception of W. After I and E, W is usually pronounced like V.

A is pronounced like **AH** in **Father.**

E is pronounced like **AY** in **Fake.**

I is pronounced like **EE** in **Peel.**

O is pronounced like **OH** in **No.**

U is pronounced like **OO** in **Tattoo.**

Vowels are each pronounced individually when one after the other. For example, **"ali'i"** is pronounced **AH LEE EE.**

1950'S ART BY TRYEE

'ekahi/'akahi................................One, or once.

'elua/'alua....................................Two, or twice.

'ekolu..Three, or three times.

'eha..Four. or four times.

'elima ....Five. or five times.

Ahiahi..Evening

Aloha!..Love, luck, and happiness.

Aloha Nui ....Lots of aloha

Aloha Oe.......................................Aloha to you

E Mea Maitai Roa ....This is very good

Hala..The pandanus tree

Halau ....A long house for canoes or hula instruction. Hula troupe.

Hale..House

Haole ....A foreigner, especially blondes or caucasians.

Hauoli .... Happy

Here Vau la Oe .... I love tou

Hina Aro Oe E Inu .... Do you want a drink?

Honu .... Turtle

Hui .... A club, association, or group.

Hui Pu La .... Brew

Hukilau .... Fishing feast

Inu .... Drink

Kahuna .... A priest, minister, or expert in any field

Kai .... Sea, or near the sea.

Kama or Keiki .... Child, or kids.

Kane .... Male

Lei .... A flower necklace

Lewa .... Sky

Lua .... Bathroom, or toilet.

Lilepu Oe .... The same to you

Mahalo .... Thank you

Maitai .... Good, or "the best."

Malihini .... A newcomer or visitor

Mana .... Spiritual power derived from the gods

Manuia .... To your health

Mauoli Hanau .... Happy birthday

Mauoli Makahiki .... Happy new year

EDWARD LEETEG PAINTING

Mele Kalikimaka.........................Merry Christmas

Moana Kai ....Ocean

Nani Wahine ....To a beautiful woman

Okole Maluna ....Bottoms up

'ohana ....Family

Ola Ola ....Very alive

Opu ....Stomach, or belly.

Pape...Water, or juice.

Paraparu......................................Weak

Pia ....Beer, or ale.

Pohaku...Rock, or stone.

Polu...Blue

Ta'ero..Drunk

Wahine ....Female

PHOTO CREDiTS

All photos by James Teitelbaum

All scanned images of Tiki-related ephemera are from James' archive.

Except:

Page 09 (lower left) and page 20 (upper right) photos by Billy Hawell, courtesy of Kurt Blakesley

Page 09 (upper right) courtesy of Shepherd Brown

Page 10 (lower left) and page 20 (upper right) courtesy of John Forsythe

Page 13 (upper left) courtesy of the Snead family

Page 14 courtesy of Mike Stutz

Page 32/33 courtesy of Caliente Tropics

Page 78 (bottom) courtesy of Kirsten Archives

Page 95, photo by: Sally Finger

Page 135, used by courtesy of Brucemore National Trust

Page 168, courtesy of Freddie Kekaulike Baker

Page 172, courtesy of Waikiki Wally's

Page 208, photo by Pamela Dawn Cunningham

Page 210 through 214, photos courtesy of Kat Borosky

Page 220-221 courtesy of Politiki

Page 256 courtesy of Tiki Room

Page 279 (middle) courtesy of Shag

Pages 17 (top), 76 (bottom), 111, 260 (top), 265 (top), 269 (bottom), 283 (bottom) courtesy of Don Brown.

ABOUT THE AUTHOR

James Teitelbaum's seemingly unrelated interests in both mid-20th century American culture and in primitive art fused together at some point in the 1980s to inspire his love of Tiki. As a professional in the music industry, James has been able to explore classic Tiki bars worldwide while on tour with bands as diverse as Ministry, Pigface, and Royal Crown Revue. To chronicle his exploits, he launched the "Tiki Bar Review Pages" in 1994, and has since been interviewed and profiled on the subject of Tiki in several dozen publications. James is also the mastermind behind Left Orbit Temple, who create CD/CD-ROM discs containing original music and art with a tribal theme. James lives in Chicago with two tortoises.

JAMES TEITELBAUM

BOOKS AVAILABLE FROM SANTA MONICA PRESS

Blues for Bird
by Martin Gray
288 pages $16.95

The Book of Good Habits
*Simple and Creative Ways
to Enrich Your Life*
by Dirk Mathison
224 pages $9.95

The Butt Hello
*and other ways my cats
drive me crazy*
by Ted Meyer
96 pages $9.95

Café Nation
*Coffee Folklore, Magick,
and Divination*
by Sandra Mizumoto Posey
224 pages $9.95

**Discovering the History
of Your House**
and Your Neighborhood
by Betsy J. Green
288 pages $14.95

Exploring Our Lives
*A Writing Handbook for
Senior Adults*
by Francis E. Kazemek
288 pages $14.95

Footsteps in the Fog
Alfred Hitchcock's San Francisco
by Jeff Kraft and
Aaron Leventhal
240 pages $24.95

**Free Stuff & Good Deals for
Folks over 50, 2nd Ed.**
by Linda Bowman
240 pages $12.95

**Jackson Pollock: Memories
Arrested in Space**
by Martin Gray
224 pages $14.95

James Dean Died Here
*The Locations of America's Pop
Culture Landmarks*
by Chris Epting
312 pages $16.95

**How to Find Your Family
Roots and Write Your
Family History**
by William Latham and
Cindy Higgins
288 pages $14.95

How to Speak Shakespeare
by Cal Pritner and
Louis Colaianni
144 pages $16.95

**How to Win Lotteries,
Sweepstakes, and Contests
in the 21st Century**
by Steve "America's Sweepstakes
King" Ledoux
224 pages $14.95

The Keystone Kid
Tales of Early Hollywood
by Coy Watson, Jr.
312 pages $24.95

Letter Writing Made Easy!
*Featuring Sample Letters for
Hundreds of Common Occasions*
by Margaret McCarthy
224 pages $12.95

**Letter Writing Made Easy!
Volume 2**
*Featuring More Sample Letters for
Hundreds of Common Occasions*
by Margaret McCarthy
224 pages $12.95

**Nancy Shavick's Tarot
Universe**
by Nancy Shavick
336 pages $15.95

Offbeat Food
*Adventures in an
Omnivorous World*
by Alan Ridenour
240 pages $19.95

Offbeat Golf
*A Swingin' Guide to a
Worldwide Obsession*
by Bob Loeffelbein
192 pages $17.95

Offbeat Marijuana
*The Life and Times of the
World's Grooviest Plant*
by Saul Rubin
240 pages $19.95

Offbeat Museums
*The Collections and Curators of
America's Most Unusual Museums*
by Saul Rubin
240 pages $19.95

Past Imperfect
*How Tracing Your Family Medical
History Can Save Your Life*
by Carol Daus
240 pages $12.95

A Prayer for Burma
by Kenneth Wong
216 pages $14.95

Quack!
*Tales of Medical Fraud from
the Museum of Questionable Medical
Devices*
by Bob McCoy
240 pages $19.95

Redneck Haiku
by Mary K. Witte
112 pages $9.95

**The Seven Sacred Rites
of Menarche**
*The Spiritual Journey of the
Adolescent Girl*
by Kristi Meisenbach Boylan
160 pages $11.95

**The Seven Sacred Rites
of Menopause**
*The Spiritual Journey to
the Wise-Woman Years*
by Kristi Meisenbach Boylan
144 pages $11.95

Silent Echoes
*Discovering Early Hollywood
Through the Films of Buster Keaton*
by John Bengtson
240 pages $24.95

Tiki Road Trip
*A Guide to Tiki Culture in
North America*
by James Teitelbaum
288 pages $16.95

What's Buggin' You?
*Michael Bohdan's Guide to
Home Pest Control*
by Michael Bohdan
256 pages $12.95

ORDER FORM 1-800-784-9553

	Quantity	Amount

Blues for Bird (epic poem about Charlie Parker) ($16.95)

The Book of Good Habits ($9.95)

The Butt Hello...and Other Ways My Cats Drive Me Crazy ($9.95)

Café Nation: Coffee Folklore, Magick and Divination ($9.95)

Discovering the History of Your House... ($14.95)

Exploring Our Lives: A Writing Handbook for Senior Adults ($14.95)

Footsteps in the Fog: Alfred Hitchcock's San Francisco ($24.95)

Free Stuff & Good Deals for Folks over 50, 2nd Ed. ($12.95)

Jackson Pollock: Memories Arrested in Space ($14.95)

James Dean Died Here: America's Pop Culture Landmarks ($16.95)

How to Find Your Family Roots... ($14.95)

How to Speak Shakespeare ($16.95)

How to Win Lotteries, Sweepstakes, and Contests... ($14.95)

The Keystone Kid: Tales of Early Hollywood ($24.95)

Letter Writing Made Easy! ($12.95)

Letter Writing Made Easy! Volume 2 ($12.95)

Nancy Shavick's Tarot Universe ($15.95)

Offbeat Food ($19.95)

Offbeat Golf ($17.95)

Offbeat Marijuana ($19.95)

Offbeat Museums ($19.95)

Past Imperfect: Tracing Your Family Medical History ($12.95)

A Prayer for Burma ($14.95)

Quack! Tales of Medical Fraud ($19.95)

Redneck Haiku ($9.95)

The Seven Sacred Rites of Menarche ($11.95)

The Seven Sacred Rites of Menopause ($11.95)

Silent Echoes: Early Hollywood Through Buster Keaton ($24.95)

Tiki Road Trip ($16.95)

What's Buggin' You?: A Guide to Home Pest Control ($12.95)

	Subtotal _____
Shipping & Handling:	CA residents add 8.25% sales tax _____
1 book $3.00	Shipping and Handling (see left) _____
Each additional book is $ .50	TOTAL _____

Name _____

Address _____

City _____ State _____ Zip _____

☐ Visa ☐ MasterCard Card No.: _____

Exp. Date _____ Signature _____

☐ Enclosed is my check or money order payable to:

Santa Monica Press LLC
P.O. Box 1076
Santa Monica, CA 90406

www.santamonicapress.com 1-800-784-9553